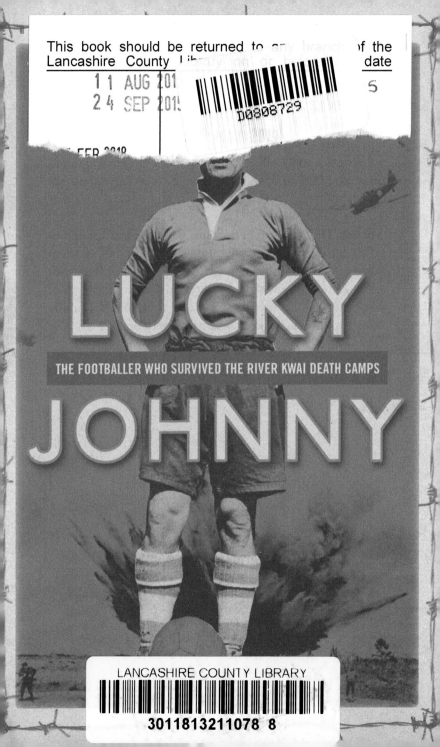

D0808729

LUCKY

THE FOOTBALLER WHO SURVIVED THE RIVER KWAI DEATH CAMPS

JOHNNY

Johnny Sherwood was one of eleven children, and played professional football for Islington Corinthians, Middlesbrough, Reading, Aldershot and Crystal Palace. During the war, he was a Sergeant in the Royal Artillery. Johnny suffered life-long effects from his POW years, but nonetheless went on to become a pub landlord and successful bookie. He raised three children and was the proud grandfather of six grandchildren.

Michael Doe grew up in Reading and lived near his grand-father. He discovered his grandfather's manuscript hidden in the attic of his mother's house in 2013. Michael lives with his wife, step-son and twin daughters in the Wirral, Cheshire, where he runs his own business and continues the family tradition through his keen interest in football.

Lucky Johnny

*The footballer who survived the
River Kwai Death Camps*

Johnny Sherwood and Michael Doe

HODDER

First published in Great Britain in 2014 by Hodder & Stoughton
An Hachette UK company

First published in paperback in 2015

A CIP catalogue record for this title is available from the British Library

ISBN 978 1 444 79033 7

Typeset in Sabon MT by Hewer Text UK Ltd, Edinburgh

Printed and bound by Clays Ltd, St Ives plc

Hodder & Stoughton policy is to use papers that are natural, renewable
and recyclable products and made from wood grown in sustainable
forests. The logging and manufacturing processes are expected to
conform to the environmental regulations of the country of origin.

Hodder & Stoughton Ltd
Carmelite House
50 Victoria Embankment
London EC4Y 0DZ

www.hodder.co.uk

For all the family

Contents

Contents

INTRODUCTION

by Johnny's grandson, Michael Doe

Grandad was the eldest son of eleven children and always on the go. They were a close-knit, happy family who always stuck up for each other. It sounds like they were a boisterous lot, so they must have been quite a handful for their poor mum when they all lived above the May Duke pub in Reading, which Grandad's parents ran for more than forty years.

Apparently, he was quite a rascal and full of fun from the start, often getting into . . . and out of . . . trouble. His real name was Henry William, but his mother soon nicknamed him 'Lucky Johnny' and it stuck.

When he was a teenager, Johnny was playing football with some mates in the park, when his talent was spotted . . . twice. The first time it was a Queens Park Rangers scout who saw him and said he would come back the following weekend. But during the week, the Reading Football Club manager came by and noticed him kicking the ball about in his hand-me-down boots.

'How can you play football in those boots, lad?' he asked, looking at the flapping toe on one of them.

Reading was the local club, so the manager, Billy Butler, came to see his parents to ask if Johnny could join them.

'But he'll need a new pair of football boots if he does!'

So his mum and dad took him into town and bought him his first ever new pair of football boots. That was it – the beginning of Johnny Sherwood's career. He went down to the club and signed the papers the next day, on his way to becoming a professional footballer.

Johnny struck lucky again when he was invited to join a world

1

tour team, the Islington Corinthians. They toured a lot of countries in four continents and played ninety-five matches in all, winning most of them. Johnny was centre forward and he used to tell me and my brother how many goals he scored in each match. I remember the pride in his eyes when he told us about being the top goal-scorer of the whole tour, with more than seventy goals in the seventy games he played, but he was modest about his success. He always said he couldn't have scored so many if it hadn't been for the other players being so good.

The football world tour was in all the papers. My aunt found Grandad's scrapbook after he died and it's full of newspaper articles and photos of their matches across the world. We've reproduced some of the pages from the scrapbook within the text of this book. A journalist from *The Times* newspaper followed them all the way, so there are several articles from *The Times* in his scrapbook. Most of them mention Johnny's talent and his goal-scoring. One of *The Times* articles even tipped that Johnny 'could be centre forward for England'. So he had the world at his feet . . . until the war put a stop to all that shortly afterwards.

Reading FC, 1938-39. Johnny Sherwood is in the front row, third from left.

The tour lasted six months in 1937/8, after which Johnny happily went back to his club, the 'Royals' at Reading, where he was still playing at the outbreak of the Second World War on 3rd September 1939, his twenty-sixth birthday. That soon changed everything. Johnny joined the Royal Artillery as a PE instructor and was quickly promoted. He was an excellent sergeant, who would do anything for his men. He was based in Northumberland in the first two years of the war, so he was snapped up to play on his Saturdays off as a professional for Middlesbrough in the war league. He took all the men in his unit along to watch him play, then spent all his pay on taking them out to the pub afterwards.

In late 1941 his regiment was posted to the front, in the Middle East. On the way, Pearl Harbor happened, so they were diverted to Singapore, and that spelt the end of Johnny's freedom in February 1942. His next three and a half years were filled with horrors and starvation in the death camps along the river Kwai.

Grandad always told us bedtime stories when we were children, but there were no nursery rhymes or fairy tales for us. They were all about his football or his wartime escapades. We loved it when he came to stay, every other weekend, and he would sit in our bedroom for hours, telling us stories. His stories about the football tour kept us riveted, when he described the exotic places they went, the matches they played and the adventures they had along the way.

He told us stories too about the Siege of Singapore, the waves of Japanese bombers flying low, a girl and her baby he helped, people running in fear, and his big ack-ack gun shooting at the planes. As boys with toy guns and aeroplanes, he kept our attention for hours.

On other occasions he told us stories about marching in the jungles, the jobs he had to do on the railway, the awful things they had to eat, the wild animals he saw and the brave things he did for his men. He sometimes told us about incidents he probably shouldn't have done, but mostly they were upbeat, like he was, and we soaked it all up.

My brother Sean remembers him telling us one night about his ship being torpedoed and having to jump into the sea, being adrift all night and the next day till he was rescued. My favourite story was about the Americans flying low over the Japanese prison camp, waving at the prisoners and dropping a barrel of chocolate bars for them.

After those weekend story sessions, I would go to school and paint pictures of aeroplanes dropping bombs, guards with rifles, or lines of very thin men marching in the jungles. My teacher was quite alarmed about my 'obsession' with the war, so my mother had to tell her about Grandad's bedtime stories.

After Grandad died, my mother and her sister cleared his house. Mum brought home a suitcase of old photos she found in his attic. Many years later, I helped her when she moved to a smaller house. I found the battered case in her loft and brought it down. When I looked inside, underneath the old photos I found a typed manuscript, with some handwritten notes tucked inside.

I took it home to read and quickly realised this was my grandfather's memoir, written by him – a collection of all his familiar stories from my childhood bedtimes, and many other harrowing tales that I had never heard before, all in one book. I knew it was something special.

In his manuscript, my grandfather says that when he wrote this book, he wanted it to be published for everyone to read. So now at last I feel that I'm the lucky one, to help his dream come true.

1

The Siege of Singapore

February 1942

'Things are going to be very grim,' said Lieutenant Jackson, calling me to one side. He spoke in a low voice, with a face as stern as his words.

'Yes, sir.' I was shocked at his pessimism. But I didn't know then what an understatement it would turn out to be.

As the sergeant in charge of a Bofors light ack-ack gun, I realised things were going badly. We didn't have a single aircraft left in the sky and the Japanese were bombing and shelling us like crazy, flying so low they were almost diving down the barrels of our guns.

'But we'll fight to the finish,' the lieutenant assured me. 'We must defend Singapore at all costs.'

It was the night of 14th February 1942, during the Siege of Singapore, the major British military base in Asia. It was supposed to be an 'impregnable fortress', but the Japanese had been bombing the island on and off since the end of December and we had arrived in the thick of it all. It was only a week before that the air-raids had developed into a full-scale battle, when the Japanese sank our warships. Their aircraft had completely outnumbered ours, and they soon destroyed the few we had left. So we were left trying to defend the civilians and our territory with nothing but anti-aircraft guns and rifles.

The situation that night seemed almost hopeless, but not quite. If the Japanese dive-bomb pilots had been half as good as ours, I and my gun detachment would have been killed off quite easily. Luckily that was not the case – not yet anyway.

5

The Japs had already knocked out the Singapore water supply. Across the city there was panic and chaos as thousands of people ran all over in fear and dread, trying in vain to find any places of safety from the heavy shelling and mortar bombs being thrown at us by the Japs.

Added to the Singapore civilians were thousands of Malays who had been driven from their homes up-country. Can you imagine the pandemonium? Bombarded from all angles, these normally stoic people screamed in terror. There was nowhere safe to go.

I walked into the blazing centre of Singapore just after midnight with two lads from my gun detachment. The night sky was bright with tracer fire and blazing buildings. As we turned a corner we stopped in our tracks. There in the middle of the road, a British army lorry was engulfed in flames with two men inside the cab. It scared the hell out of me. We ran over to try and get them out, but the intense heat drove us back. I don't think I had ever felt more helpless in my life. My insides lurched as I suddenly caught sight of the driver's face, his mouth screaming in agony, before the flames swallowed him up. It was only a moment, but it seemed like an age.

The smell of burning flesh sickened me to my stomach as we turned our backs and walked away. Even now, I can't get either that image or the stench out of my head.

There were women and children running helter-skelter, not knowing what to do or where to go, as they rushed to and fro between the bodies strewn everywhere along the roads.

'Help us,' they pleaded, again and again when they saw us. 'Where can we go?' Their hysteria and desperation tugged at our hearts.

'What can we do, Sarge?' said one of the boys.

'Is there anywhere safe for them to hide?' asked the other.

I had a sudden brainwave. 'The storm-drains,' I said. 'We must tell them to hunker down in the monsoon-drains at the sides of the roads. They're solidly built of concrete, and large enough to squeeze into. They'll all be pretty safe in there, as long as they don't receive a direct hit.'

So we split up and roamed the city, trying to calm people down, and directed them to the nearest monsoon-drains. The word spread and soon they were all filled up with desperate civilians.

A beautiful young girl of about seventeen came up to me, carrying a small child in her arms.

'Sir,' she cried. 'Please help me.' The tears fell fast down her face and her toddler screamed, clutching on to his mother in terror. 'Can you protect us?' Her soft brown eyes beseeched me and I melted with fear for her.

'Come with me,' I said, taking her by the hand. 'The drains are all full now, but I know a place that should keep you safe.'

She tried to smile through her tears and let me lead her and her child through the streets.

'Here,' I said as I took her to the corner of two thick walls, partially covered by the jutting overhang of an adjacent building. 'I think you'll be as safe here as anywhere. Now sit down against the wall. I'll go and get you a blanket to lie on.'

I went off to a British detachment about thirty yards away and borrowed one of their blankets.

'What's it for?' asked their sergeant.

'A young girl and a small child,' I said. 'I've found them a place to lie down.'

'Here,' he said, rummaging about in his stores. 'Take these. I don't expect they've eaten for days.'

'Too right,' I grinned. 'Thanks, mate.'

I took the tins back with me, along with the blanket, which I laid down on the ground for her and the child. Then I opened the tins, one of condensed milk and the other of bully-beef, and handed them to her.

'Thank you sir.' She began to cry again, this time with gratitude as she smiled through her tears.

By now it was very late and I picked my way through the streets back to my own detachment, sheltering from the renewed Jap bombardment. It was a constant storm of shells. As I arrived, dog-tired, just in time to shelter with the lads from another wave of planes, we were showered with leaflets falling from the sky. I picked one up and scanned it.

'Hey, look at this,' I said. 'It's a picture of an American soldier with his arms round an English girl.'

'What a cheek!'

'Does it say anything, Sarge?'

'Give in so you can go home to your women,' I read aloud. Well, you can imagine how I felt. I wished I hadn't picked it up, but it was too late now, so I tried to make light of it, for the men's sake.

'Take no notice,' I said. 'It's just propaganda. They want us to lose our morale so they can defeat us. And we're not going to let that happen, are we boys?'

'No bloody fear . . . too right we're not,' they all agreed.

'The rotten devils,' I said to my corporal later. 'However did they manage to think that one up? Do they think we'll really take it seriously?'

Of course we tried to put this out of our minds, but it only highlighted the fact that we were seven thousand miles from home and all our loved ones, and that hurt. We had not seen them for four months now, since before we left for the front. When we embarked on the transport ship at Gourock, Scotland in November 1941, we thought we were going to Basra in Iraq, but on the way the Japs bombed Pearl Harbor and everything changed. We were re-routed to Singapore, and now here we were, just in time for the last days of this terrifying Japanese bombardment.

We had only been here a few days, and as I tried to get comfortable and snatch some sleep that night, all I could think of was my family, especially Christine, my lovely beauty-queen wife, and my little toddler son Philip. He'd been poorly when I left, so I worried about him a lot and missed them terribly. How were they getting on without me? Would they manage all right? I knew Christine must have had the new baby by now. Was it a boy or a girl? Oh, when would I get back to see this precious new member of our family? It hurt so much to think of them getting on with their lives without me. And I can't tell you how down I felt that night, knowing I might not get back to them for quite a while. *If only I could will myself back there*. With that thought weighing on my mind I drifted into a fitful sleep.

When the dawn light woke us a few hours later, the first thing I did was to walk back to the wall where I had left the girl and her child. There was a lull in the bombing and I was keen to make sure they were all right and to give them what little comfort I could. I even smuggled out a tin of good old Ambrosia rice pudding for them to share for breakfast. I smiled to think of how pleased they would be.

Suddenly I froze. My heart lurched as I took in the sight. Sometime during those few night hours they had been blasted by a Japanese shell. They were both lying dead in a pool of blood, clasped in each other's arms.

I had seen a lot of dead bodies in the past few days, but the sight of this girl's and her toddler's corpses lying there shocked me. Her open eyes stared straight at me, but there was nothing behind them. My stomach churned as an irrational feeling of guilt overwhelmed me for a few moments. Was this my fault? Could I have prevented it? I knew I couldn't, but would they have been safer if they hadn't met me?

A few paces away I found an abandoned chunkel, a kind of pointed shovel, and dug them a shallow grave by the side of the road. I gently picked up the light bodies of that lovely girl and her child and laid them out, then covered them over with sandy soil. I said a little prayer for them, then realised I didn't even know their names.

Feeling empty inside, I walked back to my Bofors gun to wait for the next wave of Jap dive-bombers.

* * *

'Sherwood,' called the lieutenant as he approached our placement on his motorbike and cut the engine.

'Yes sir,' I saluted him.

'At ease, Sergeant,' he said. Then in a quieter voice: 'Remember this date, 15th February 1942. Forget what I said last night about fighting to the last man.' He looked pale, dejected, his face more lined than I'd noticed the day before.

'We can't stand by any longer and watch all these innocent women and children being killed,' he continued. 'We have new orders.'

'New orders, sir?'

'We are going to capitulate.'

'You mean surrender, sir?'

'Yes, but we don't call it that. It's for the sake of the ordinary citizens of Singapore, you see. The British command has decided we cannot let them all be killed. We have to stop the bombing now, before it's too late.'

I wondered whether that was really the reason, but it didn't matter either way. I was shocked that we Brits would give in so quickly, but we all knew we were losing the battle and, without more reinforcements, it was only a matter of time. It was like lambs to the slaughter, watching all those civilians being killed by the relentless bombing, and so many of our own lads too.

I wanted to ask the captain, and of course the senior officers who had supposedly planned this bit of the war, why they sent our lot, the 18th Division, into Singapore only seventeen or eighteen days before capitulation, when they must have realised we couldn't defend the place for long. Even I could see it coming, so surely it was obvious to everyone that Singapore must fall.

These are questions I have never had answered. I just hoped and prayed that those who suffered and perished in Singapore did not die in vain and that higher powers would learn a lesson from all this, eventually.

Lieutenant-General Percival and his party carry the Union Jack on their way to surrender Singapore to the Japanese, 15th February 1942.

Later that day, 15th February 1942, our lieutenant gathered us together to confirm the bad news.

'We have today capitulated to the Japanese Imperial Army and I have new orders. We must gather all our arms and ammunition together in a pile for them to take away.'

'We'll see about that,' whispered one of my comrades.

'Yes,' I replied with a smirk. 'They may get our guns, but we'll make damned sure they won't be able to fire them!'

We spent the next hour or so gathering and sabotaging our weapons. I buried most of our rifles, damaged the ammunition to make it useless and took the breech-block out of my Bofors gun, so it couldn't be fired.

'They may have had a fair capture,' I said as we piled everything up. 'But they won't gain much from it.'

* * *

A few hours later, in the early evening, the Japs arrived at our arranged rendezvous, yelling and screaming at us as though we were a pack of animals. But we stood proudly and said nothing. It was the Japs themselves who behaved like animals, howling and baying at us in high-pitched voices.

'You British demi-demi,' screeched one of the guards, pointing at us. 'British no good,' he translated triumphantly, trying to make us squirm. He might have succeeded if he hadn't made himself look so ridiculous.

Presumably they were trying to impress us in their own way from the start, now that they were the masters. Of course, their hysterical behaviour had the opposite effect, and we laughed about them later and aped their ludicrous antics.

'You prisoners,' shrieked their officer at us in his pigeon English. 'You go parade. Speedo-speedo.' It didn't take much to guess what that meant.

We duly lined up on a field nearby, where they searched each one of us to make sure we had not concealed any arms or ammunition and that we had no radios or electrical equipment, as that also had to be handed in.

'You give tin food,' ordered the officer. So we gathered all our tins of food and piled them up too. This was becoming absurd. Some more orders were issued in Japanese to their soldiers, who came and removed all the tins to store them. Apparently these would be issued to us as our rations each day. When they heard this news, many of our lads believed it, but I couldn't help being sceptical and, to be on the safe side, I hid some of my detachment's tins in my haversack.

I held my breath as the Japs did a peremptory search . . . and I got away with it. During the next few days, this small food supply was to be a godsend to my pals and me.

Now came the serious news. I was one of the unlucky NCOs (non-commissioned officers) picked out by our captors to clear up the hundreds of dead bodies from the streets, dig holes and

12

throw them in. I was horrified at the thought of this task, but I had no choice. I retched repeatedly as I gathered the mutilated bodies of women and children and put them in the holes others were digging. I tried to place them down gently, despite the shouts of the guards and the prods from their guns. These had been human beings and I had to give them what dignity I could, despite the Japs' rough treatment.

A few days later, we were ordered to sit in groups along the road-side, with our armed guards keeping a close watch on us all. Along came a group of about twenty-five natives, tied to one another by their wrists and herded along by their irritable Japanese captors. Following a few minutes later came another group, then a third.

'Where do you think they're taking them?' whispered one of my pals.

'Probably an internment camp,' I answered, watching them all go by.

Suddenly we heard a splatter of machine-gun fire reverberating through the humid air, as the birds fled in shrill terror from a clump of trees nearby. This shooting lasted about twenty-five seconds, then silence.

I was shocked rigid. Was there some connection? No, I must have jumped to the wrong conclusion.

After a few minutes, another group of natives were led past us, and another, their heads bowed.

I tried to get up. I didn't know what I could do to stop this, but it was an instinctive reaction. I got a rifle butt to my head for that, drawing blood from my ear, and I was forced to sink back down on my haunches, fuming.

Another long round of machine-gun fire echoed through the still air.

Now I was raging mad inside. How could this be allowed to happen?

Everyone was dumb with shock and one lone bird of prey shrieked as it wheeled above our heads. I too shrieked silently inside as we sat mourning these poor civilians' fate.

At this point, one of our own guards stood out in front of us and started to gesture with his rifle, using his hands and pointing, that our turn would be next. I was horrified. My mind was in a turmoil. The men all reacted in different ways, but they were true Brits and nobody gave in to their emotions or betrayed their fear. I was proud of them all.

2

Changi POW Camp

February 1942

A couple of days later an interpreter came to talk to us on the parade ground.

'You march to Changi barracks,' he barked at us.

Changi was a British army camp a few miles up the road.

'You take haversacks. Leave everything else. We bring to Changi in transport.'

Before we set off, our officers gave us some orders of their own.

'Under no circumstances must any of you drink water from a tap or a stream, nor any water given to you by locals on the route, as it will more than likely be contaminated and this could make you very ill.'

So off we marched the fourteen miles to Changi, our new detention camp. As we marched we became increasingly hungry, but we had no food, and on this scorching hot day we were all very thirsty, but the Japs had not allowed us to bring any water to drink. As the sun beat down and the day wore on, we became desperate and I'm sure it will not surprise you that we all began to accept drinks offered to us by the friendly villagers in the places we passed through. They were all smiles and we were so relieved to be able to quench our thirst.

At last, worn out from marching in that heat, we arrived at the camp.

'It all looks quite clean and tidy, Sarge,' said my corporal as we marched through the gates. 'That's a good start.'

'No thanks to the Japs,' I added. 'It was our boys who were billeted here. Only the Brits could have kept it so well.'

We were sorted into groups for the various billets, each with an officer in charge.

This was a good start for us, as the officers soon got to work, organising tasks and activities as only British officers could. Every man who was fit enough was detailed his particular jobs to do around the camp.

'Do you think our things will turn up like the interpreter said, Sarge?' asked one of the boys in my unit as we settled in that evening.

'They'll probably arrive tomorrow,' I assured him. I was dubious about this myself, but I didn't want to let on.

As it turned out, I needn't have worried. For once, at least, the Japs kept their word, almost, and the day after we arrived our belongings did turn up . . . with several items missing. Of course, there was nothing we could do about that, but I was glad I had hidden my precious British football in my haversack to carry with me, so the Japs didn't get their hands on it.

At this stage of our captivity, the Japanese guards left us pretty well to ourselves, which was a great boon to us, though we had only meagre rations which left us permanently hungry and thirsty.

After a couple of days, my problems really began. I started to suffer awful cramping pains in my stomach, as if it were being squeezed and twisted round. First of all I thought they must be hunger pangs, but I'm afraid they turned out to be much worse than that.

It was the start of a terrible attack of dysentery. Not knowing how serious this could be, I kept my discomfort to myself, wandering about the camp with the bouts of pain becoming worse and worse, and my visits to the latrines more and more often.

Eventually, I became so weak I could no longer walk and I began to pass blood. I sat in the latrines for long intervals throughout the day and the night, crawling in and out to try and snatch some sleep for a few moments in between.

At last I recognised that something was very wrong with me and I struggled over to see the army doctor in the officers' hut.

'You have a nasty case of dysentery,' said the medical officer. 'If you had left it even another day, you would have been beyond my help. You would have died.'

'Really sir?' I gulped. 'I was hoping it would get better.'

'I'm afraid not.' He was a kindly man, but said this with a stern expression, making sure I understood. 'This is very serious, Sergeant Sherwood. But hopefully we may be just in time.'

I was laid on a stretcher and carried to the barracks hospital. Fortunately for me, at that early stage, our doctors still had a few medical supplies left, so they were able to give me the proper treatment. But it was to be no easy recovery.

After about ten to twelve days of absolute agony, and virtually sleeping outside the hospital's lavatory door, I began to feel a little better.

'You'll be pleased to know,' smiled the medical officer, 'I've taken you off the critically ill list this morning.'

'Thank you sir.'

'You must thank your lucky stars that you are a strong, fit young man. Many soldiers would not have survived the stage of dysentery that you had reached when you came here.'

'I used to be a professional footballer,' I told him.

'Well, that undoubtedly gave you the stamina to beat this illness. You'll soon be feeling much better.'

'Thank you sir.'

'But you'll need a lot more time to regain your strength and make a full recovery.'

Sure enough, when I was discharged from the hospital and started getting around the camp again, I felt very weak and I tired easily. I had so little energy that I just sat or lay around, doing nothing. This wasn't like me at all. I don't remember a day of illness in my life, though I suppose I must have caught the odd thing when I was small. Not having enough of the right food didn't help and it took me a long time to regain anything like my former health and strength. A couple of my pals used to take me for a steady walk each evening, when they had finished their tasks. It was cooler then, so those walks helped me a lot.

As we walked, we chatted about our families and our lives before the war.

'You were a professional footballer, weren't you, Sarge?' asked a young gunner called Ray who I'd got to know at Changi. 'I always wanted to be a footballer, but I guess I wasn't good enough.'

'You're young enough to give it another go when we get home,' I said, always keen to encourage promising youngsters. 'You never know when something good might happen. I was just spotted by a scout, kicking a ball about in the park with my friends one day.'

'Bloody hell, Johnny,' said Bill. 'You get all the luck!'

'That's what my mother used to say,' I laughed. 'She was the one who first called me Lucky Johnny, and now everyone does back home.'

'Why was that, Sarge?'

'Well, I was always rather a scallywag when I was a nipper. I never did anything really bad, but I was the eldest boy in my family and I got myself into a bit of mischief now and then. I suppose I just pushed my luck.'

'What things did you do? Did you get into trouble?'

'Yes . . . and out of it as well,' I laughed.

'Didn't you tell me you once got in trouble with the police?' asked my pal Patrick.

'Yes, but only the once.'

'Did they put you in jail?' asked Ray.

'Not quite,' I laughed. 'I was only about thirteen or fourteen at the time.'

'Tell us what happened.'

'Well, I was a bit of a demon in those days, always fighting and getting into trouble. But on this particular occasion it didn't start out like that at all. I just went fishing in the Thames one evening with my pals, near Caversham Bridge. We didn't catch anything, so we stopped trying and started throwing stones in the water instead, then up into the air. Somehow, I managed to smash a light on the bridge and that fused all the other street lamps.'

'Did you scarper?'

'Yes, but a man from the boathouse saw what happened and came after us. He must have been a good runner because he caught me and took me back to the boathouse, where he rang for the police. When the policeman came, he took a statement from me, then drove me home in his police car.'

'What happened then?' asked Ray, quite excited at the thought.

'My parents asked him in and we all sat in the room behind the bar. I remember my dad and the policeman having a good talk and the policeman said he might have to charge me. But my dad talked him round and paid for the damage, so it was settled out of court.'

'That was lucky, Sarge.'

'Yes, that's what my mum said when the policeman left. "Lucky Johnny breathes again," she smiled, with a twinkle in her eyes. "But you'd better not use up all your luck – you might really need it one day." She was right. It was a close shave, and I made sure I never got caught again.'

'What was it like having so many brothers and sisters?' asked Ray. 'Your mum must have had a lot of cooking to do to feed you all!'

'You're right there,' I nodded, thinking of my poor mum slaving away all day to make sure we were clean and fed.

'Was she a good cook?'

'Yes, a marvellous cook. I often think of her Sunday roasts, and all the puddings and cakes, and . . .'

'Stop! You're making my mouth water too much, Johnny,' complained Patrick, laughing. 'Our miserable rations make me think about food too much as it is!'

'I can't bloody well stop thinking about it,' agreed Bill, holding his shrivelled tummy.

'I bet you miss her now.'

'Of course. What I'd give for even a crumb of her fruit cake.'

'Me too, Sarge,' nodded Ray.

'But I don't think I ever appreciated her enough in those days. We just took it for granted there would always be food for us. Like the time I was so hungry when I came in from football practice, just before bedtime, that I peeked into the pantry and saw a whole chicken my mum had roasted for dinner the next day. It looked delicious, so without a thought I ate both legs and part of the breast.'

'I bet that got you into trouble?'

'Not half! My dear mum worked hard all day in the kitchen to feed all eleven of us children, then she would count us all into bed and go to work in the bar every evening. She's a saint, but she doesn't miss a thing.'

'So what happened?'

'She asked us all next morning if we'd been in the pantry, but none of us owned up. Then she swung round to look straight at me. "You look well fed, son," she smiled. "So you won't be needing any dinner today, will you?" Well, I knew she knew. "Sorry Mum," I said. "You always say I'm a growing lad, and I just didn't think." She wagged her finger at me. "You're a rascal and no mistake," she said with a wink. "Lucky Johnny, that's you. Always charming your way out of trouble!" And the whole family has called me Lucky Johnny ever since.'

It was all going too well for me health-wise. As soon as I became fit enough to return to a more normal routine in the camp, I started to suffer from blackouts. I had sudden faints or collapses, when I would pass out on the ground and take a few minutes to come to again. I had no idea why this happened, but I'd seen a few of the other lads do something similar, so I thought perhaps I had caught another illness. These blackouts were sporadic but quite frequent at times, so they gave me a fright and I didn't wait so long to seek help this time.

'I keep having blackouts, Doc,' I said, and I explained how they happened and how often. 'Could it be an after-effect from the dysentery?'

'Not directly, Sergeant, though I think that might have depleted your body of some of its natural minerals and other things we all need.'

'So what do you think I've got?'

'I think the cause of your blackouts is more likely to be the same as for some of the other men. None of us are getting enough of the vitamins we need to keep our bodies healthy, so I believe it's a sign that you have a disease caused by deficiency. It could be beriberi. I don't have any medication for that, so the only cure would be to try and make sure you take any opportunity to balance your diet with green vegetables and fruits, but I know that is almost impossible here, so we'll have to keep an eye on you. Come and see me again if it gets worse.'

At about this time, feeling rather down in the dumps, I started to attend the occasional Church of England services that were held every other day in the Changi camp chapel. We had quite a charismatic padre at that time called Noel Duckworth and all the men liked him, so a lot of us went along.

Whether this did anything for me long term, I still don't know. But attending church seemed to help me deal with my depression in those early days and I suppose the singing lifted our spirits for a while.

3

Football at Havelock Road

May 1942

Even at this early stage, I looked a shadow of the young Johnny Sherwood, who only a few weeks earlier, on his Saturdays off from army duties, was playing professional football for Middlesbrough. But at least, despite the food shortages, I was now regaining some strength and feeling brighter.

Word went round Changi that one of the Japanese guards was going to stand at the top of the tower in the centre of the camp each evening and throw down tins of food to the prisoners. My pal Patrick was cock-a-hoop.

'Let's go and see if we can catch any,' he suggested, goading me on, though I didn't need any persuasion.

'You bet,' I said with a grin. 'I'm not called Lucky for nothing.'

Well, you can imagine. The first night there were about five to six hundred men and, no matter how high we jumped, we couldn't catch a thing. Undaunted, we went earlier the next evening to bag a better position and a miracle happened.

'I got one!' I yelled above the shouting.

'Me too!' Patrick mouthed.

We were unable to move for a few minutes, until the throwing had stopped and the outer groups had dispersed, most of them walking away with leaden feet, downhearted that they had nothing. We held our tins down, so as not to flaunt them, but when we got back to our billet we showed each other our prizes.

'Mine's bully-beef,' I crowed.

'And I've got jam!'

There was great excitement, as if we'd won the football pools. When we collected our meagre rations, an hour or two later, we shared our booty between us, stirring the bully-beef into our watery stew, and the jam into our rice to have as a sweet. A banquet by recent standards.

When we had first arrived at Changi camp, conditions were basic, but tolerable, as the Japs pretty much left us alone and allowed us some medical supplies as well as the limited food allocations. But now things changed and they seemed to become much more resentful and enjoyed being cruel to us.

I expect you've seen big Shire horses pulling carts. Well, the Japs began to use some of us prisoners in the same way as farmers would use horses. They had four-wheel tractors to deliver supplies and transport building materials or machinery around the camp. But now they could no longer get any petrol or diesel to fuel these tractors, so we became the horses to pull them, with ropes, hauling them along under the unrelenting sun. The slightest slope or bump in the ground aggravated our taut muscles, or what was left of them, and the slower we became the more furious the guards were, yelling and screaming at us. They didn't care how hard it was for us, and thought nothing of digging their rifle butts into our ribs or backs.

Our rations were cut again and we all began to feel weak. The lack of nourishment badly sapped our energy, so the harder we worked, the less we could do and the more the guards tormented us. Appalled at this state of affairs, and by now stronger again than many of my pals, I decided I had to get hold of more food from somewhere, though I had no idea where, and my only option was to try and barter what few belongings I had.

Two or three of the other men had the same idea as me, to try and break out of the camp at night, when there were only a couple of guards on duty. I suppose I must have realised this would be punishable if I was caught. After all, they had told us that anyone who tried to escape would be shot, and most of the prisoners were too anxious to chance it, but I didn't think twice. We desperately needed more food, so it was worth the risk. I just remembered my dear mother calling me Lucky Johnny and that carried me through.

At what seemed like a good moment, I sneaked out of my billet and, keeping in the shadows as much as possible, I ran light-footed towards the nearest stretch of barbed wire at the perimeter. Feeling my way along the ground, my eyes got used to the darkness and I found a section where there was less wire. This would be my exit route. It may seem strange, but it hadn't occurred to me to try to escape outright, as the whole island of Singapore was overrun with Japs and the people were terrorised almost as much as we were.

I got through the wire all right and made my way into the edge of town. As soon as they saw me, the friendly locals brought out their surplus foods and they even offered me money. I bartered a couple of items of clothing I had managed to keep with me for some eggs, fresh vegetables and fruit, and a few coins. Within the hour I was back in camp and hiding my treasures to share with my pals the next day. There was a little more food than we needed, so I let some of the other boys have that in exchange for their spare clothing or other belongings, which I could take outside next time to barter with. I did this trip a few times, gradually building myself up as I had lost about two stone by now. There were several others doing the same and I didn't hear of anyone being caught.

At this stage, the guards ordered various working parties, me included, to be taken into Singapore to help clear up all the debris. Well, as you can imagine, this was a welcome new opportunity to barter for extra food. Our camp rations were still very low, but I was now regaining some of the weight I had lost and some of my energy too, though I was still undernourished and hungry most of the time.

* * *

New orders came through at Changi camp that all fit men, about fourteen hundred of us, were to be moved to a new camp at Havelock Road, Singapore. This happened almost immediately and we were marched off to our new camp nearby. On arrival, we settled in very quickly and at once started to organise some sort of recreation for the men.

'Sergeant Sherwood,' said an officer who approached me. 'Weren't you a professional footballer?'

'Yes, that's right sir.'

'Who did you play for?' He sat down with me and seemed genuinely interested.

'I played for Reading and I went on the Corinthians world tour in '37.'

'Did you come to this part of the world, Sergeant?'

'Yes sir, we played several games in Singapore and somehow we won every match we played.'

'Well done, Sherwood.'

'After we came back from the world tour and docked at Southampton, I found out later that there were chaps from six of the top clubs waiting on the quay to sign me up, but I didn't know they were there and I just went straight home. Anyway, I wanted to stay with Reading, so I played for the Royals until the war started. That's when all the leagues were changed, sir, so that the top local clubs could play each other and save on fuel.'

'What did you do then?'

'I was posted to Middlesbrough as the battery PE instructor.'

'Did you get to play any football up there?'

'Yes, I was asked to organise some teams from different batteries to play each other. My team got to the final at Middlesbrough's ground, Ayresome Park. Somebody must have seen me play, as the next day the manager at Middlesbrough Football Club put in an official request for me to play for his club on Saturdays, until I was posted overseas.'

'That worked out very well, didn't it?'

BRITISH ARMY PHYSICAL TRAINING INSTRUCTOR 1941

Sergeant Johnny Sherwood, centre, army PE instructor, 1941.
From Johnny's scrapbook.

'Yes, very well indeed, sir. Major Bullock gave me permission.
It was a great thing for me and my pals because I was allowed to
be paid one pound and ten shillings for each match. I pooled it
with the men and it bought us a few beers on Saturday nights, and
a night or two in the week as well.'

'Well done, Sergeant. I know the war office wanted the football
to continue in order to keep up morale.'

'Yes sir. Thank you sir.'

He looked thoughtful for a moment. 'Now, I wonder whether
you could do an even more important morale-raising job for us
here?'

'What's that sir? I'll help if I can.'

'I know you were very ill a while ago, but you look well recovered. Do you feel strong enough for a challenge?'

'I always like a challenge sir,' I smiled.

'Good, that's the ticket. Now, what I have in mind is this. We
have quite a bit of spare ground in this new camp, so I thought

that if we could clear it well enough we could try to make a football pitch of sorts. What do you think?'

'What do I think?' I could not conceal my excitement at the thought of it. 'I think it's a grand idea, sir. When can we start?'

'Straightaway, Sergeant. As well as leading the clear-up detail, I want you to organise the fit men into teams and play some games on the new pitch. The only problem is getting hold of a ball.'

'That's no problem at all, sir,' I grinned. 'I have a ball with me, hidden in my kit.'

'I knew I'd got the right man,' he said, patting me on the shoulder.

So that was it. I had a dozen light-sick men (ill but mobile) allotted to work with me every day, and within a couple of weeks we had completed our task, and made goalposts as well. The fittest men now started to play football in the evenings, including young Ray, who soon showed his talent. It felt amazing to be playing again and I enjoyed sorting out who should play and in what position, giving everyone that wanted to a turn.

Meanwhile, working parties had started to march into Singapore to help clear the place up. While they were there they met with British POWs from another camp nearby called River Valley.

We all got one day off, the same day every ten days, so we arranged with the lads at River Valley camp to play a match against each other. The Japs gave permission and it was something that both camps looked forward to. It certainly boosted the morale of the boys, whether they played or just watched the game.

It was a happy coincidence that at River Valley camp there was another pro-footballer called Albert Hall, who used to play for Tottenham Hotspur FC. So we had one professional on each side.

These matches cheered us all up no end and they continued for a while, every time we had a day off.

* * *

		THE POLYTECHNIC		
Branch Offices BRADFORD, 39 Well Street BRISTOL 67ᵗʰ Park Street		TOURING ASSOCIATION LTD 309 REGENT STREET, LONDON, W.I		Branch Offices MANCHESTER Royal Exchange LUCERNE Polytechnic Chalets

TELEGRAMS: POLYTOURS, WESDO, LONDON
TELEPHONES: MAYFAIR 8100 (8 LINES)

No. B/HR/13

27th September, 1937.

SPECIAL ITINERARY FOR
THE ISLINGTON CORINTHIANS FOOTBALL CLUB
WORLD TOUR 1937/1938.

DATE		PLACE, HOTEL, EXCURSIONS, ETC.	TIME
October 4th	dep.	LONDON (Liverpool Street Station)	9.30
		Reserved seats on train	
	arr.	HARWICH (Parkeston Quay)	10.55
		British passport examination	
	dep.	HARWICH (Parkeston Quay)	11.00
		Lunch on steamer	
	arr.	FLUSHING (Quay)	17.00
		Dutch passport & customs examination	
	dep.	FLUSHING	17.38
		Reserved seats on train	
	arr.	THE HAGUE H.S.M.	20.04
		Transfer of passengers and hand luggage between station and Grand Hotel Victoria, 16 Spuistraat.	
		Two nights' hotel accommodation at the GRAND HOTEL VICTORIA commencing with dinner on arrival and terminating after breakfast on departure.	
October 5th		Evening Match at The Hague	
October 6th		Transfer of passengers and hand luggage from Hotel to Station	
	dep. arr.	THE HAGUE H.S.M. AMSTERDAM C.S.	11.26 12.14
		Programme of Matches and hotel accommodation to be arranged locally.	

The first page of the itinerary for the Islington
Corinthians world tour, 1937–38.

The numbers of sick men began to increase and the guards did not like this at all. They demanded so many men each morning to go into Singapore and work. We all had to be on parade at 7 a.m.

I shall never forget my first journey out of Havelock Road on one of these working parties. The Japs unlocked the gates and marched us through. Right outside the gates, we were shocked beyond belief at the sight of five civilians' heads, decapitated and hoisted on the spiked railings for all of us to see. The blood was still running down the railings and along the pavement beneath each head. This death parade had the desired impression on us. I shuddered just to look at them. To make sure we understood why they were there, the Japs had written a caption in English under each head with whatever their trumped-up charge was supposed to be. One said 'This man was a thief.' Another read 'This man tried to give food to the prisoners.' Each one was clearly calculated to shock us. But the little bastards didn't realise it would take more than that to break our morale.

As we marched on, the Japanese interpreter stopped us again to speak to us all.

'You must not talk to others while you work. If you talk, we catch you and punish you.' Well, that was clear enough. When the Japs did catch one man talking, later that day, they made us all stop and watch as they made him hold a block of stone above his head at arms' stretch. He had to march back to camp with us like that, screwing up every sinew in his body to try and maintain that hold. When we finally got back to camp and his arms sagged with the effort, the guards laid into him with a vengeance, hitting him repeatedly with everything they could find, till he dropped to the ground, where they still continued to kick him with their heavy boots.

We were getting no extra food coming into the camp now and we had precious little nourishment from our daily rations of watery stew, which had almost nothing in it, and the lowest grade of rice. We were all malnourished and beginning to suffer from a number of complaints through vitamin deficiencies. Nearly everyone in the camp now had beriberi. This was a condition that caused severe swelling, especially in our legs. I could press my thumb right in and its indentation would remain for some time afterwards when I took it away.

Another thing we all had to deal with on a daily basis was chronic diarrhoea. Most of us had to go to the latrines at least ten times a day, which made us very weak and dehydrated.

The boys at River Valley camp were just the same and our games became slower as we grew weaker every match and had to have lots of rests in between. The medical officers at both camps were increasingly concerned about our health. In fact, our doc came to see me after the match was over one day. He looked me up and down with a stern expression.

'You've lost a lot of weight again, Sergeant. Are you still having those blackouts you told me about?'

'Not often, sir, only now and then.' I looked down at my skinny frame. I realised that I barely had the stamina to play for ten minutes these days.

'You won't like this, Sherwood, but it's an order.'

'Yes sir?' I dreaded what he was going to say.

'You're not in a fit state to play football for more than a few minutes at a time and if you continue like this, malnourished and riddled with beriberi, you are in effect committing suicide. We have no medicines to help you now, so I'm sorry, but I must order you to stop playing football.'

'Please sir, don't ban me altogether. I could just start the match off next time and let one of the lads take over,' I pleaded, but I could tell from his face he wouldn't budge.

'If I find you on this football pitch again' – he shook his head – 'I will have you court-martialled, and any charges will be confirmed when this war is over.' He paused. 'I'm sorry, but there it is. My first priority is to keep you alive.' He turned and walked away.

You can imagine how wretched I felt. I could have cried.

4

'Cattle-Trucks' to Thailand

August 1942

It was sweltering mid-summer 1942 and we were now getting one or two deaths in the camp every day, which was only to be expected in our current situation. All 'fit' men were made to work and, as most of us were suffering from one thing or another, it was hard going. Only those men who worked were allotted any food, so our measly rations now had to be reduced still further to be shared with the sick.

We had to work ten hours a day, and all we could come back to camp for was usually a bowl of inferior-quality rice with some watery pumpkin stew, or very occasionally a piece of hard, dried fish.

When we got back from a day's work, the weaker men usually just collapsed on to their lice-infested sleeping platforms, where we all slept side by side. It was now going to be the survival of the fittest.

The only thing that we got a real kick out of was talking about our homes and our families. It gave us something to live for, so it was very important to keep the lads talking. No matter how tired we were, I would sometimes start off a conversation, just to get everyone going.

'Did I ever tell you I married a beauty queen?'

'Pull the other one, Sarge,' said one of the boys, while Patrick threw a rag at me and Bill did a wolf-whistle, which must have hurt with his cracked lips.

'It's true,' I insisted. 'She was Miss Reading in 1936.'

'Ooh, get you, Mr Reading,' joked somebody from the darkness.

'What does she look like, Sarge?' asked Ray.

'Beautiful, of course,' I said. 'Especially her eyes. But it's not just how she looks.'

'What is it then? Or can we guess?' grinned Bill.

'Well, that too, of course,' I laughed. 'But one of the best things is that we're friends as well as married. We talk a lot and share everything.'

'You're a lucky feller!'

'Yes, I know. And that's what keeps me going.'

'Well, my wife's probably got her hands full with our four nippers,' someone said. And our tiredness seemed to fade as we talked and listened, helping each other to keep our hopes alive.

During our stay at Havelock Road camp, the officers tried to put on activities in the evenings to raise the men's morale. I was asked to give talks on my 'famous' football world tour. I talked to the officers as well as the boys and I know they all enjoyed hearing about my experiences, including the King of Egypt's practical joke on us, meeting Charles Laughton and David Niven in Hollywood, going on Opium Den raids with the Hong Kong police and being attacked by the British army in the Khyber Pass. It all took their minds off things for a while and made them laugh. For a few moments everyone stopped thinking only of England and their loved ones at home.

I remember very clearly one evening, when I was talking to a hut full of officers and got on to the Malaya and Singapore part of my story. I began to tell them about our social life in Singapore, when during the days and nights we were allowed to go sightseeing, meeting VIPs and attending parties laid on for us.

Well, quite casually, I happened to mention how friendly I had become with a beautiful Eurasian schoolteacher, whose father was British.

32

Johnny, second from left, in Malaya during the Islington
Corinthians world tour, January 1938. From Johnny's scrapbook.

'This lovely girl's name was Eileen, and she used to take me on
sightseeing trips all over the island in her car. We spent some wonderful evenings together,' I told the officers, much to their approval.

'She was an angel.' I smiled at the memory of her sweet face.
'She even took me to her school, where she introduced me to her
fellow teachers. Then she took me to her classroom to meet the
children she taught.' I paused to think. 'I still remember the name
of her class. It was Nelson.' There was a cheer from the back and
a few laughs.

'Go on, Sergeant,' another officer encouraged me.

'Well, by now we had become really close. It broke her heart
when I told her it was time for us to leave for the next place on our
football schedule.'

I continued my talk about other highlights of our ninety-five-match world tour, and at the end several of the officers came up to speak to me. I noticed one of them hanging back, waiting till the others had all gone and I was picking up my notes, ready to leave.

'I wanted to talk with you in private,' he said.

'Yes, of course, sir,' I nodded.

He leant forward and shook me by the hand and began his story. 'That beautiful girl you were talking about . . .'

'Yes, sir?'

'You won't believe this, Sergeant. That beautiful girl called Eileen . . . well, she is now my wife.'

'Really?' It seemed unbelievable. What a coincidence that would be, but surely not? 'Are you certain it's the same Eileen?' I asked in astonishment, thanking God that I'd only said good things about her, and nothing to upset him.

'Yes, I met and married her before the war. She told me all about you – what your name was and everything, so I'm sure you must be the same Johnny Sherwood.'

'Gosh, sir. That's amazing.'

'Yes,' he laughed. 'If only we could tell her, eh?'

Things seemed bad to us, imprisoned in Singapore, but we battled on, working and suffering with only our memories and dreams to console us. It gave us a lot of hope, just talking about home and our precious families. Many of us still had tattered photos of our wives and sweethearts that we showed each other proudly, talking about them, sharing our stories.

One evening, after we had returned from our work at the Singapore docks, we cleaned ourselves up as best we could and began to line up as usual for our paltry rations of rice and stew – jungle stew we called it. It was now impossible to get any extra food, so we were all very hungry and every grain of rice counted. There were three men in front of me. The POW at the front collected his rice and stew and hesitated, standing his ground. There was a painful tension in the air as we waited to see what would happen.

Suddenly he let rip at the poor cookhouse worker.

'You gave that man in front of me much more rice than you gave to me! I want the same as him.' His face turned red and I could see a muscle throbbing in his neck. 'Give me more rice, or I'll do you in,' he yelled.

'What are you on about?' argued the cookhouse worker, one of our own men – a cockney by the sound of him. You had exactly the same as everyone else.'

'No I didn't. You short-changed me.'

'No, mate, I'm sure I didn't. Now move on there and let the rest of 'em get their food.'

'You're a cheat,' accused the angry POW. 'I'm not moving anywhere till you give me the same as him.'

'Get out of it,' called someone behind me. 'We want our food too.'

'You see what you've done,' said the cookhouse worker. 'Now, take your rations and clear off, mate.' He leant across and gave him a shove to move him on his way.

'Don't you bloody well shove me! Who do you think you are?' He aimed a punch that started an all-out fight between them, with one or two of the lads goading them on, but most of us watched this terrible sight in horror. They were both so thin and weak, they could ill afford to waste their energy on a stupid brawl like this. After a short while, we managed to separate them, but not before they were both covered in blood and feeling very sorry for themselves. It was sad and frustrating to see something like this happen, but please remember that we were all suffering from continuous hunger, which saps a man's sense of decency, so anything could happen over the suspected loss of a grain or two of rice.

* * *

Now the Japs sprang another surprise on us. They got us all on parade and handed out pieces of paper.

'You sign forms,' shouted the interpreter.

We all took our forms away and read what they were about.

'Here, Sarge, have you read this yet?' asked one of my lads. 'It says we promise not to try and escape!'

'Not at any time,' added another.

'We can't sign that, can we?' asked the first lad, with an anxious expression.

'No, you're right. We can't sign anything like this, no matter what the words say. We're British soldiers and we have a duty to try to escape if any sensible chance comes our way. I'll check it with the lieutenant, but I'm sure he'll agree with us.' And that is what I did.

'You're damned right,' he said. 'The CO has given us orders to make sure that nobody signs.'

So that was it. We all refused and nothing happened for a few days.

After a week, we all had to gather on the parade ground again. We knew it wouldn't be pleasant.

'You no sign forms,' shouted the interpreter in his angry staccato voice. 'You have less food. No medicines.'

The message was clear enough. Half starved already, this was a bad blow to us, but we were told again not to sign, while our officers tried to work something out. We were all frightened how we would cope. With no medicines and almost no food, it wouldn't take more than a day or two for the deaths to escalate.

Finally the decision came through and I had to pass it on to the lads.

'We've been ordered to sign these forms, under great duress,' I explained.

'What does that mean, Sarge?'

'Apparently, the rules of war say we can only sign away our rights under great duress, which means if they force us against our wishes.'

'But, Sarge, why do we have to sign it now?'

'It's orders. We have no choice.'

'This "under duress" – doesn't that mean we have to sign it but we don't have to obey it?'

'That's right,' I replied. 'Our officers have tried everything to get the Japs to change their minds, but they refuse to budge on this one. If we don't sign, the sick will all die first, and with half-rations of almost nothing we will all follow them pretty quickly. So what choice do we have, boys? I don't like it any more than you all do, but our first duty must be to survive. That means we have to sign.'

So, with heavy hearts, that is what we did, in the knowledge that saving our lives was even more important than escaping. But it nearly choked me.

After we had eaten our stew one evening, we were ordered to go on parade to hear an announcement.

'All fittest men,' began the Japanese interpreter. 'You be moved soon to camp in Thailand where you do light work and plenty food for you.'

'Do you think this is real?' asked Bill.

'It could be,' I shrugged. 'Who can tell? Maybe we'll be moved, but I'm not sure I can quite believe the light work bit, or that we'll get plenty of food, though God knows we need it.'

'You can say that again!'

'Let's hope it's all true.'

Sure enough, in early September 1942, we were ordered to assemble and the Japs picked out all the men who they thought were the fittest and ordered us to stand by, ready to leave for the camp in Thailand.

We prepared ourselves in high spirits for what we presumed would be a move for the better. Surely it couldn't be any worse than Singapore?

Meanwhile, although half starved, our officers were somehow

managing to smuggle in a few medical supplies to help our sick men for a while. It really cheered us up to know that there were so many pro-British natives in Singapore. It was the local civilians who found ways to help us, but they were taking horrible risks to get these medicines and other supplies into camp. If they had been caught it would most likely have resulted in their deaths. Their courage did not go unnoticed by us and I know that many lives were saved by their ingenuity.

I remember a game the guards used to play, while we were waiting to move on. They made a circle on the ground, about six feet in diameter, and one would challenge the other to a match. The object was to wrestle the other man out of the ring, with lots of other guards looking on. They used to get themselves really hysterical over this game. They loved winning and simply hated to lose, so some of our fitter men saw a way to cash in on these games.

You see, they loved to show us how superior they were to us, although I know that some of our men, especially the Aussies, could have slaughtered them. A POW would simply go into the circle with a guard, play around for a short while, then let the Jap throw him out. We used to make it look good, of course, and these guards screamed with delight when our man was thrown out. They were so delighted they had beaten us that they used to give us a couple of Japanese cigarettes or a little of their food.

Quite a few of us did ourselves a bit of good by this clever acting. I shall always remember one big Australian who really hated the guards. He strode into the circle and threw them all out, one after the other. The guards all got into a filthy temper. Had it not been for the fact that a couple of his Aussie pals made him lose after that, I'm sure he would have been killed. But it was good while it lasted, just to see the Nips humiliated for a change.

By now, we were learning a few Japanese words. I wanted to understand as much as I could of the language, so I made a point of it, as I thought maybe it would stand me in good stead. Of course the first words we worked out were swear-words, but I did manage to pick up some useful words too, like *benjo* for toilet and *mishi* for food. *Nunda* meant 'what do you want?' and *demi-demi* meant something was very bad. We all had to learn the numbers for when we were ordered to count ourselves off in the line. *Itchi, nee, san* was 'one, two, three'.

Shortly before we were due to leave for Thailand, I was working on the outskirts of the city one day when I noticed some guards at bayonet practice, or perhaps they were using swords, in a field some distance away from the road. I couldn't see them very clearly, but I could hear them screaming and yelling at the tops of their voices as they ran towards figures tied to a series of posts. At first I assumed they were dummies, but then I realised they were trying to move and the true horror of the situation struck me. I retched as the screaming continued, knowing that there was nothing I could do to save these poor people from their terrifying fate. It was bloody awful. I suppose we were lucky it was not us being brutalised in that way, but what's the difference? These poor human beings, whose lives were just as important as ours . . . how could any man do this to another, whatever their nationality? How could such a horrific thing happen in this modern world of ours? No wonder the hatred began to burn inside us POWs when we witnessed such terrible events.

When it was time to leave Havelock Road, in September 1942, we were ready and optimistic about our future, but sad to be leaving so many sick men behind. What happened to them, I don't know. I never saw any of them again, but please God they didn't suffer and die.

After a few farewells and handshakes, the fittest of us formed up and marched out of camp singing 'Rule Britannia', followed by 'Roll out the Barrel'. When we arrived at the Singapore railway station, we lined up on the platform to hear the interpreter speak.

'You all go on train,' he shouted, trying to make himself heard to so many of us against the sounds of the station. 'Train is coming soon. But first you have new guards.'

Through the entrance to the platform came a lot of pompous-looking little men in different uniforms.

'They from Korea,' explained the interpreter. 'They look after you now.'

These new guards immediately set about prodding us and snarling at anyone out of line. This wasn't a promising start.

Within an hour a train pulled into the station, but it was only pulling what looked like metal cattle-trucks so we took no notice. As it came to a halt, we had a rude awakening. We were counted into batches of about fifty men, then loaded into these steel box-trucks, shoulder to shoulder. It was bloody awful. Most of us were already suffering from malnutrition, beriberi and various degrees of dysentery, so we knew that a journey in intense heat and under these conditions could only result in death for at least some of us.

In this way, we began our journey into the unknown. It was unbearable. The scorching sun made the steel walls of our truck burning to the touch, and there were far too many of us in a truck for comfort.

After travelling for about five hours, men began to pass out and, being packed so tightly together in these trucks, it was almost impossible to fall to the floor, let alone sit down. Anyone who did manage it was at risk of suffocating.

Some men couldn't help themselves and urinated in the trucks. Others had almost constant diarrhoea. By this time, many of us were in a terrible state and the stench had become intolerable.

One man died in our truck and on our first stop some of us were allowed to carry him to a room at the station, where we had to leave his body. We were allowed to relieve ourselves and we each collected a small ball of rice and a hard piece of dried, salted fish, together with a bowl of smelly water they called stew.

After about half an hour, we were herded back into our trucks like animals, and with the heat, the smell, and them now being full of flies, our plight was even worse than before – awful; not fit for humans. Once we set off again, men started to pass out, really ill, and our officers were getting no better treatment than us. We were helpless to do anything for those who fell sick, and we had no medical supplies with us at all.

Allied POWs beside their train, one of the rare stops on the long journey to Ban Pong, Thailand. Approximately fifty men were crammed into each stifling truck.

During our first stop, our new Korean guards had told us that when we arrived in Thailand, at a place called Ban Pong, there would be plenty of food and medical supplies for us. But now we suspected they were lying.

5

Ban Pong and the Jungle Marches

September 1942

After a nightmare journey lasting five days, we were emptied out of our trucks, gasping for air on the earthen platform of Ban Pong station, a simple bamboo hut covered with atap leaves for a roof. We were herded like cattle and made to march as well as we could manage along the dirt track, through the little town of Ban Pong, past the colourful market traders and the groups of yellow-robed Buddhist monks. On out of the town again we went, in a long straggly, staggering line, towards the camp beyond, with our guards constantly poking our weaker men with their rifles or bamboo sticks. Finally we reached Ban Pong camp, where the Japs were waiting for us.

'You rest here,' said a little Japanese guard in a high-pitched voice as he poked us into line, going through the camp gates.

'Do you think they'll have a swimming pool, Sarge?' whispered the lad next to me, with a grin.

'And a massage parlour?' smirked another.

'Just a regular feather-bed will do me,' I sighed, trying to remember the luxury of a good night's sleep.

To be honest, we were so exhausted from our trip that we couldn't have done anything else but rest.

Half dead with hunger, dehydration and dysentery, and a lot of other problems too, we took our sickest men to the hospital hut that had been set aside for them. To our great surprise, the Japanese had supplied the camp hospital with a few pills and some medical equipment.

* * *

While we were at Ban Pong, the rainy season started. I had no idea it could rain so much. It rained all day and all night, pouring through every gap in our atap-thatched roof, soaking everything, us included. The whole camp turned into a swamp of mud and excreta that we had to walk through to get anywhere. Of course all this was a heaven for flies, especially mosquitoes, and boy, didn't we know it?

After two days' rest, we were called on parade and the guards picked out the fittest men. I was astonished to be included. I had probably been one of the fittest men in England before the war, but I didn't feel anything like fit now.

'You stand by,' began the interpreter. 'You go on little march.'

'How long is little, Sarge?' whispered Ray. 'I can't march even half a mile in this state.'

'Me neither,' I replied. None of us was strong enough to walk far. 'But I reckon they have other ideas.' I was right, but they kept their plan to themselves.

As we prepared to leave, there was an incident that shocked me to the core. Two men were being beaten up by a group of vicious Korean guards for some minor misdemeanour. I had no idea what. I remember the beating very clearly though, because we were forced to watch the action. Wretchedly, we stood there, desperate to stop the pounding these men received, but unable to intervene for fear of even worse retaliation, for them and for us.

The guards were being goaded and whipped up into a frenzy by a *gunso*, a sergeant in the Japanese army, who stood at the end of the circle, shouting and screaming at them. The more hysterically he yelled and threw his arms about, the fiercer the beating became. It was horrific to watch our lads being lashed to a pulp like that. My helplessness to prevent this brutality was a desperate pressure that weighed me down.

If only looks could kill, I would have cut down that *gunso*, but as I stared with loathing at his screwed-up face, I had a strange feeling of recognition. He definitely looked familiar to me, but how could that be? I couldn't think when or where, but I was absolutely certain that we had met before.

I went to bed that night on my bug-infested bamboo sleeping platform, racking my brains to try and think where I could have met that Japanese *gunso* before. As I began to drift off to sleep, it suddenly struck me. I sat upright with shock. The tyrant was one of the Japanese football team I had met and played against in Yokohama, on our 1938 world football tour. No, I thought. It couldn't possibly be the same man. I must be mistaken. But when I saw the split-minded devil again the next morning, I was convinced. It was more than a million-to-one chance, but it was true. I could hardly believe that the player I remembered as a man of the utmost grace and courtesy had turned into this sadistic monster.

I considered, for a moment, going over to introduce myself to him, but decided against it. I didn't know which way he would take it if I reminded him of those pre-war days, when we were equals in the friendly rivalry of a football match. That was another world. If I spoke to him about it now . . . well, that could have been my lot.

Here we go again, I thought. Unwell and unkempt, we 'fit' men were a sorry sight as we bundled up our flimsy rags and lined up to march out of what we later realised was the relative haven of Ban Pong camp into the most terrifying ordeal any of us had ever encountered. We were, at that point, ignorant of our fate, and the guards were indifferent, joking among themselves as they poked us into a tidier line.

When we set out that day, frail as we ourselves were, we knew we were leaving behind us some very sick men. I have often wondered what their fate was. All I know is I never saw any of them again.

Right from the start, the guards urged us on at an impossible pace, sticking their rifle butts into us if we lagged behind for a moment. The paths turned into streams in the pouring rain and we didn't have the strength to march even two or three miles, let alone the distance the Japs had in store for us. But they kept it to themselves, the cunning swine.

At the end of that first day, as we collapsed to the wet ground, we were instructed to rest and given a bowl each of low-grade rice and watery pumpkin stew, completely lacking in any nutrition or vitamins. This filthy muck was better than nothing, but only just, and when we had finished it we lay flat on the jungle floor, out in the open and in the sweltering heat, prey to all the millions of insects that were drawn towards us.

I looked at my own emaciated body and at the men lying all around me, our bones poking through our wrinkled skin, and I remember thinking how difficult it would have been for any of our loved ones to recognise us. Would we survive to see them again, I wondered, as I wrapped my lousy rag around myself and fell into the deep sleep of exhaustion.

The guards had us awake again at dawn the next morning and gave us a few spoonfuls of rice and a cup of weak tea, without sugar, milk or nourishment. With nothing in our stomachs, we set off again on our journey through the almost impenetrable jungle, keeping as near as we could to the river Kwai. As some of our lads began to drop behind, the guards knocked them about mercilessly, trying to make them keep up. They were wasting their time. These wretched men had no energy left. They could no longer fight their weary battles against sickness and exhaustion.

'Leave them alone,' I pleaded, and was rewarded with a sharp dig in my ribs from a Jap's rifle butt.

'No talk!' he shrieked at me.

As the stronger POWs at the rear of the main group, we tried our best to help these poor lads keep up, some men carrying their packs while others of us put our arms round their emaciated bodies to help them along. All the time the guards jabbed at us, shouting 'Speedo-speedo'. We tried all we could, but it was hopeless. The guards allowed us no leeway and in the end we were forced to leave our comrades behind where they lay on the jungle track, probably dying a slow, distressing death. We never found out what happened to them, or their bodies. God only knows. I tried not to think about it, but their desperate faces haunted me for days.

On and on we trudged, day after wretched day, hacking our way through the dense, virgin jungles of Thailand, until we arrived at a place the guards called Kenburi. This turned out to be our first destination. It was a fairly large camp and we were sorted out into the sick on one side of the camp and the semi-fit on the other. Here they let us rest for a few days, which seemed like heaven to our exhausted bodies.

On the third or fourth day at Kenburi camp, the Kempi-Tai, Japanese police, arrived with a vengeance. Believe me, they were heartless and brutal. They knocked us around as they searched our small bundles of kit for any items that could make a wireless set, or for any small arms or ammunition, as if we could have got that far without them being found.

When they discovered nothing, they took two of our officers away to another part of the camp, where they beat them up, not just once but over and over again. Whether the Kempi-Tai were still searching for something, or maybe trying to obtain information from them, we never found out, because the following morning we were ordered to leave on the next stage of our journey.

'You cowards will build railway,' screeched the interpreter, under the beady eyes of the camp commandant. He pointed at us. 'You build railway join Siam and Burma,' he continued, using the common name for Thailand in those days. 'You build Japan army railway.'

'Come on boys,' I said as we lined up to leave the camp. 'Let's show them what we're made of.'

'But, Sarge,' replied the corporal. 'That's against the rules ain't it? We don't have to build a railway for their army, do we?'

'Bloody criminal if you ask me,' mumbled another lad under his breath.

'I don't think they have the same rule-book as we do,' I shrugged. 'The most important thing for us is survival. If we don't do what they say—'

'OK, Sarge,' interrupted the corporal. 'I get the picture, but it's all wrong ain't it? We shouldn't be made to do anything to help the enemy.'

'Well said,' I nodded. 'But we have no option. We work or we die.'

Just then the guards jabbed us into action. 'You leave kit here,' shouted one of them. 'We bring to next camp.'

'I bet they don't!' moaned Bill. 'They're bloody liars, the lot of them.'

So we reluctantly piled up our bags, smuggling just a few things out of them to tuck into the rags we wore, and marched out through the gate, leaving most of our few belongings behind us.

As the morning wore on and our marching turned to staggering, the guards forced us forward, deeper and deeper into the jungle, where the rudimentary path cut through for us by native labour became a quagmire in the constant rain of the monsoon season. Softer and squelchier it became with every step, until we had to drag our weary feet out of the oozing mud.

As before, some of our men could not be forced on any further and fell away, dropping in their tracks and left behind, at the mercies of the unbearable heat and the jungle wildlife. I shall never forget their sunken eyes and pleading faces, tearing out our hearts as we trudged away.

Every step was a trial of what little strength we could still muster, with the interpreter goading us on.

'You nearly there.'

Miles more and several hours later, we did finally reach a clearing, which was to be our camp for the night. Once again, we dropped to the ground with exhaustion and gulped down a lump of dried fish, dipped in black tea with a few small spoonfuls of rice. I remember finding the driest spot I could, between the roots of a tree, rolling myself in my filthy blanket and fighting my fears until I fell asleep.

Next morning, after the usual meagre breakfast, we were herded off again to shouts of 'Speedo-speedo'. We had to leave behind some very sick men in that makeshift camp.

'We look after them,' said the Japanese interpreter when I asked him.

I knew as well as he did that medical supplies were non-existent and I doubted that any of the guards cared, so we could all imagine how hard it was going to be for the lads we left behind.

By this stage, we were so weak that we moved forward very slowly. The guards prodded the slowest men repeatedly with their bayonets, and we knew these were not empty threats, but all this bullying and driving by our persecutors could not move us faster. Our energy was badly drained and we looked like a bunch of skeletons.

As the day wore on, once again our lads were dropping down, weak and exhausted, some of them with malaria and others with dysentery. We were all suffering. After endless days and nights of struggle through this jungle in the torrid heat, our pitiful party reached the banks of the river Kwai, where six or seven barges were moored, waiting for us. We almost fell into these barges, cramped together on the decks, our bones sticking into each other or into the hard, wet wood, making it impossible to find any comfort.

As I tried to sleep that night, under the stars instead of the dense jungle canopy, with the murky waters lapping against the sides of our barge, all kinds of awful things ran through my mind. *Johnny my boy, you will never make it*, I said to myself. But then I thought about all the other poor men who had been left behind, men in a worse state than I was. This seemed to steel my resolve. *Keep going*, I encouraged myself. *Maybe when we get to our final destination we will be looked after all right*. Of course, I could see through our cruel guards' lies, but I didn't allow myself to dwell on that as I drifted off to sleep.

49

6

Punishment at Tarso

October 1942

Over the next few days, we were allowed some glorious, though uncomfortable rest as the barges took us up-river to a clearing where there were a few bamboo huts. These huts had been newly built by Thai civilians who had been lured into working for the Japanese by vain promises of plenty of food and money. Of course, this proved to be their undoing as they were treated just as badly as we were. Indeed, cutting their way into virgin jungle, they were bitten by snakes and disease was rife among them, so they died like flies. It was an appalling waste of life.

This camp was called Tarso and our first job there was to build more huts to sleep in. Before moving into them, we had to bed down on the floor of the clearing, maybe two or three hundred of us. At this time I made friends with a lad called Geordie Ashbridge, who turned out to be a good pal to me. This boy was full of courage. He really hated our guards with a vengeance.

As I lay down to sleep that first night at Tarso, I looked up at the stars twinkling in the clear sky and wondered whether Christine could see those same stars. But then I realised we were hours apart and thousands of miles away, so it was still daytime in England, and at night her starscape would be different to mine. But I took some comfort from the fact that she might sometimes look up at the night sky from our bedroom window in Reading and think of me.

The following night, after a day's hard labour, we settled down to sleep in this clearing. Suddenly, to our complete surprise, our possessions were brought up from the river and dumped in the middle of our clearing. We wearily leant up on our elbows, thinking we would have to go and sort them out straightaway, but one of the guards made signs at us to lie down.

'Tomorrow, tomorrow,' he said.

So we took him at his word and went to sleep. The next thing I knew was a rough awakening by two guards at about three o'clock in the morning, well before dawn. They screamed their heads off and prodded Geordie and me to get up. In our bleary state, we wondered what the hell was going on, but we very soon found out.

The guards held up a kit-bag each. 'You stole,' shrieked one of them at me.

'No I didn't,' I replied; then more slowly and clearly, 'I no stole.'

'You stole! You stole bags,' shouted the two guards, both looking straight at me.

'Why you stole?' asked one of them.

'I NO stole,' I repeated.

At this, they both lunged forward, lifted me up from the ground, gripped my arms tightly and marched me across the clearing. By now, several of the lads had been woken and were shouting their indignation on my behalf, knowing that nobody had touched the bags before we slept.

Above all the voices, I heard Geordie's strong Newcastle accent bellowing out. 'Leave him alone, you bastards!'

I expected him to be punished for his loyalty. Fortunately, I don't think the guards heard it, or perhaps they didn't understand, as they ignored him. I was the one they had singled out with this trumped-up accusation and I was the one they were going to make suffer for it. They were probably in need of some entertainment, as they saw it.

I was marched about fifty yards away to the guardroom, where a group of Japs and Koreans gave me a good beating up with bamboo sticks, ripping my flesh with every strike. I lost count of how many as I struggled to stay silent. I knew any noise I made would provoke an even greater frenzy of physical abuse.

I don't know how long this punishment lasted, but finally they tired themselves out and I crumpled into a bloody heap on the ground. The two guards stood over me, their steel-tipped boots only a couple of inches from my head. They made it clear to me, in no uncertain terms, that I would be beaten up every day until I admitted I stole the kit-bags.

Of course, I knew I hadn't stolen them and wondered through the fuzz in my brain how I could get out of this. They tried to persuade me, with a few words and a lot of wild gesticulation, that all I had to do was own up and they would stop. But I couldn't own up to something I hadn't done. And anyway, I suspected that if I did take the easy route and owned up to it, they'd almost certainly break their word and punish me even more for stealing. I'd already seen what they were capable of, so I refused, which made them livid.

'You tell you took bag,' one of them yelled, pushing his face into mine.

I looked straight back at him, but said nothing.

They yanked me to my feet and continued their beating with renewed vigour. It was a no-win situation, so I just had to try to stand and take it. The beating went on and on that night, until finally they wore themselves out. I was in a terrible mess, with blood all over me from my open wounds, and the more I pleaded my innocence the more they beat me.

They threw me into a pen for the rest of the night. This pen was so small I couldn't stand or lie down straight, but I was in such a distressed state that I craved only to be transported away from this horror, to sleep.

The guards' brutal treatment went on several times a day, for the next three days, but no way was I going to admit to a crime I hadn't committed, even though I was pretty senseless by the end of some of those beatings. Boy, was I obstinate, or maybe foolish, but the more they beat me up, the more determined I was to maintain my innocence. It was only later that I realised how easily that could have been the end of me.

I burnt with pain all over, covered in a pulpy mess of wounds and bruises, and felt desperately weak, having had hardly any food or water throughout that time and precious little rest.

I was at my lowest ebb, desperate for this to end and semi-delirious, when a new Japanese interpreter came into our camp. When he came to the guardroom, he saw me kneeling down in front of it, as I had to do every day between beatings, in the searing heat. I was wavering to and fro in a daze when he came over to me and spoke, thank God, perfect English. I couldn't believe it. His voice was calm and cultured. He seemed human and was obviously well educated.

'What are you doing, kneeling down here?' he asked me, as if genuinely interested.

'It's a punishment,' I replied carefully, through swollen lips, trying hard to concentrate my mind. I was unsure if he had been sent to make me confess or, worse, to trip me up in anything I might say.

'A punishment for what?' he asked. 'What did you do?'

'I didn't do anything. The guards accused me of stealing two kit-bags. But I didn't do it.'

He gave me a thoughtful look and I returned his gaze.

'Why did they think you stole the bags?'

'I don't know. They weren't there when I went to sleep, but the guards woke me up and told me they had found them near my feet.'

'And you didn't put them there?'

'No. It might have been somebody else who had it in for me, or maybe the guards didn't like me and wanted to get me in trouble.' I gulped, realising I might have said too much by now.

'It's a rotten business,' he sympathised in his impeccable English. I was astonished at this – both his compassion and his language skills. Fortunately, he didn't push things any further about the kit-bags and changed the subject.

'What rank are you in the British army?' he asked.

'I'm a sergeant.'

'And what did you do before the war?'

'I was a professional footballer.'

'A footballer? That is wonderful. Who did you play for?'

'I was playing for Reading when the war started.' The whole conversation seemed very strange, with me still kneeling down in front of the guardroom as we talked together.

He stood in thought for a few moments, then walked into the guardroom and started to speak in Japanese to all the guards who were on duty, having a rest before my next beating. As he was an officer, they had to listen to him. By now I knew a few Japanese words, but I understood very little of what he said to them; not enough to know which way this would go.

When he had finished talking, he came out to me again.

'I am sorry for what has happened. There will be no more beating.' He reached into his pocket and pulled out a full packet of Japanese cigarettes, which he gave to me. 'Now go back to your friends.'

I trembled with fear as I struggled to stand up. Was this some kind of trick? I accepted the packet from him as I knew some of the lads would appreciate these cigarettes.

Nothing more was ever said about this episode. I went back, hurting all over, and cleaned myself up as best I could. Then I stretched out for a glorious rest on the damp earth until Geordie and the others finished their hut-building work. Nobody ever owned up to stealing those kit-bags, but I suppose they wouldn't, would they? I mean, they could obviously see what the consequences were. This was a situation I did not wish to go through again, and I never did find out what really happened.

* * *

Despite my physical state, I was ordered straight back to work, and my first job was to help dig several large holes in the ground. Then we were ordered to throw in the bodies of the native workers who had died of malnutrition or disease, while they were clearing the jungle and building the first bamboo huts.

It was a sickening job. These bodies had lain festering for several days and it made me retch at the stench of blackened, putrefying corpses and the swarms of flies. We weren't allowed to give them any dignity or respect at all, not even to say a prayer over the appalling mass graves, but they couldn't stop me saying one in my head. The difference between the dead and the dying was at times very hard to determine.

At this camp, there was one curious thing. For the first time, the Japs gave us some quinine tablets to help us fight against the dreaded malaria. I think they were at last beginning to realise that if they didn't give us a little medical help, they would soon have no one left to build their railway.

By now, our sick outnumbered the fit, and were put into some of the bamboo huts set aside as overflow quarters for the camp hospital. Our medics did a grand job with the very few medical supplies the Japanese had grudgingly allocated to them. With endless patience, day after day, they comforted and helped the men as much as they could, although they were far from well themselves.

Daily and nightly we all suffered the greedy attentions of plagues of blood-sucking insects and mosquitoes. We did not of course possess the luxury of mosquito nets to sleep beneath, so it was just one long, endless slapping and swiping of these winged killers. We were close to being driven insane by them and what they did to our bodies. There seemed to be no end to our trials in the jungle.

7

Slave Labour – The Dead and the Dying

December 1942

The guards ordered all 'fit' men, which meant all those who could walk, on parade at 6.15 every morning, after an early breakfast of the same old things, rice and sugar or rice and fish. As I'm sure you can understand, we struggled to work on that through till lunch, which consisted of rice and a mug of watery 'jungle stew' at one. Then it was more hard labour in the unbearable heat of the day, right through till six or seven in the evening, and often with no water to soothe our parched throats and cracked lips in between.

This was slave labour of course, and men weakened and fell ill as they worked, becoming thinner and frailer than ever, though it hardly seemed possible. We were all bags of bones as it was. We were easy prey for diseases and, for anyone who succumbed, their chances of recovery were not good. Every POW knew it was only a matter of time for any of us, so I just concentrated on keeping on going, completing this or that task, one thing at a time.

You know, I often sat with some of our poor, sick lads in the jungle hospital during the evenings, after working on the railway, and they were absolute skeletons, very weak and with almost no chance of survival. For many of those who suffered, death was their only hope of relief. Some of those poor boys were only twenty or twenty-one, and I saw several of them turn grey overnight.

Yes, I cried for them, more than I have ever cried in my life. What a waste of good young lives. If only the Japanese and Korean guards had been a little more human, and treated us as prisoners of war in the proper way, thousands of British and Australian POWs would have survived this terrible ordeal.

I don't know if it was an order from the Japanese powers that be, or just a rule made up by our sadistic camp commandant, but we were all assembled on the parade ground one morning and ordered to salute the rising sun, the symbol of Japanese supremacy. It was the order of the day, every day, and God help you if you didn't comply. It was sickening to have to watch those who refused to make this menial gesture receive vicious beatings for their British or Australian pride.

At this time, our officers were getting no better treatment than their men and, like us, looked in a very sorry state. But despite everything, they continued to put around rumours.

'We're winning the war, chaps . . . We'll soon be rescued . . . It can't be long now.' Anything to encourage the men to battle on, and boy how we wanted to believe it all.

By now, men were dying at an alarming rate, for want of nourishment and medical supplies. The officers kept asking for more and better food, and the medications we needed to keep us going, but for months it was no use. Nothing changed, until our captors again realised that if we didn't have more supplies, there would not be enough of us left to get the railway built on time. This was the deciding factor and soon extra dry food and medicines arrived, transported up the Kwai river on barges and carried into camp.

Those of us detailed to collect and carry these goods had a terrible job. The barges were tied up at the bottom of steep banks of grey mud. We slid down this slimy skid-pan so fast that we often collided with the barges, or fell into the river. But coming up was a nightmare, trying to carry heavy barrels or chests, while at the same time trying to get a grip with our bare feet on the mud. I lost count of how many times I dropped the supplies and slithered back down the bank after them. It was a bruising and exhausting task for a fit man, and none of us were up to it. But the guards didn't care, laying into us every time we fell. The only thing that kept us going was the knowledge that this was food and medicine, and we somehow wrestled everything up the bank in the end.

The guards were now instructed to allow local natives into camp with fresh bananas and duck-eggs. Even more unexpectedly, the Japanese began to pay the working POWs a few yen so that we could buy some of these life-saving foods, and the light-sick men bartered any clothes or shoes they had left to increase their rations.

The Thais would take anything in exchange for their produce, and they were particularly keen on items they could sell. If you still had a watch or ring left, well you could do yourself a bit of good, although it was very hard to have to part with a wedding ring or a wrist watch that happened to be a present from your wife or girlfriend. We hung on to such links with our loved ones as long as we could, but sometimes they had to go, when we knew our survival was at stake.

Of course, those in the camp hospital could not join in this market trading, so we shared whatever we could get with them and we all managed to fill our stomachs a little fuller for a few days and build ourselves up a bit. But of course it wasn't to last for long. The pay stopped and so did our extra rations.

The work here at Tarso camp was harder than we had ever done. We hacked our way into the dense, virgin jungle to cut down straight bamboos for building huts up-river, to make new camps. It sounds simple enough, but have you ever tried to pull a bamboo out of the ground? Their roots make it almost impossible. We had to get a lot of men roped together to pull up just one bamboo tree. And the ground around them was full of short spiky plants that cut the skin of our feet to shreds.

Our Korean guards set each man a task of cutting and carrying to the river so many bamboos a day. And of course these quotas were ridiculously high, even for the fittest. No man could dodge the column, as he was checked each time he returned with his cut bamboos. According to the POWs' levels of fitness, some men took hours longer than others, but still these swine forced them to complete their tasks. No one was allowed to stop work until he had brought in his full quota of bamboos, so it could be as late as midnight before some of our men finished work for the day. When the guards weren't looking, I tried to help the weaker ones, but I often got beaten for it and it pulled at my heart to watch some of the men struggling so badly.

On days when I worked myself close to collapse, almost ready to give up any hope, and worrying what would happen to us all, a saying of my mother's used to come into my mind. 'Hard work won't kill you,' she used to tell us children when we complained of doing some chore or other. 'It's worry that kills you.'

That brought me to my senses every time.

When we were moved into our first main camp, we noticed a small native hut, built over the side of the river. It was about fifty yards away from our boundary and we saw that there was a Thai family living there – a man, his wife and two children. One of the children was a young boy, about five years old, and the other was a pretty young girl. I would think she was about fourteen and she had beautiful, long hair, reaching right down her back.

We prisoners used to sit at a distance and gaze at her in adulation as she moved about, unaware of our interest, helping her parents with their chores and playing with her little brother. It seemed as if we had never seen anyone so beautiful, or so innocent, and we took every opportunity in those first few days to sit and watch her graceful movements that inspired such longing and desire in us. We knew this was wrong of course, but we also knew she was safe. It was fantasy – our yearnings could never be fulfilled. We could only admire her charms from afar, but her purity lit up our ugly existence for a few days.

Very soon, however, things started to go wrong. This innocent young girl had not gone unnoticed by our guards, who started to molest her family at first, but with all their eyes and their lusts focused on this teenaged virgin. She was no more than a child, but not for long. She didn't have a chance.

I will leave it to your imagination what went on after that. But I can tell you that within a few months that child, and that's all she was, became a complete wreck at the hands of the despicable guards, who savaged and raped her continuously, day in and day out, to satisfy their cruel cravings. Her face lost its beauty, taking on an expression of utter fear and hopelessness, and her shining hair lost its lustre as she turned from an innocent teenager to a ravaged hag in a very short time. We never saw her smile again.

Exactly what that poor girl went through, no one will ever know. It must have been heartbreaking for her mother and father, knowing what was happening, perhaps even being forced to watch it all, yet being helpless to intervene, for fear of their lives.

Yes, the saki-fuelled guards would probably have loved the chance to torture and kill them had they protested. It would have been merely another pastime.

I did hear later, as the story went round the camp, that the girl had a baby, poor soul. I shall never forget how those bastards ruined her life.

Sadism always found an outlet and the guards now dreamt up another way to spend their fortnightly afternoons off. They would collect about ten of our weakest men and make them race against each other. These men could hardly walk, never mind run. It was pitiful to have to watch as the drunken savages gambled with one another as to which man would be the winner.

Then they set them off, hitting them with sticks to make them run, screaming and shouting at whoever they had placed their bet on, then bursting their sides with laughter to see the men stagger or fall. They would run over and drag the poor wretches to their feet, giddy and weak, and try to force them on again. This was a good day's sport to the guards, but to us it was a horrifying spectacle.

We were forced to watch, but we hated those guards with a vengeance for what they did to our poor friends. We desperately wanted to intervene, to stop them, but we couldn't, as it would not have saved our lads, and would have led to terrible punishments for anyone who tried.

At about this time, a bunch of Aussies who had been working up-river came to join us and told us about an incident that took place in their camp.

'Someone stole some food from the Jap cookhouse, the "sweegie-bar",' said Dale. 'When the Japs found out about it, they waited for us to return to camp, after we'd spent all day clearing a new passage through the jungle.'

'Then they ordered us to line up in the camp compound,' continued his mate.

'What happened next?'

'Well, they asked us who had stolen the guards' food.'

'Did anyone own up?'

'No. So the guards were furious and they made us all get down on our knees, and that's where we had to stay.'

'How long for?'

'Hours in the heat, with the flies zooming in on us, right the way through until late evening.'

We sat and listened in silence.

'As you pommies can imagine, first one or two, then more and more of our men were collapsing with thirst, hunger and fatigue. It was a dire situation for us all.'

Another Aussie took up the story. 'Finally, three brave men staggered to their feet and admitted to the crime they didn't commit.'

'Why?' asked one of our lads.

'Just to save their two hundred comrades from this terrible ordeal.'

'What happened to them?'

'The guards lammed into these three men and beat them with long bamboo sticks – vicious as can be. Our mates tried their best not to show their pain. They knew that if you stood up for your beating as long as you could, it would go better for you than if you straightaway dropped and squirmed with pain on the ground.'

'By God, it must have taken a lot of guts to go through that voluntarily, for a theft that wasn't theirs,' I said with genuine admiration.

I must say, they were great men, those Aussies. They had bags of courage and were absolutely fearless. Please God they recovered to see an end to this ghastly business.

When the Aussies settled into our camp, I made friends with one of their boys. His name was Roly K. Hull and I believe he came from St Arnaud. We became very good pals and, as a survival team, we did very well. It was amazing how he would suddenly turn up with food he had stolen from the Japanese, and he always shared it with me. He proved to be a real life-saver to me at this time, and helped me through a very bad period.

Unfortunately, as they say, all good things come to an end. Roly was moved to another camp up-country, and I never saw him again. I knew that, with luck, he would survive – he was that kind of man, taking terrible chances where others would not and usually getting away with it. I did make enquiries after the war, when I came home, and as far as I could make out he survived the lot.

If you ever came home, pal, and read my story, please remember that I often think about you. Thank you for being such a pillar of strength to me when I needed it most, on the railway of death.

Work was relentless, and the heat was almost impossible to endure. It sapped what little remaining strength we had and labouring in it for twelve hours a day was unbearable. Always hungry and desperate for water, we looked for any way we could to slake our thirst. I remember one afternoon, when two of the lads working in my party felt they were dying for lack of water, they decided to drink a few drops of their own urine. Under such terrible conditions, you are inclined to try anything once, so we all watched them, waiting to see if this could help us, but we soon had our answer. They were violently sick and looked like death. Believe me, it nearly drove them mad. We realised then that we could not, under any circumstances, drink our own water.

It was heartbreaking to see the pitiful condition of so many of our men: just bags of bones, dashing to the jungle toilet every few minutes, as I had often done, only to pass blood and mucus. This was usually the early stage of dysentery, and most of the lads were experiencing a fair amount of pain with it. I was fortunate enough to be free of dysentery at that time, but I felt sick to my stomach to have to watch the suffering of my pals, several of whom died from this slow killer. Still they would be made to work. We had to be half dead for the guards to class us as sick, and then, no longer being of any use to them, they would wash their hands of us. But if we could somehow keep on working, we had a small chance of survival, as long as disease and malnutrition didn't kill us.

Our doctors fought for us all, but they could do little to help us without medication. They were in an awful predicament, but they tried their best.

8

Night-Time Torments

March 1943

I was always on the lookout for ways to improve our chances as I knew this could be the only way to stay alive. I realised early on that we had to be willing to take risks and, if necessary, endure the consequences, to keep going, and this is what I tried to do, not just for me, but for my lads too. Sadly, the average POW was not prepared to take such gambles for their lives, in fear of retribution, which was of course understandable.

You could tell by looking around which men were getting some extra nourishment. It was by now very clear that the ones who got through the ordeals of every day in the death camps were the good thieves, or their friends. The cleverer and more courageous the thief, the better were his and his friends' chances of pulling through. Some of our men, including the officers, behaved themselves impeccably at all times, but in eight cases out of ten, they were the ones who died first.

As I was the only sergeant in our unit, lads would come and seek me out from time to time to talk about their problems. Now this situation at Tarso camp was escalating, and boys were coming to me every evening with one worry or another, or to spill out their despair. Often they were depressed, as I had occasionally felt myself, and they needed someone to tell their troubles to.

'I feel too ill to work. I can't go on,' groaned one young lad.

'I can't take this any longer,' wept another, later that evening. 'There's no end to it.'

'Yes there is, there will be, one day soon.' I put my arm round him and comforted him. 'The war can't go on for ever. I'm sure it will all be over soon, then we will never have to work "speedo-speedo" ever again.'

'Thanks, Sarge,' he sniffed, wiping his eyes with the back of his hand.

'It will get better. You'll see.'

Of course, I knew there wasn't anything I could do to change their situation. Unless they were half dead, there was absolutely no way I or anyone else could lighten their workload and the terrible toll on their bodies. If the guards said they were all right for work, then they had to work, no matter what. All I could do to help these lads was to listen to their problems, to humour them and keep them going at least for a little longer.

'I don't think I can cope with any more of this,' said the youngest boy in my unit, with tears in his eyes.

'As long as you keep breathing, you can cope.'

'But I can't.'

'Yes you can. You have to keep trying.'

'I physically can't do any more. I'm ill, can't you see?'

'Yes, I know. It's very hard, but take one day at a time; one hour at a time. Just focus on getting through one thing, one minute, and then the next.'

'But why? What's it all for?'

'For you, for your future . . . and for your loved ones.'

'But they've probably forgotten all about me by now.'

'No, I'm sure they haven't. How could anybody forget you?' I gave him a slight smile to see if he would respond.

There was a pause as he took that in . . . then he looked up at me with a tinge of hope. 'Do you think so?'

'Yes I do. You have to fight so that your loved ones will get you back. I bet they're all worried sick and desperate to see you again, so you've got to keep going to make them smile again. Just think of their happiness when they welcome you home.'

'Thanks, Sarge,' said the boy, unhunching his shoulders a little. 'Can I come and talk to you again tomorrow?'

'Of course you can. Just one day at a time, remember?'

'Yes, one day at a time. If only it wasn't so hard.'

'It's hard for me too. It's hard for us all. But it will be worth it – just think of the smiles on your family's faces when you get back to them.'

The guards' daily cruelties and humiliations continued. I didn't think it could get any worse, but it did, in a sinister and dangerous new twist to their attentions. One night a couple of Korean guards came over to us, using crude sign language to try and make us understand what they wanted. At first, we didn't realise what they meant, but they started to mime with each other and we were horrified. How were we going to get out of this new situation? They clearly wanted to use our bodies, making it clear they would rape us if necessary.

My God, didn't they realise that they had done enough damage to us already, mentally and physically, without this new threat?

We had to think quickly and made it clear that we were not interested in what they were suggesting. Fortunately, there were quite a few of us and the guards probably realised they were not going to get anywhere without reinforcements, so they went off to find other victims. This was a frightening time for many of our lads and we all tried to stick together in groups as much as possible to avoid their attentions. But I don't think everybody escaped this fate so easily.

Meanwhile, the sadists always managed to find some excuse to carry out their frenzied beatings. One evening I was sitting outside our hut with my pal Geordie, when a Korean lashed into one of our lads with a bamboo stick, hitting him repeatedly, shrieking at him with every stroke. The unfortunate victim was already so weak that we knew he could not last long.

In a flaming temper, Geordie stood up and screamed at the guard. 'You cruel bastard! Leave him alone or I'll kill you.'

Fortunately, although he heard it, the guard didn't understand what Geordie had said. He stopped his beating and marched across to us.

'Nanda?' he yelled at Geordie, angry at being disturbed.

'Nanda means "What do you want?"' I whispered.

Geordie was always a quick thinker, so he held his backside and said '*Benjo*-speedo?' meaning 'Can I go to the lavatory quickly?'

The guard, thinking this was what Geordie had called him for, gave him permission.

'Phew, that was a close shave,' I said as the guard walked away.

'Well, I had to distract him somehow,' grinned Geordie, sloping off to the latrines, in case the Korean turned around to check.

By this time, the man who was being beaten had been carried away by some of his mates and his thwarted attacker went off towards the guardhouse. I couldn't stop smiling – Geordie had saved a man that day.

The POWs who were deemed to be 'light-sick' had the job of keeping our huts clean and tidy, while we worked as slaves on the railway. They did as well as they could, but with all the humidity and insects, and without any disinfectants most of the time, it was an uphill task. Night-times had always been a battle with armies of blood-sucking and poisonous insects.

As well as the dangerous mosquitoes, we were plagued by giant red ants, the size of bluebottles, that climbed all over us as we tried to sleep. If there was a crumb of food, especially a grain of sugar, or any sweat-soaked blanket or garment on the floor of our hut, or on our bamboo sleeping areas, the ants would come in their thousands. And, of course, our sweating bodies used to attract them and they bit us like hell. They sucked the blood out of us all night long, but we were so desperate with fatigue that we had to sleep and this was just another torment we had to live with.

But the rats were the worst of our night-time visitors. In the quiet darkness, they invaded our hut. Where they all came from, I don't know, but they would pour in through every gap and run all over us. They sent shudders through me as I felt their scratchy paws scrambling over me in the darkness, up and down my body, often several of them at a time.

Some of these rats were as big as small cats. When I could stand it no longer, I used to jump out of my lice-ridden bed, wearing just a tattered pair of shorts, which was my only remaining item of clothing, or later a ragged loincloth, and scream at them, jumping about and flailing my arms to try and frighten them off, but if they moved away at all, they soon came back to plague me anew.

Some of my friends were either too ill or too weak to jump out of their beds, and these rats had the time of their lives in our hut. What most of us had to do was to wrap ourselves as completely as we could in what was left of our blankets and try to ignore them. But I can still feel now the creepy sensation of those rats with their scratchy claws, crawling all over me.

Occasionally, some of the fitter lads used to catch them, when they were quick enough. They skinned them and stewed them up for some protein. I have to say that, although at different times I ate almost anything and everything, rats were never on my menu – I just couldn't bring myself to eat such disgusting vermin. The thought of swallowing any part of these filthy rats made my stomach heave, and we couldn't afford the risk of letting anything we ate or drank come up again. Our bodies needed to retain what little nourishment we could get and, being so sore and weak, we couldn't take any more digestive upsets.

One morning on work parade, I was picked out, along with four other men, to go to the Japanese workshop. We had to resharpen axes that were used for felling trees and bamboos. That afternoon, as I was in the middle of sharpening an axe blade, a metal splinter sheared off and flew up into my left eye, which immediately caused me a sharp, severe pain and tears began to run down my cheek. I went over to the Korean guard who was in charge and tried to explain what had happened. He promptly dug my exposed ribs with his rifle and ordered me back to work, 'speedo-speedo'.

By the end of the day, I was almost writhing in pain and didn't know what to do with myself. My eye was now so swollen it had closed up. All I wanted to do was to crawl into my bed, like a wounded animal, and hide. As my pals came into the hut and saw the state I was in, they were quite concerned.

'That looks bad, Johnny,' said one of the boys. 'I reckon you should go and see the doc with that.'

'Do you want me to look in your eye and see if I can find the splinter?' suggested another of my pals.

'No!' I almost shrieked, then realised how ungrateful that sounded. 'No thanks. It's so swollen and painful that I don't think I could open it.'

'Well, you really should have it seen to,' said my corporal.

'Yes, I know,' I groaned. 'But I can't go now. I'm not dying. I'll go in the morning.'

'That's the ticket, man,' said Geordie, the tough guy who never went to see the medics if he could avoid it. 'You don't want to lose your eyesight.'

As I lay awake that night, unable to sleep with the pain, I worried what would happen if I did lose sight in that eye. Would I ever be able to play professional football again? Football was my life. How could I score goals with only one eye? I had to get back to fitness somehow and play again for the Royals at Reading Football Club. It was one of the things that kept me going through those terrible POW years, the thought of being back on the home-ground with the lads in the cool English air, training and playing the beautiful game.

The following morning, bleary from lack of sleep and still in agony, I went to see the medical officer, who bathed my eye and tended it as best he could, though he was unable to find the sliver of metal that was giving me such intense pain. I put up with this for two or three days and kept away from the hospital hut, but it was still as bad as ever, so I decided to go back to the doctor.

'I've tried to ignore it,' I explained. 'But the pain is constant and so bad that I just had to come back.'

'Tell me about this pain. Have you had anything like it before?'

'No. Only since the metal splinter went into my eye. It's agony – just the same as when it first happened.'

'Mmm,' he said as he attempted to lift my swollen lid and I desperately tried not to squirm.

'Maybe you could bathe it again with something soothing?' I pleaded.

'I don't have anything soothing,' he said. 'We have no supplies – only warm water. That's all.' He paused. 'Don't you think we have enough on our hands, Sergeant Sherwood? The hospital is already full of the sick and dying, without us having to worry about you with a little something in your eye.'

As I slunk away, I knew he was right, but I did feel very sorry for myself. I lay down on my bed and hid from the world under the cover, crying with pain. Whatever happened, I knew I could not go back to see him again, no matter how bad my eye became. Of course I realised he was overworked and under great pressure, and in the scale of things an eye wound should be the least of his worries, but my morale was so lowered by the pain that I did feel selfishly indignant at being turned away.

After several more days of this agony, with my eye still so swollen that I could not open it, I despaired of it ever improving. But then a miracle happened. I went off to sleep with my eye watering like hell and feeling as if it would burst. When I woke in the morning, to my utter surprise and relief, the pain had practically gone. How this happened, I will never know. I can only suppose that the metal sliver rose to the surface and fell away with my tears. Over the next three weeks, the swelling went down and my wound must have healed itself, but to this day I still carry the scar in that eye.

'Hey, Johnny. We heard you lost an eye,' said a friend of mine in the next camp up the line, a few weeks later.

So that's how things sometimes became distorted on the jungle telegraph, and this is the story that went around. It seemed that though I lost pals at various times to disease and death, I also made new friends, and so it went on throughout my POW years. But I never forgot those I had lost and thanked God every day for the luck that somehow kept me going . . . until the next problem came along.

9

Collapse at Kanu

April 1943

Now that we had cleared the passage through the forest, we were marched to our first main camp upriver, unnamed as yet, where we had to begin the terrible task of building the railway itself, the railway that would become the notorious 'railway of death'.

There were about 250 men in our party, and it took us a week's weary trek to reach a clearing in the jungle, about a hundred yards long and sixty yards wide. Here we found three newly completed huts, built by native Thai labour, once again lured by empty Japanese promises – all lies. They had encountered new diseases to which they had no resistance and had been made to work until they dropped. There were bodies everywhere, some in the clearing and many more rotting corpses in the jungle, where the poor men had gone to die.

Our first job was to collect and bury these poor blighters. This was the second time I had been ordered to take on this grim task and it was even more gruesome than before. The putrefying bodies, with their stick-limbs at hideous angles, were riddled with maggots and thousands of other insects, covered with flies and left to rot. I couldn't stop retching, but the fanatical guards kept prodding us to work harder and faster, so we had no choice but to get on and do the best we could for these hapless wretches who had never had a chance. Death, it seemed, was their only relief.

The clearing was dotted with piles of bamboo and atap, cut ready by the ill-fated Thais, for building our huts. This was to become Kanu camp, later known as one of the worst death camps, but thankfully we weren't aware of it at the time.

Our sickest men slept in the three new huts, while I and the rest of us had to hunker down and sleep rough in the open air, until we built more huts for ourselves. Of course, that meant some of our 'least sick' men had to stay in the camp and work themselves half to death to complete these huts, while the rest of us started on the harder labour on the railway.

The huts were a standard design, built with two sides of sleeping spaces on bamboo platforms and maybe four feet of open space running down the middle as a gangway. The sides were separated off into sections, to hold six men in each, with about eighteen inches' width per man. It wasn't much, but we were so thin that it was just enough.

When we were finally able to sleep inside one of these new huts, I selected my space, with a group of my pals, in a section halfway down the long hut, with a path running along parallel on the outside of the hut.

On our first evening in our new hut, we were given the usual bowl of rice, with a piece of dried fish. As we were eating, surprise, surprise, along came some guards with an allocation of quinine tablets for each one of us.

'Why are the Japs giving us quinine tablets again?' one of the lads asked me.

'I suppose they must have realised that if they don't do something to preserve what little health we still have, they won't get their railway built on time.'

'So it's not really for our benefit, just for theirs?'

'Yes. That's the size of it.'

Whatever their reason, we were glad to take the quinine, or at least most of us were. There were a few who were so suspicious of our guards by now that they couldn't trust them.

'I'm not taking any pill those bastards give us!' protested one lad.

'Yes, how do we know they won't kill us?'

'I wouldn't put it past them.'

'Surely they won't try to kill us if they want their railway built,' I said.

'They're trying to kill us slowly anyway, so why not in one shot?'

'Sorry, Sarge. I'm not taking anything I don't have to.'

Before lights out, one of our officers came around each of the huts to speak to us.

'I want you all to take your quinine tablets to protect you from malaria. This place is swarming with mosquitoes and I don't want any of you going down with diseases unnecessarily. You must all try to get a good night's sleep. You will be starting work on the railway in the morning.'

At dawn, the guards had the fittest men on parade, the fit men being those who could still stand up. What a depleted, miserable body of beings we were as we waited to be allotted our chores – painfully thin, with hardly any clothing or footwear, having bartered most of it away for food. A few still had something on their feet – if only rags wrapped around them – and many had tattered shorts or rags for loincloths, but most of us, thank God, still had some kind of covering for our heads – the most important thing of all in that piercing sunlight and steaming heat.

The Japanese interpreter at this camp was rather an uncouth-looking individual, I thought, as he came to talk to us.

'The sick men erect tents for more men come from Tarso camp. They come help you.' He puffed his chest out with pride. 'Many camps being built, same as Kanu, through jungle, all way into Burma, close by river Kwai to carry Imperial soldiers.' He paused and looked along our ranks, as we waited to start work. 'All men must work very hard. All men who stand must work. All men in all camps make railway meet up.' He stopped and smiled, a gold tooth glinting in the early sunlight.

We were given axes, picks and chunkels, and we got down to

the real job of clearing a new part of the virgin jungle, keeping as near as we could to the river Kwai. Although the work seemed extremely arduous to us that day, it was not as bad as what would follow. At least here, the terrain was fairly flat and the ground not too hard or rocky. But we had to watch out for venomous snakes and kill them before they killed us. We started by chopping and cutting bamboos, all the straight ones being taken back to camp to help with the hut-building or as poles for tents.

Before long, the few lads with nothing on their heads started to waver and were soon down with sunstroke. Many others of us were also affected by the intense heat as the morning wore on. The temperature was about a hundred and twenty degrees and the humidity was unbearable. Working in such heat was pure torture.

Once we got into this daily working routine, that's when our troubles really began. Although we were still being given regular doses of quinine, increasing numbers of men started going down with malaria as well as our old enemy, amoebic dysentery. One morning Pat, a friend of mine, collapsed in the jungle and died within a few hours. Then, later that day and almost without warning, I too passed out.

Usually we were not allowed to take any ill men back to camp until the end of our working day, but maybe they realised they were losing too many workers and changed their minds. Anyway, I must have been in a bad way because the guards allowed two men to carry me back to the camp hospital. I knew nothing of this, or of the following days, until the medical officer and hospital orderly told me the story when they were doing their rounds about a week later, once I had finally regained consciousness.

'Well, Sergeant Sherwood,' began the doctor. 'How are you feeling?'

'Not too good, sir,' I replied, with my head still reeling and my body sweating like a feverish pig.

'Do you realise that only about thirty-six hours ago I thought you were certain to die?'

'Really sir?' I was shocked. I didn't even know what was wrong with me, though I suspected it must be malaria.

'Yes, Sergeant. I gave this orderly strict instructions that if you died he was to make sure to have your body tied up in a rice sack and laid outside the hospital unit, ready to bury the next morning. I told him not to wait until it was light, as it would upset other patients that were very sick.'

'I had the rice sack ready,' agreed the orderly, nodding gravely.

'Now,' continued the medical officer. 'You're out of the worst of it and, with a bit of luck, you will pull through it all right. You should be up and about in a couple of weeks.' He smiled.

'Thank you sir.'

'It was a seriously close shave, Sherwood. You must be a very lucky man.'

Well, as they continued on their rounds, I smiled to myself and thought of my dear old mum and that nickname of hers for me: 'Lucky Johnny'. If she could only know how lucky I had been this time.

Perhaps I would be able to tell her one day. Oh I hoped so – I missed her and all my family so much. Now I was on the mend, I felt sure I would see them all again one day soon, God willing.

Sadly, other men were not so lucky as me. The death toll rose and our little cemetery had to be expanded to fit in all the new graves with their home-made bamboo crosses. Our officers detailed the light-sick men, which included me in those weeks following my collapse, to keep our graveyard clean and tidy. Even when I was fit enough to go back to work on the railway, I often used to go and sit in that peaceful cemetery in the evenings, with its open view up the hillside, and its cool shade, just gazing at all those little crosses. So many of my friends had died and all the men buried there were men I knew. I used to cry like a baby when I thought of the pals I had lost. Quite often I would sit there, whispering to myself. 'How much longer can I be lucky? Will it be my turn soon?'

To raise morale at Kanu camp, some of our officers decided to organise short concerts, about twice a week, around a large camp-fire. Although our resistance was pretty low at this time, the fittest of the men stood up to sing songs, tell jokes or recite pieces of poetry they could remember from their school-days. Then, of course, there were the lewd pub-stories and songs. It's strange how people in the direst circumstances can laugh so hysterically when they get the chance. Those evenings were life-savers as they were great entertainment and helped us to forget how bad things were for a few hours.

Over time, I had begun to learn some Japanese words and phrases, thinking it might help us, and it certainly proved to be so. One day I was chopping down bamboo when a *gunso* came across and started to speak to me, in very good English. Indeed, his English was as good as that interpreter who had rescued me from the kit-bags incident at Tarso.

'I have been watching you,' he began. 'You are a very good workman.'

'*Domo*, thank you.' I smiled, astonished that a Jap should pay me a compliment.

'You speak Japanese?' he asked in surprise.

'No, but I have learnt a few words.'

'That is good. You deserve a reward,' he said, handing me a packet of Japanese cigarettes.

I gave him a slight bow as I took the pack from him. I had often seen the Japanese do that and I thought it would be a sensible gesture to make. '*Domo*,' I repeated.

He beamed with delight and I clutched the cigarettes gratefully. I didn't smoke, but I knew a lot of the lads would be very glad to share these out.

'Are you a wood-cutter?' he asked me.

'No,' I smiled. 'I've only learnt to cut bamboos while I've been here.'

'What did you do before the war?' he continued.

'I was a footballer. A professional footballer.'

'Really,' he grinned. 'I love football.'

'Well, I have played football in Japan,' I added.

His eyes widened. 'In Japan? When?'

'Yes, in 1938, when I was playing on a world football tour. We played a match against a Japanese team in Yokohama. And while we were there, we were introduced to all your top people. One of them was a general in your government, called Hideki Tojo. He had a chest full of medals and stars. I remember he wore round glasses and a neat moustache. I shook hands with him.'

Well, you never saw such a change in a man!

'General Tojo is now Prime Minister of Japan.' He beamed even wider than before.

That was another lucky break for me. From that point on, this Japanese sergeant would do anything for me. As a matter of fact, I'm sure he saved my life one night.

It was about 9.45 when we returned from a concert party and we had just got on to our lice-infested, beaten bamboo beds. The lads, as usual, were smoking anything they could find, which that evening meant dried leaves, wrapped up in discarded Japanese newspaper.

My pal, Tommy, offered me a puff of his home-made cigarette, which I accepted. I had a couple of puffs and it nearly choked me! Just at that moment, the bugle sounded for lights out. This of course meant no lit cigarettes, so I threw the tipper out into the path that ran along the side of our hut.

For once, I must have been very unlucky, for at that moment, two Korean guards were walking along this pathway on guard duty. They stormed into our hut and shone their torches at our faces, blinding us, while one of them held up this still smouldering roll-up.

'Who?' shrieked one of the Koreans. 'Who cigarette?'

'No light, no light!' yelled the other guard, pointing at the tiny red spark.

Well, we were so shocked that nobody answered them at first, and the devils were getting themselves all worked up about it.

'You out,' screamed the first one, gesticulating that he wanted about twenty of us to get off our beds. This was the point at which I realised I had no option but to admit that it was me who had committed that awful crime.

'Go sleepo,' one of the guards said, ordering all my hut-mates back to their sleeping platforms, while the other one grabbed my skinny arms in a tight grip. Together they half dragged me out of our hut, took me thirty or forty yards up the pathway into a small clearing in the jungle and began to lay into me, beating me up.

There was a strange thing about these uncouth Korean guards. Like their Japanese allies, if you took whatever they did to you, being hit or beaten, without cowering away or falling down, you were more likely to get away a little lighter, so that's what I tried to do. However, these swine were hitting me with their rifle butts across my bony shoulders and back, and my nose was pouring blood that was now all over me. I could see they were really enjoying themselves and finally, in a dizzy spell, I could withstand the blows no longer and dropped to the ground.

Now they readjusted their attack, slamming their rifle butts into me, and kicking me with their steel-capped boots, so that I was sure they would break my bones. Suddenly I thought of the Japanese sergeant who had befriended me just a few days before. I saw the slightest chance when they paused for a breather and, more in hope than anger, I pulled myself up and made a run for my life, down the pathway about sixty yards, with the guards shouting and running after me. Even in that weak and terrible state, my football training came to my aid and I was able to outrun them. I knew where I was going and ran straight to the hut where this sergeant slept.

I burst open the door, desperately hoping he would be in. Fortunately for me, he was. His candles were lit and he was sitting up in bed knitting, of all things. He looked up and saw me standing in front of him, covered in blood. I had been beaten so badly that I believe he didn't recognise me. This frightened me as I expected the guards to come rushing in, grab me and thrash the hell out of me, but they didn't come. I was just thinking how strange this was, when the Japanese *gunso* realised who I was.

He put his knitting down and jumped out of his bed. 'What a state you are in,' he said, helping me towards a chair. 'Sit down and tell me what happened.' I began to explain, while he listened patiently, tut-tutting, then shook his head.

'I'm sorry about this beating,' he sympathised. 'Now come with me and I will talk to the guards to put them right.'

He held my arm gently and led me back up the path to the clearing where I'd been beaten up. But when we got there, funnily enough, neither of the guards was anywhere to be seen.

The sergeant shouted out to them in Japanese, and both appeared out of the darkness. As they stood before the friendly *gunso*, I was astonished to witness him giving each of them six hard slaps across their face with the flat of his hand. He said something curt to them in Japanese, then turned and put his arm around me.

'I am very sorry,' he said again to me, in his excellent English. 'Now go back to bed. You will be all right now.'

Well, to me that seemed like a miracle. I would not have believed it if anyone else had told me, yet I witnessed it for myself. I was stunned. I went back to my hut and quietly cleaned some of the blood off with a little water from my water-bottle. Some of the boys were still awake.

'What happened?' whispered one of them.

When I told them all the details, they couldn't believe it either.

'He really slapped their faces?'

'In front of you?'

'It's true,' I assured them.

'Boy, that's a miracle!' said Tommy, whose cigarette had started it all off. 'You're a lucky blighter, and no mistake.'

I slept as soon as I lay down my head and didn't wake again until five o'clock in the morning. As soon as I tried to move, I felt stiff as hell and my whole body was sore from all the cuts and bruises. I could see now that I still had quite a lot of dried blood on me too, so I needed to clean that off.

After the bugle had sounded for us to collect our small portions of tea and rice, this Jap sergeant who had saved me came into our hut and walked over to where I was sitting. I must have still looked quite a mess.

'I have come to tell you that I give you permission for you to have the day off work. So you can go back to bed and rest.'

All the men had gone quiet as he spoke to me, their mouths half open with surprise.

'Thank you,' I said. '*Domo.*'

He gave me the slightest smile and an almost imperceptible bow of his head, before turning and walking out of the hut. You should have heard some of the names the lads called me that day as they went off to work parade, leaving me to have a peaceful day, relaxing in the hut.

10

A Job In the 'Sweegie-Bar'

May 1943

About half the camp were now stricken down with various complaints. The usual dysentery and malaria of course, and most of us had either beriberi or dengue fever and other vitamin deficiencies such as pellagra, but now some of the men were suffering horribly from ulcers, mostly on their legs – huge, raw ulcers, some the size of saucers and so deep you could see their bones. They were very painful and the medics had no way of healing them, other than cleaning them out as best they could and packing them with salt, if they had any, and that was excruciating to bear.

The officers went to the Japanese commandant to plead for more food to build us up and medical supplies to help our boys get their strength back and keep working, as they put it, but this inscrutable figure always gave the same answer: 'Men work hard, get more food.'

It never happened, of course.

Despite these problems, work was progressing and the Japs now brought in their engineers and technicians to instruct us and supervise the building of the railway itself. Make no mistake about it, they knew their job. And what was even better, they seemed very well educated; much kinder and more human towards us, though they couldn't get us any more food and water than the starvation rations we were on. While they were there we managed to complete the railway embankment right the way through our section, though not a line or sleeper had yet been laid.

It was at this stage that we all began to suffer from a terrible soreness in certain parts of our bodies, especially in between our legs – the worse place for a skin disease. The irritation was relentless and distressing, to say the least, chafing me until my scrotum was red-raw, cracked and swollen. Indeed, it was so severe that many of us had difficulty in walking and some could barely move one leg in front of another. This was apparently a fungal infection called tinea, but I heard some of the men give it more colourful names. The usual one was 'rice-balls'.

Despite our illnesses and our generally frail state, there was no stopping the guards. They had no time for our problems or delays, and their only answer was to beat us into submission.

'Speedo-speedo' was the constant cry, all day long and well into the night. This railway had to be completed on time, at all costs. The cost in human lives meant nothing to them. But they did finally agree to some of the jungle natives coming up-river to our camp with extra food to barter or sell. By now, we had nothing left to exchange for the life-saving duck-eggs and bananas, but the Japs paid us a pittance once again for working, so the fit were able to buy a little extra to eat for themselves and their mates. Meanwhile, the officers had a whip-round to buy food for the sick in the camp hospital.

No praise would be high enough for our medical officers and their orderlies, who performed daily miracles, despite the lack of medical supplies. Being a witness to some of the things they did, I can honestly say that if ever Oscars could have been awarded, then, by God, those medics deserved one apiece.

Despite the occasional extra morsel of nourishment, the punishing labour, diseases and deficiencies were taking an increasing toll on my body and I was thinner than I had ever been, my skin creasing like dry parchment over my stick-like bones. So I thanked my lucky stars at the good fortune that befell me, just when I needed it most. Indeed, it's likely that this saved my life, as well as the lives of a few of my pals.

The Jap *gunso* sergeant who had befriended me came over to

my hut one evening before lights out. After the initial greetings, with all those nearby listening to our courteous conversation with astonishment, he handed me the olive-branch of my dreams.

'We need a new man to work in the sweegie-bar, someone who can kill and skin pigs. Do you think you could do that? If you can, the job is yours.'

'In your cookhouse? Yes of course I could do that. No problem at all.' I had never skinned a pig in my life, or even met a live one as far as I could remember, but I wasn't going to let that get in the way. I was sure I could learn to do anything if it meant a job in the Japs' sweegie-bar, where all the food was prepared for their officers and guards.

'Good. Report there at dawn tomorrow morning.' He turned and walked out, leaving the whole hut in silence.

'You lucky bastard!' exclaimed Geordie.

'Can you get us some extra food, Sarge?' asked one of the boys.

'Champion!' cheered our Yorkshireman, realising this could be his lifeline.

'I'll do what I can,' I grinned, still unable to believe it. 'I reckon I can be a pretty good smuggler when I need to be.'

'You can say that again, Johnny,' laughed Geordie. 'If smuggling is what you call it!'

What a godsend this new job turned out to be. The Japanese had plenty of food: eggs, chickens by the hundreds, about one pig every four days, and plenty of greens – all the things we couldn't have and desperately needed. What an opportunity, I thought, to build myself up again and, as it turned out, a chance for me to help some of my pals and hut-mates, and our jungle hospital too.

I had to be at the sweegie-bar at four o'clock every morning to cook the guards' rice and boil the water for their tea. Then I would go into the chicken pen and kill six chickens, which I promptly boiled and cut up into tiny pieces to mix with their rice and diced vegetables. Then I had to fill up sixty guards' mess tins for their day's rations on the railway.

I soon got into the swing of things, with two POWs working under me, and of course it was all under Japanese supervision. I always used to be the first man in the cookhouse in the mornings, early enough to steal a dozen eggs and some uncooked rice; I would take it back to the boys in the hut and they would hide it until they returned from their day's work on the railway, when we could go off together and hide somewhere in the jungle to have a good cook-up.

The Japs had a real fetish about not eating chicken unless it had been freshly killed, so they wouldn't touch any dead chickens. I would kill two or three, leave them on the floor in the chicken-run until they were practically cold, then call the Japanese supervisor and show him the dead chickens in the hen-house.

'Throw in Kwai,' he ordered, whenever this happened. So I would take the carcasses to the river bank, alongside the sweegie-bar, to pass them on to some of my pals who were hiding there.

The same thing happened every time we had a pig-skin. I used to cut the pig's throat first and let the blood run into a bucket. One of the POW kitchen-hands used to take the pigs' blood to the hospital to give to the very sick patients to drink. My next job was to skin the pig, which I did, always making sure I left plenty of fat on the skin. I was supposed to throw that into the river as well, along with the pig's carcass from the day before, but I had arranged for Geordie and some of the lads to be in the river, just round the bend, where it was shallow. At the pre-arranged time, I threw away the pig's skin and carcass into the Kwai. Just a few yards downstream, the boys would lift out the treasure trove.

After taking a bit for ourselves, all the rest went to the POWs' cookhouse, where the chickens, pig's fat and scrapings from the carcass would be cut up small and boiled in our jungle stew. That way, everyone got at least a morsel of protein and a little fat, which their bodies so desperately needed.

I know they all really appreciated it.

* * *

I must tell you about an exciting experience that occurred while I was working in the sweegie-bar. The Japanese had lots of live chickens brought up the river Kwai on barges, maybe two hundred a week, and they were put into the chicken house we had built on the side of the cookhouse.

One week we kept finding dead chickens and feathers all over the run, and many of the birds had been ripped to pieces. I knew this time it was nothing to do with me, so I was puzzled at how this had happened. The *gunso* in charge of the sweegie-bar called me over.

'Me come night,' he said, trying to explain his intention to investigate what or who was responsible. 'You,' he pointed at ten on his watch. I understood. He wanted me to sit guard with him from ten o'clock that evening.

When I arrived, we hid ourselves and kept as silent as possible, waiting to solve the mystery of the mutilated chickens. I had never imagined I and this guard would be allies together, lying in wait. But there must be strange moments in every war.

We sat and we sat. We waited for hours, until finally, at about 2.30 in the morning, we heard a slight movement outside the chicken pen. We held our breath in utter amazement as a beautiful leopard sprang over the wire fence and began to play havoc with the poor hens, who were like sitting ducks on their perches in the dark.

As we had pre-arranged, I shone the guard's strong torch straight into the pen and, in that split second, the *gunso* shot this creature of the wild. And to make absolutely certain, he fired another shot into it.

We went and lit a couple of lanterns in the cookhouse, returned to the chicken pen and dragged our stunning specimen back with us, strung him up and retired to bed.

As I arrived in the sweegie-bar for work an hour or so later, all the guards were examining the leopard and congratulating the *gunso* for killing it. He ordered me and another POW to skin it, taking great care not to damage the pelt, as he was going to keep that for himself, like a hunting trophy.

'Take you sweegie-bar,' he said, gesticulating that we should carry the skinned leopard to our own cookhouse.

'Thank you,' I said. '*Domo.*' I realised he was doing this because I had stayed up with him and gone without sleep to help him catch this stealthy chicken-killer.

We took it across to be butchered in our cookhouse and that same evening we all had the luxury of leopard stew for our dinner. Although one leopard shared between nine hundred men didn't go far, I can assure you that this particular stew was quite tasty and we were very glad of it.

11

Cholera!

June 1943

Well, as you know, all good things come to an end, and the inevitable happened. Something went wrong in the Japanese sweegie-bar and after fourteen weeks we POWs were thrown out, but we'd had a good run of it.

When I started at the cookhouse, I must have been at least three or four stone underweight, probably more. Working all day in a place where I was surrounded by food was like winning the pools. As I worked I ate and ate, putting on the pounds at an alarming rate. I must have looked enormous by the time I finished there.

'You've put on a lot of weight, Sarge,' said my corporal the evening I was fired. 'You must be twenty stone, I reckon.'

'Steady on, Corporal,' I laughed.

'And waddling like a duck,' grinned one of the lads.

'Well, it didn't last long, but at least I made the most of working in the sweegie-bar,' I said. 'I know I must look like Billy Bunter now, but all this weight will soon disappear.'

'Well, it isn't just you,' added the corporal. 'We've all done well out of your bit of luck, so now we're fitter than we've been since this lot started in Singapore.'

'You're right there,' I nodded. 'It was only a few weeks, but it made a lot of difference, didn't it?'

I was feeling really fit and strong now, although well under my pre-war weight. My giddiness had gone and my sores disappeared. I was probably the fittest man in Kanu camp, so at least I had something to fight the future with, unlike most of the men in other huts, who still looked pitifully thin and ill. If only I could have helped everyone the same.

After leaving the sweegie-bar, the guards made us clear and dig up a plot of land quite close to their sleeping quarters so that they could grow their own cabbages and pumpkins. Believe me, they grew them to prize-winning sizes and this is the way they did it. Every night, they urinated into buckets. When they had gone to supervise work on the railway, some of our light-sick men were ordered to collect the buckets and pour a mugful of urine under each plant. As you can imagine, this was not a pleasant task, but it did seem to stimulate the cabbages and pumpkins, so much so that they grew enormous. I have never seen vegetables flourish like it.

Some of the Japs used to let us have the outside leaves of their cabbages, which we cooked to give us precious nutrients, and we drank the cabbage water as well. We wasted nothing, convinced these small extras helped to alleviate our various diseases. I must admit that we always used to feel queasy after we had dined on those cabbage leaves, when we thought about how they had been fed. But I think, at this stage, we would have eaten anything to help us survive.

In fact, I shudder at some of the things we did eat – snakes, monkeys, lizards, stray dogs and cats, rats, mice, maggots, insects, boiled flies and once we even found a newly dead horse. Nearly all of our men were so weak, ill and in constant pain by this time that we often found ourselves thinking about how death would bring us peace. Yet, the will to survive is so strong that we took every chance to keep ourselves going, somehow.

After my fourteen weeks in the sweegie-bar, I had gone back to work on the death railway, alongside the other men. I found it very hard to get back into that hard labouring, but at least I had something in me to fight with for a while. Every day our inhuman guards drove us on in the torrid heat and humidity, parched and hungry every minute. I was either cutting the railway track, carrying earth in heavy baskets or breaking up stones. Whatever my task, I was not allowed to return to camp until I had completed my quota. While I was the strongest, I helped my friends complete theirs too whenever I could, without being seen.

I thank God that, being a footballer, I wasn't a smoker. But several of our boys craved a cigarette. The Korean guards saw the furtive looks some of our lads gave them when they took out their packets of cigarettes. So they would deliberately light up, where everyone could see them, take a few puffs, exhale in the direction of nearby POWs, then throw down the remainder of their lit tab among our poor men, who scrambled and fought for it in the dirt. I don't blame our lads, but to watch those uncouth guards laughing their sadistic heads off used to make my blood boil.

By now our camp, Kanu, had become about the largest one on that stretch of the Kwai and, as we progressed with our jungle clearance and railway building, two other, smaller camps were built by Thai natives. These camps, one and two miles up-river, were named Kanu 1 and Kanu 2. Our own workforce had now become so depleted by illness and injury that our guards tried to beat more and more work out of those of us still able to stand. But, of course, it was physically impossible to get us to work any harder. Only the most severely sick were left in camp or in the hospital huts. But now, the Japs and Koreans would regularly tour Kanu camp in search of any additional men they could force to work.

I did admire our medical officers for fighting off these cruel guards. Often they would get smacked around the face or beaten for telling these bastards that this or that POW was incapable of working. Our commanding officer, Colonel Lilley, in particular stood up to them. We all admired him greatly for that.

'That man deserves a medal,' said Geordie as we passed him on our way across the camp. 'But I don't suppose he'll get one.'

With all this relentless work, and rapidly losing my healthy weight, I sank into another of my depressions and most evenings I strolled slowly down to our sacred little cemetery. I remember one of those evenings, when my eyes filled with tears as I gazed up and down the lines of graves, each with its small bamboo cross. The most awful thoughts went through my mind. Then I remembered my precious wife and son, and the eighteen-month-old child I had never seen. I came from a big, happy family of brothers and sisters and I wondered how they all were, and my mum and dad too. Since we had first met, when she was a barmaid, I'd only had three years of happiness with my beloved Christine before war started, and only three months of those living as husband and wife. The thought that I had been away from her now for half the time I'd known her made me feel even worse. We were seven thousand miles apart, and I knew my chances of survival were not good. Would I ever see her, or any of them, again?

Johnny's future wife, Christine was 'Miss Reading', in 1936. They met when he had just returned from the Islington Corinthians world tour. From Johnny's scrap book.

I pictured my home – my own little palace – with my lovely Christine, formerly Miss Reading, the title Christine had won three years before the war began. Did she still keep a place in her heart for me?

'Johnny, you know it takes two or three hundred men to make an encampment,' I said to myself. 'But only one woman to make a home.'

As I walked back, dragging my feet, to my lousy bamboo hut, I saw my loved ones' faces in my mind and remembered all the love and happiness they had given me. I fell asleep that night, mentally and physically exhausted.

I was surprised and grateful to wake up the next morning feeling brighter and thinking only of good things. I don't know what it was that changed my mood, but now I was ready to face another twelve-hour day of back-breaking work in the jungle.

So many of our men were going down with serious cases of malaria and beriberi that you can imagine what our dedicated doctors had to contend with every day. I found out that Colonel Lilley went to the Japanese commandant with demands for supplies. Some of our lads overheard them speaking.

'These very sick men will all die if we do not receive medicines and better food for them,' he pleaded.

'It be all right if sick die,' the interpreter translated for the Japanese commander. 'There be more food for working men to eat.'

'But if the sick men get better, you will have more working men,' persisted the colonel, bravely.

I bet that stumped the Japs, but it made no difference. If anything, our rations got even worse.

So, once again it was impossible to carry on without some kind of fiddle going, to help us survive. Sadly, some of our more upright, gentlemanly officers didn't make it, but by and large there were enough rascals in the camp, myself and Geordie included, to think up ways to keep us going from one day to the next. That and a bucketful of luck on our side.

As before, we had to resort to night-time antics. Some of us took any opportunity to break out of camp in twos or threes to look for food. We realised the dangers of course, and not just the Japs this time. One or two of the lads had seen tigers in the jungle nearby, and we couldn't spot the deadly snakes so easily in the dark, but we had to find additional rations somehow.

The obvious thing was to barter with the natives, as we had done before. But all we had left now to do business with were our rings or wristwatches, the last links with our loved ones. Even when things seemed to be at their worst, I couldn't bring myself to barter the ring Christine had given me when we got married, though I often came close to doing so. Most of my pals felt the same, so we had to look for other opportunities.

Occasionally we would come across a patch of cultivated ground to raid, near a Thai village. We were in desperate need of vegetables and fruit, and I didn't think twice about taking what I could, though I always tried to leave some of it intact for the poor grower to harvest. After all, they had to live too. Occasionally, if we were really lucky, we might find a stray chicken or two.

A few of the fittest and most enterprising lads somehow managed to obtain whole bags full of illicit food and take them to our officers, who wrote them letters of credit, made payable by the army, if and when we returned to England. Of course, most of these letters of credit would never be honoured, as so many of us passed away in captivity. But I guess that some of these men and officers returned home safely, and the few surviving sellers, if they had somehow managed to hold on to their receipts, might have made themselves a tidy packet.

Finally, there came a time when none of us had anything left to barter, except the piece of rag wrapped around our loins.

The Japanese used palm oil for cooking, and our bodies were crying out for some kind of fat in our diet, which we never had. I remember very well one day when a lad in my unit was caught stealing this precious oil from the Japanese cookhouse. He had filled his water-bottle with it, to share out sips around the hut later on. But he was caught leaving the sweegie-bar.

The Japs took him to their guardroom, bashed him around until he was almost dead on his feet, then ordered five nearby POWs, including me, to come inside. We were made to watch while the guards forced our bruised and battered comrade to drink this palm oil from his water-bottle. All of it. He did his best to drink the thick oil, but when he paused and started retching, the Japs held him and forced the rest of it down his throat.

I desperately wanted to step forward and stop them, and it was hard to hold myself back, but I knew that would only make things worse for him, as well as for me.

By the time they had finished with him he was in a terrible state and was violently sick. The guards stood and watched him, laughing their heads off. This incident was obviously the highlight of their day.

It was only after he had collapsed that the guards allowed us to take this poor wretch away. Fortunately, he did recover from his torture, but humiliation was the name of their game and this was only one of many such incidents, with more disastrous results for some of their victims.

The Japanese officers began to fear they wouldn't get their railway finished on time with the workforce dwindling, so once again they began to give us quinine tablets each morning. But it was too little too late and the death toll was mounting daily. Because the Japs couldn't now get enough of the men working, even with those standing sick lads forcibly taken from the hospital, they ordered our officers, many of them very weak, to make up a working party between them and work alongside us.

When this wasn't enough, the guards made us carry out some more of the sick men on bamboo stretchers. They reasoned that, though these men no longer had the strength to walk, they were still able to use their hands, so could break stones all day.

Every ten days, the guards had an afternoon off, so that meant we did too. First we cleaned up our camp, while the guards got themselves drunk on saki-wine. God help us if we got in their way, as we would be in for trouble, so once the cleaning had been done we used to go off and hide in the jungle with our friends.

I remember one time that a lad called Harry Dance from Barrow-in-Furness, an army boxing champion before the war, was badly beaten up by these drunken guards on their afternoon off. He was a highly strung individual. One of the guards upset him in some way and, in a sudden rage, Harry struck this guard an upper-cut to his chin.

Before he knew what was happening, he had been tied by his arms to a tree by four guards, with his toes just about touching the ground. They then proceeded to beat him without mercy, using anything they could lay their hands on. When they had finished with him he was covered in blood and hardly recognisable. After the guards had enjoyed a good laugh and walked away, some of his pals came and cut him down and took him to the hospital hut for medical attention.

As things turned out, I reckon he was very fortunate to get away with his life, as I'm sure that, had they been out of sight, deeper in the jungle, the guards would have finished him off.

On another of our rest afternoons, four of us lads went to the river Kwai to cool down and have a swim. Suddenly, five drunken Japanese guards appeared out of their tool-shed. They collared us and made us go into the tool-shed with them. They had found a little puppy dog from somewhere, probably belonging to the jungle natives, and had put its paw in a large vice. It made me feel sick just to think about what they intended to do. They made us watch while they slowly tightened this vice, until the little dog's foot was almost pulp. They laughed their heads off in a drunken frenzy. They tried to make us laugh too, but we couldn't even pretend. It was revolting and we were desperate to get out of that torture-chamber. Even Geordie went pale. When they finally let us go, we couldn't get out quick enough and several of us were physically sick on the river bank. What eventually happened to that poor animal, we never found out.

One afternoon off, splashing and swimming around in the Kwai, where it was only about six feet deep, we noticed there were a lot of fish around us. All of a sudden, one of the lads cried out in pain. Another friend and I went over and helped him out of the water. It was only then that we saw the reason – one of these fish had bitten him on the end of his penis! It was bleeding quite heavily and gave him trouble for days after that.

From then on, we always made sure to wrap something round our loins when we went for a swim in the river, in a mixture of fear for ourselves and laughter at this lad's plight, after he was fully recovered.

We had now been prisoners for about eighteen months and, although most of us were in poor health, the morale of the semi-fit men, including myself, was exceptionally good, despite the terrible conditions we lived in. But just as we found a way to cope mentally with everything, we were plagued more and more by flies and mosquitoes, carriers of malaria and dengue fever, both rife in the camp. The jungle seemed to be full of flying insects, so much so that it was impossible to eat our rice without also eating flies. They were almost tame and we had to pull them out of our mouths in case they were poisonous to us, though I suppose they were a handy source of protein when we did swallow them.

The mosquitoes played havoc with us at night, reducing still further our few sleeping hours and making hell of our lives. On top of this, dysentery, always a problem for us, flared up into a real epidemic throughout Kanu camp. Men were in and out of the jungle toilets all the time.

To make matters worse, if you can imagine it any worse, we had to salute the guard and say '*Benjo*-speedo?' – meaning 'Can I go to the lavatory, quick?' – before they would let us go.

We had to hope he would reply 'oh-ka-ga', or 'yes', and we could make a desperate dash to get there on time.

Of course we hadn't had any lavatory paper since our first imprisonment, and any leaves we collected didn't last long, so we had to follow the natives' way and use water out of bamboo containers called 'boats' to try and clean ourselves up each time. An almost impossible task with constant diarrhoea.

But dysentery, bad as it became, was nothing compared to the next shock. We heard about it when we got back to the camp one evening.

'Cholera!' exclaimed one of the sick men who did light work around the camp.

'Here?' I asked, trying to hide the fear in my voice.

'It soon will be,' he said with a downcast expression. 'Cholera has broken out at Kinsaiyok camp, just ten miles up-country. Lots of men are dead already, and many more are dying.'

'Thank God it's not in our camp!' I sighed. 'Not yet anyway. But how can we stop it? It's the rainy season.' It was true, the rain lashed down several times a day and the ground was slushy underfoot. We were down-river, so it could only be a matter of time.

'Collect your rations as usual,' he told us. 'After we've eaten, at eight o'clock, all the men who can walk must come to the compound in the centre of camp.'

'What for?' asked Geordie.

'So that the officers can instruct us about safety precautions in case this plague strikes us.'

'Or *when* it does, more likely,' added another lad with a hangdog face.

As we all gathered at eight o'clock, an anxious silence settled heavily, like a cloud overhead.

'I don't wish to cause any panic among you,' began our senior officer. 'But I feel I must be blunt on this occasion, as we are all in terrible danger and need to work together to ward off a disease worse than any we have encountered so far.'

I went cold all over, despite the evening heat.

'To begin with,' he continued. 'Every one of you must sterilise everything you use in boiling water for ten minutes. And you must keep your hands clean at all times. I know that is not easy in our situation, but you must be especially careful to wash your hands thoroughly in boiled water before picking up any food to eat.'

Whether these instructions helped us to ward off this evil threat for a few hours or so, I don't know. But before we knew it, cholera struck our camp . . . and we were in real trouble.

Within two or three days, men had started to die, and the whole of Kanu camp was in turmoil. I didn't realise quite how sudden and severe cholera was until it surrounded us. One day I would be working alongside a man on the railway, and the next day he died. It could be that quick, sometimes just a few hours. I suppose our weak physical condition hastened its effects but nobody could resist it, once they had contracted the disease.

We all sank into a potent mixture of fear and depression. Morale hit rock-bottom again. It seemed to us that it could only be a matter of time before we were all struck down with it. We were already walking skeletons, and now we were waiting to succumb and die. The future, however short it might be, looked black. Death had always been a daily presence in our lives as POWs, but now our outlook was bleaker than ever before. And yet, death was the only relief from this relentless life of work, beatings, starvation and disease.

Every evening, when we returned from work on the railway, we had to set to and bury the dead, a terrible and dangerous job. First we looked among them in case we recognised any of our friends, which sometimes happened. It was overwhelming, but we always tried to give each dead man a thought and a prayer before we buried him. We tied every body up in a rice sack, if we had enough, and attached a little note saying the man's name and rank.

'Whatever you do,' I told my lads as we lifted the bodies down into their graves, 'don't touch your faces with your hands, or any part of your body that has touched one of these corpses.'

A few sleeping huts on the edge of the camp had been set aside for the cholera patients, to keep them as far as possible from the rest of us, and we were advised to keep well away. We were all scared stiff, seeing for ourselves how contagious cholera was and how quickly it killed. After the first few days of anxious tension, I walked around the camp like an empty vessel, all emotions drained away, which was probably just as well.

More and more I wanted to be on my own and I often went down to that holy spot, the cemetery. This was the only time when I allowed myself to feel anything. I would put my head in my hands and say a little prayer for each of the men. What a waste of good young life, I thought. What's the use? It could be my turn soon. My luck can't hold up for ever.

12

The Hammer-Tap Boys

July 1943

One morning during the early days of the cholera outbreak, we were going out to work on the railway, in sweltering heat, when one of my pals collapsed right in front of me, drenched with sweat and his face grey with the look of impending death. I took one step forward, then stopped myself. This must be cholera, I thought. I mustn't touch him.

No more than a second passed while I hesitated, then I took the risk. So much sweat could mean malaria, and I would never forgive myself if I didn't help him, whatever it was. A couple of the other brave lads helped me to lay him down as comfortably as we could beside the railway track. I was desperate to get him back into camp and take him straight to the medical officer and give him the best chance of recovery, or even survival, so I went over to the nearest guard, a Korean, and pointed at my pal Joe.

'Man very sick,' I began, in simple words that he might understand. 'Me take man, get help?'

His face turned red with rage as he stepped forward and slapped my face with the flat of his hand. 'Man good,' he screeched, and slapped me again.

As always, I had to stand and take it, without showing any response. I was aware that he was holding up his rifle, ready to clout me with its butt, or worse, so I knew I would have to leave poor Joe where he was.

'You work. Speedo-speedo!'

It was a very long day, in the scorching sun, with very little food and water between us. This heat was a killer and I was very worried about Joe. I kept an eye on him as best I could, as he drifted in and out of consciousness, and I gave him sips of water from my water-bottle when the guards weren't looking, so there wasn't much of it left for me. One time the little Korean saw me and rushed over to lash me with a bamboo cane.

'Don't worry, Joe,' I tried to reassure him when I was moving between tasks. 'We'll get you back to the doc as soon as we can.' I only hoped we would be in time. As the day wore on and he was still with us, just about, I was relieved to think that perhaps it wasn't cholera after all.

At last it was six o'clock and time for us to return to camp. Between us, we carried this poor, feverish boy back to the camp hospital. When we left him there with the medical officer, I could see he was in a bad way and barely conscious.

After eating my usual jungle soup, I had a quick clean-up and went back to the hospital hut to see how this lad was getting on.

'How is he, Doc?'

'Well . . .' he began slowly, weary to his bones.

'Is it cholera?' I had to know.

'No, thank God. We have lost enough men to that killer already. However, your man is lucky to be alive. I don't know how long he can last, with no strength left in his body to fight it.'

'Is it malaria?' I asked.

'Yes, malaria with a high fever, and also a bad case of dysentery.'

I sat with the boy for about an hour, holding his hand and telling him all kinds of lies to try and cheer him up.

'I've just heard we're winning the war. The Americans are coming to free us soon, so you have to keep going. I want you to be there when the Yanks arrive, so you've got to do your best to get well again. It's only a touch of malaria. You've beaten it before, and you'll beat it again now. A good bit of rest – that's all you need.' He was delirious, so I wasn't sure if he could hear me. 'In fact, I could do with a good bit of rest myself,' I joked. Was it my imagination – I thought I saw the glimmer of a smile.

I visited him again the next night, but I don't think it did any good. He died a couple of days later. I sometimes wonder, even now, whether he could have survived if that cruel guard had let me take him straight back, out of the searing sun, for treatment. Perhaps it was possible, but I will never know, and there will always remain a slight doubt in my mind . . . could I have saved him?

Suicide was very much on men's minds during this period. It seemed like a quick way out. But thank God I remained sane and put that thought right out of my head . . . or maybe I never had the guts to do it anyway. But I understood the few that did.

Cholera raged on, taking a heavy toll. Our previous day-to-day live-or-die basis now became hour-to-hour. The slightest ache, cough or bout of diarrhoea spelt death tomorrow as far as we were concerned, and since most of us had diarrhoea anyway, we were all very fearful.

We endured this state of affairs for several more days, until the epidemic began to subside. We could barely understand this.

'If it's so contagious, Sarge,' said one of my lads, 'how come the cholera huts have fewer men in them now?'

'I don't know. Maybe we are building up immunity to it.'

We might have been losing fewer men to cholera now, but we were still losing them to a string of other complaints. It was work, work and more work.

As I lay on my bamboo sleeping platform one night, trying to get off to sleep, I remember turning everything over and over in my mind. Then I wondered for the umpteenth time about trying to escape, but how could I? It was an impossibility. I was too thin, weak and weary to get far. I had no medical supplies or food and would not be able to forage for sustenance in this virgin jungle where so many things were poisonous and could kill me quicker than the railway. I didn't even know where we were – just somewhere between Thailand and Burma, but I would have no idea how to plan an escape route, other than along the river Kwai, which was where I would be sure to be caught by the Japs and killed. And if any of the natives tried to help me, it would mean certain death for them too. The outlook seemed grim. All we could do was carry on until we dropped.

Then, with the snores of the lads resounding around me, the insects biting and various creatures running over me, I pulled up my ragged cover and my thoughts turned to all those men who were lying ill in the camp hospital, men who were fighting for their lives with little chance of survival. It was then, in the middle of the night, that I remember giving myself a talking to. *Johnny boy, you mustn't give up hope. You must fight on.* That was when I finally drifted off to sleep in my lice-infested bed.

In addition to all the usual medical problems pulling us down, large, deep ulcers were especially bad at this time. Some men had two or three of them on each leg, horribly infected with pus, and seething with maggots. Our medical orderlies had to use a spoon and scrape out the pus, along with the maggots, which was excruciating for the men, without anything to numb the pain. Once every last vestige had gone, they would swab out the ulcers with rags and hot water, which had been boiled by volunteers like me. Then they would put a handful of washed maggots into the gaping hole in the man's flesh and let them eat away the infection. Occasionally it worked, and other times it didn't.

Make no mistake, these men suffered, and sometimes gangrene set in, which meant certain death without quick action. Indeed, many lives were saved by immediate amputation, but remember, this was nothing like a hospital operation under anaesthetic. It was a crude task, performed without the benefit of any kind of painkiller, so the poor victim was aware and in fearful agony throughout.

There was one Australian medical officer who performed

absolute miracles, with the most primitive tools and utensils, while the poor orderlies held the screaming patients down. It used to send a chill through my spine every time, just watching these men having their limbs literally chopped or sawn off.

Work on the railway had now reached Hellfire Pass, sheer rock faces we had to cut through and an area of enormous boulders we had to remove. The only way was blasting them with dynamite. So the Japs organised a body of men known as the hammer-tap boys. To our horror, Geordie and I were put on this work for three months. What we had to do was to pair ourselves off in twos, one man with a long chisel or drill length and the other with a sledgehammer.

The guards would then march us out and set each pair the task of hammering and tapping. This meant that each pair had to work together. Luckily, I managed to grab Geordie as my partner. I couldn't have chosen better. One man would wield the sixteen-pound sledgehammer and the other a drill-bit, a short one at first, then longer, to the longest. As the man with the hammer pounded it down on the slim drill-bit his partner, who was holding the rock, had to twist it. Hammer-tap and twist, all day long, to a depth of eighteen inches every time, jarring our bodies with every blow of the hammer, with never a moment to rest, twelve hours a day.

As you can imagine, many suffered wounded hands or fingers, or on rare occasions heads, from inaccurately aimed sledgehammers. We had to trust each other in our pairs, which fortunately Geordie and I did, and take whatever rudimentary precautions we could to avoid potentially disastrous consequences for us and anyone nearby.

These holes we made were to put the explosives in, which we had to prepare ourselves, along with the short fuses. A guard would give us a lit cigarette to light the fuse, leaving us only a few seconds to literally run for our lives from the blast each time.

'Speedo-speedo', the guards constantly hurried us on, and yet rushing the delicate work of preparing and igniting the explosives could have killed us. I know that many POWs died doing it.

We were not allowed to return to camp until we had blasted enough rocks. This was very unfair, as sometimes we would encounter a particularly hard boulder, which would take longer to drill. But whatever our fortune, if we were given a certain job to do, we had to complete it.

'Bastards!' muttered Geordie. 'So that's how the crafty guards are working things now.'

They certainly squeezed every last ounce of effort out of us. Whatever our tasks, whether we were digging, blasting or building the railway embankment, we were worked almost to death. And if the guards felt we were getting behind, we would soon feel the sharp sting of a bamboo stick around our backsides.

Once back at camp, we were all in, desperate with hunger and especially thirst. We could barely summon the strength to go to the cookhouse and collect our rations. After that we would occasionally go down to the river that ran alongside the camp and swill ourselves down, but often we were too worn out. All we could do was just collapse on to our lousy, bug-ridden beds and fall asleep.

At this stage I again contracted that terrible soreness and irritation, mainly between my legs, so I could barely walk, and it was excruciating when I did. It was between my toes and under my arms as well. I can tell you, it nearly drove me crazy.

I also blew up to a huge size again, but this time it was nothing to do with food – I was more malnourished now than I had ever been, but I had fluid or maybe water collecting under my skin and making me bloated. This was extremely uncomfortable, and in the intense heat and sweating heavily I felt as if I could burst. I was in agony. But my condition was not sufficient for the guards to allow me to go for treatment in the jungle hospital. They saw me as big and 'fat', therefore fit for work. Perhaps the medics couldn't have helped me anyway, as I think it was all to do with vitamin and mineral deficiencies – a symptom of beriberi.

A few of the guards had picked up a handful of English words so that they could boss us around better. But with most of them, all they knew was 'speedo-speedo', which they shouted at us all day long, even though it was impossible for most of us to speed up at all. We could only work at one pace now, and that was slow. All the driving and beating made no difference whatsoever.

At night our huts and beds were infested with bugs and it was nothing unusual for us to wake up in the morning covered from head to foot with bites. On one of our afternoons off, Geordie and I decided to take our beds to pieces. They were made of bamboo canes that had been split and laid flat. Never any mattresses of course. Very uncomfortable at the best of times, but the insects made them purgatory.

'Let's lever all the bamboos out,' Geordie suggested. 'And beat them.'

'Good idea.' So that's what we did. We beat them as hard as we could.

'They're alive, man,' shrieked Geordie in excitement as we saw all these tiny black bugs scrambling out of the split bamboos, trying to escape our frenzied beating.

'Let's get the blighters,' I yelled, beating all the harder to make them run.

'There must be hundreds of them.'

'Yes, I'm counting.' I never dreamt our beds would be so crawling with these little black, blood-sucking devils. We both beat the pile of bamboos from my bed all the harder and carried on counting as fast as we could, trying to keep up with them all.

'I make that at least four hundred and fifty,' said Geordie.

'Yes. A lot more got away too, I reckon. I've lost count.'

When we'd got as many as we could out of my bamboos, we started on his, dancing around in our killing frenzy as we kept on beating, delighted to see the streams of frightened bugs scrambling over the battered corpses of their dead comrades and running away in all directions. The stench of these miniature monsters as we crushed them was vile.

'Your bed had hundreds of them too,' I said triumphantly, as we finally stopped for a rest.

'Well, at least we should get a better night's sleep tonight,' smiled Geordie as we gingerly picked up and shook our split bamboos, before taking them to fit back in our bed frames.

Geordie was right. We both slept better that night, but by the next our beds were overrun with bugs again, just as before.

Another constant preoccupation was the state of our latrines. They were built about a hundred yards away from the huts, on the edge of the jungle. They had to be as far away as possible because of all the insects, flies and maggots they harboured. When we built these latrines, we made a fence all around, then dug a hole about four or five feet long and about six feet deep. We placed bamboo poles all the way along, at six-inch intervals over the hole, for the men to sit on. When the latrines were newly built they were not too bad. But now, with the heat, the humidity and the awful stench, they were alive and teeming with maggots, so much so that we could not avoid stepping on them with our bare feet as we went in and out. It made me feel sick and I was loath to use the latrines if I could possibly help it, but we had no option most of the time.

Always aching with hunger and desperate to fill their bellies, a few of the most daring risk-takers continued to seek out any opportunity to steal food from the Japs. Even the theft of a few grains of rice or a cabbage leaf, if discovered, led to a brutal thrashing, or worse.

On several occasions, the guards tied men's hands behind their backs and made them kneel down in front of the guardroom, under the sun, for days on end with containers of food and water in front of them, but of course out of reach. As they roasted throughout the heat of the day, the poor blighters, choking from thirst and hunger, could only stare at these life-giving supplies. It seemed the worst kind of torture to us as we were made to walk by, to frighten us. We later found out that these men were given only a minimal amount of both food and water just once every twenty-four hours, at night. It was barely enough to relieve their burning throats and nothing more. Some men never recovered from this sadistic treatment.

It seemed the more they could make us suffer, the more they enjoyed themselves – the fanatical bastards. Even now, my blood boils every time I think about it. By God, if I ever meet any of them . . .

13

Vultures at Kanu 2

September 1943

A small but particularly daring group of POWs, mostly Australians this time, seized on any opportunity to sell our railway construction tools to natives, in exchange for food. These Aussies were devils for rascalry and they took terrible chances, with the risks of dire punishments, which just went to show the kind of courage the majority of Aussies had.

Two of these would-be heroes were caught for this serious crime. The Japs immediately shot dead the natives who had been seen exchanging their food for the Imperial army's tools. The two Aussies were dragged off to the Jap guardroom, stripped and forced to stand naked in the searing sun for several days. If they fell down, they were beaten. At the end of this punishment, when they could no longer stay upright, the Japs took them into the jungle, made them dig their own graves and shot them point-blank. We heard those shots reverberating between the trees, sending birds out in all directions, and stood silently outside our huts, heads bowed in solidarity with our murdered comrades.

The Jap and Korean guards all started to indulge in a new sport, humiliating POW officers in front of their men. They would haul one officer out at random and insult him or beat him while we were forced to watch and do nothing to help him. The valour these officers showed as they stood up to their taunting and beatings without flinching was absolutely, bloody marvellous. Never did I see a British or Australian officer shrink away from the treatment meted out to him. They always took it like a man, however bad it was, no matter how ill or weak they were, and we all felt proud to give them the credit they deserved for this show of bravery.

Sometimes our officers were punished for standing up for their men, trying to protect them. It could be fatal to interfere when the Japs started laying into someone, so we greatly respected our officers' guts for putting themselves in the firing line on our behalf.

Despite everything, our officers still managed to organise informal sing-songs and evening concerts for those who were fit or strong enough to attend. These entertainments were intended to raise our spirits and it worked – they were great morale-boosters for everyone. We would sit round a campfire and sing 'Take me back to dear old Blighty', or 'It's a long way, to Tipperary'. What a raucous crowd we were, and those songs truly made us feel closer to home on such evenings.

A good friend of mine in the camp at this time was Reg Marks, from Leeds. He was absolutely fabulous in our concerts. He had made himself a ukulele out of bamboo, and played it so well that he could almost make it talk. I well remember how he used to make up songs about the various guards we had, taking the mickey out of them, something rotten. These songs were the high point of every concert. They made us laugh till we cried. This started some of the guards off laughing too. Little did they realise they were laughing at themselves!

Every day, our officers pleaded for more food and medical supplies. The Japs made empty promises of help that never arrived. However, as our ranks became more and more depleted, we started to see small changes in their attitude. One day a Japanese doctor arrived to give us all injections which, he said, would combat certain diseases that were rife in our camps.

Many of our boys found ways to dodge these injections.

'How do we know they're proper medicines to make us better?' asked one of the lads in my hut.

'Yes, Sarge,' added another. 'The Japs might be trying to kill us off with their needles. They might be lethal injections.'

'I can see why you're worried, lads,' I said. 'But, think about it. There are so few of us left now that they are afraid they might not get their precious railway finished, so it's in their interests to try and keep the rest of us alive long enough.'

I continued to make visits to the camp hospital, so I saw first-hand how sick some of our invalids were. Dysentery wasted some of them away to nothing but skin and bones, their eyes hollow above their jagged cheekbones. The POWs with the worse cases of malaria were delirious and almost insane. It was all so pitiful to see.

I spoke with a lot of the boys and persuaded some of them at least to have the injections. What did we have to lose? We couldn't go on as we were.

The next thing was the arrival of additional food supplies up the river. I was detailed to take some men and unload the barges. We didn't know whether these supplies were intended for us or for the Japanese, but they didn't watch us very closely so it gave us the opportunity to sneak away some of the extra rations to keep ourselves going.

Well, to our great surprise, the additional foods were for the POWs. The Japs' promises had been genuine this time, but it was still not enough to restore our health or strength, just sufficient to keep the semi-fit working as long as they needed us.

We had now cleared a swathe through the jungle, so many kilo-metres each way, containing a partly-built railway track through all kinds of terrain, from thick undergrowth to dynamite-blasted rocks, from tropical swamps to bridges spanning gorges. Building these bridges involved pulling some massive tropical tree-trunks into place. Sometimes they harnessed up a team of POWs to do the haulage work, but we were too weak to pull hard enough, so they brought in trained elephants to drag the heaviest timber into position.

Allied POWs, used as forced labour, building the bridge
over the River Kwai, at Tamarkan, c. 1943.

The Japanese engineers who supervised the construction of
these astonishing bridges were very clever, in some ways. But they
seemed to have overlooked the fact that most of the wood and
bamboo we used in the erection of these viaducts was timber
felled by us, green and unseasoned. We realised what they hadn't
– that it would at some time bend or warp as the wood dried out.
We grinned at the thought of the Japs' dismay when their precious
bridges started to fall apart.

I doubted at the time that even a narrow-gauge train would
ever safely cross some of these gorges. As we later found out, a
few did, but due to the green timber, along with some clever sabotage by us at every stage, many of these bridges collapsed, some
of them taking full trains down into the gorges with them.

I was now ordered to make a second journey to Kanu 2 camp, a
couple of miles up-country, to do a bit of maintenance work.

There were about fifteen of us altogether, so I had to leave most of my pals behind and hope they wouldn't be moved somewhere else while I was away. We were told it would be for about four weeks, but what terrible memories those four weeks hold for me.

Just before we reached Kanu 2 there was a camp for Thai natives, or rather an area where the Japs had about two hundred of them working like slaves and starving even worse than we were. My God, the stench, and I shall never forget the sight of these poor wretches, lying about all over the place in their own mess, suffering from all the diseases and deficiencies we had, completely disorganised and without any medical aid whatsoever. They were fouling the ground all around them, which in turn harboured flies and maggots. It was a living hell.

Perched in the trees above their clearing were dozens of hunched, beady-eyed vultures, waiting to swoop down as soon as there was a new death. I thought to myself, thank goodness this would not be allowed in my camp, where we always frightened them away whenever we saw them.

You know, I feel sure these vultures could smell death in the air, for they were restless as they perched and waited, uneasy in their eagerness to be the first to reach the next corpse. Walking through the nearby jungle, we had seen dead bodies reduced to piles of bones, where it was obvious the vultures had had their fill.

One evening after work, three of us were having a stroll into the jungle, close to our camp, and the native camp too, when we came upon a sight that shocked us rigid. A vast hole had been dug in the ground, in which numerous bodies were lying on top of each other. The smell was indescribable. It was an unfinished mass grave. There had been no attempt to fill it in and it swarmed with flies, while scores of vultures were frantic in their frenzy to tear the flesh from the bones.

I turned away in horror, my hands to my mouth and my stomach heaving. As we walked back towards the relative safety and sanity of Kanu 2 camp, we came across two more bodies, one of them sitting against a tree as if he were having a nap. In fact that's what I thought he was doing, but when I touched him, he toppled over, his body still in its sitting position. He had obviously been dead for some time as the flies and red ants had begun to eat away at him.

When we got back to our camp, we felt so dirty that we picked up our pieces of rag that we were using as towels and went down to immerse ourselves in the river. We cooled down and cleaned ourselves up as best we could without any kind of soap. All of a sudden, down went one of my pals, down under the water. We pulled him to the bank and he was flat out, so we took him to the small hospital hut at Kanu 2, where we found him a bunk and hoped for the best.

We buried that boy five days later, and as he was from my unit I was asked to supervise his burial. I felt so low that when the burial party left, I collapsed to my knees, with my head in my hands, and cried like a child. I had lost yet another friend. Everything seemed so hopeless. I knew this wasn't like me, but I realised my resistance was low and I was in the doldrums again. I remember saying to myself, *This is hopeless. What's the use of struggling on?* Yet, even in this sorry state, I knew I had to hold on to the hope that my luck would keep me going, somehow.

14

Raucous Duets

October 1943

Whether it was luck, fate or what, I shall never know, but something must have helped me pull myself out of this depression and carry on. One evening, I returned from a ten-hour stint on the railway at Kanu 2 camp, ate my usual rice and jungle stew and lay down on my bamboo bunk, completely exhausted, thinking of home. I pictured each of my loved ones in turn, their features and expressions, as if trying to lodge their photos in my mind.

There was Christine, of course, with her beautiful smile that lit up the room. I missed her terribly. I wondered for one dreadful moment if she still missed me, but then I remembered what a loving and loyal girl she was. I was sure she'd be as worried about me as I was about her.

'Don't worry, Johnny,' she had whispered to me the night before I left that last time. 'Wherever you are, I'll always love you.'

Oh, if only I could reach out and touch her . . .

Then there was Philip, our son, born in 1940. He'd only been a tiddler the last time I saw him, and not very well, but now I wouldn't recognise him. He would be healthier, I hoped, and would be running around, aged four, causing havoc and plaguing his mother no doubt. I was sad that he wouldn't remember me. And, of course, Christine had been in the later stages of her pregnancy in the last letter I'd received from her, when our ship docked in Durban on our way to Singapore. I hoped she'd had an easy birth and wondered for the thousandth time whether this second baby was a boy or a girl. That child would now be two and a half, and we hadn't even met. I imagined the three of them, Christine and the children, in our house. I took myself on a mental tour of the house, walking from room to room, picturing where everything was, and imagining where the children's beds and toys might be. When . . . if I got back, I would hold my lovely Christine and the children in my arms and never let them go.

My mum and dad were much in my mind that evening too. We had always been a close and fun-loving family. Dad ran a pub and when we were young we children were always getting into scrapes – me most of all. I smiled as I remembered the time I was so hungry that I crept into the larder and ate all that cold chicken. Now, of course, I would give anything for even a tiny slice of chicken, but I would have to be patient.

I was really enjoying these reminiscences, my one comfort from the daily torments of my life, when a young lad of about twenty-one from my own regiment, the 35th Light-Ack-Ack, came in and flopped down beside me. Thin and weak to his bones, he curled up and cried like a baby.

'What is it, Pat?' I knew of course, but I had to ask, to get him talking.

'I can't take any more, Sarge,' he blurted out between sobs. 'I might as well end it all now and get it over with.'

'Come here,' I said, encouraging him to sit up and putting my arm around his bony shoulders. 'You must stop talking like that. I was just enjoying some memories of my family before the war. Maybe you can try and do the same. They will be waiting for you to come home. You mustn't let them down.'

'But how can I ever go home? Look at me. I'm ill; I can't survive much longer.'

'Now, come on, Pat my boy. Pull yourself together. We're all in the same boat.'

'I know, Sarge. But it's a sinking boat.' He sniffed as he tried to stop his tears.

'The war can't go on for ever,' I said. 'It will soon be over, and we'll be on our way home.'

'Do you really think so?' He used the flat of his hand to wipe the tears from his cheek.

'I'm sure. It's only a matter of time, so cheer yourself up a bit with that thought and concentrate on the positive things.'

We talked until nearly lights out, as he told me about his family. He seemed to brighten up a bit as he described them to me.

'Thanks, Sarge,' Pat said as he got up to go back to his own hut. 'Thank you for listening. I feel a bit better now.'

'Good. Come back and see me any time you want a chat.' I was glad I had given him some hope. He came back many times after that and whenever I could get hold of some extra food, I always kept a bit for him. He gradually pulled through his depression and survived our last few months on the death railway.

We were relieved when the guards took us back to the main Kanu camp. Conditions there were bad enough, of course, but nothing like what we had experienced at Kanu 2. As we trekked back down the overgrown path through the jungle, we looked forward to meeting up with old friends again, and to the concerts and sing-songs that helped us to forget our troubles for a time.

There was a Welshman in my new hut at the main Kanu camp, a sergeant by the name of Taffy Miles. He was fitter than we were, and a cheerful chap. Boy, could that chap sing. He got together with Reg Marks and his home-made ukulele, and the two of them singing raucous duets together made us all laugh like drains. They were always the highlight of our concerts, and they certainly gave our morale a huge boost when we most needed it.

'Hey Jimmy,' Reg would say to anyone who seemed depressed, regardless of their name. 'Let's go to the concert together tonight and I'll work out a couple of new songs.' And he always did. He and Taffy cheered everyone up, and the bonus is that I know they both arrived home safely after the war.

* * *

It was autumn 1943 and we had almost completed clearing and building the embankment of our section of the railway, and the final fixing of the sleepers and tracks was supervised by the engineers, so it was less arduous work for us, which was a huge blessing. All we had to do was carry the sleepers and the tracks up the embankment. I don't think they trusted us to help them much with the laying of them, so they did most of it themselves. Just as well for them, really, I reckon. We would have had great pleasure in finding ways to sabotage the railway that had killed so many of our boys. But we hadn't given up hope yet!

POWs laying the track for the Burma-Thailand 'Death Railway', c. 1943.

Towards the end of my stay at the infamous Kanu camp, I had another horrible experience. One evening, after my day's stint on the railway, I collected my usual rations and devoured these morsels like an animal, ravenously hungry. Then, instead of strolling down to the river with Geordie, Reg and the lads as usual to have a swill-down, I was so dog-tired I went back to my hut to rest.

The next thing I knew, it was about four o'clock in the morning and I woke with an excruciating pain in my right ear. It drove me round the bend, so I knew I wouldn't be able to sleep again; I was in too much pain to lie still and rest. I didn't know what to do with myself. Everybody else in the hut was still asleep, so I got up and wandered around the camp, my hand clamped to my ear, as if this might make it better, and thinking all kinds of terrible things.

A Korean guard came over to me and gesticulated to ask me what I was doing up and about at that time of the morning.

'Bad ear,' I said loudly, pointing at it, as if that would make it easier to understand.

'Sleepo-speedo,' he ordered in a shrill voice, so back I went to my hut. The pain was so sharp, I sat up on my bunk, trying to think what might be wrong with my ear. I couldn't remember doing anything to it the day before, so I thought all the worst things, as people often do in the dark hours of the night. Finally it occurred to me that this could be the symptom of a fatal illness, my worst fear . . . maybe this was the beginning of the end for me.

I put my finger into my ear, to see if that helped. But it didn't. It hurt so much I yelped with the pain and woke one of the lads who slept near me.

'What's up, Sarge?'

'I've got an awful pain in my ear. Can you take a look for me?'

He took a brave risk and lit one of the tallow candles, holding it up to try and look inside my ear.

'Can you see anything?' I was desperate to know.

'Nothing, Sarge. It all looks normal to me – a bit grubby, mind,' he grinned. Normally I'd have laughed with him, but not that morning.

The pain persisted for what seemed an age, but was only a few hours. I had to wait for sick parade, to go and see the medical officer. I joined a very long line of men, with all sorts of ailments, some of them having to dash off to the latrines every few minutes. This lengthy wait extended my agony and fear even more, until finally my turn came.

'What can I do for you this morning, Sergeant?' asked the doc, in a weary voice. He must have seen at least a hundred men before me.

'It's my ear, sir. I was perfectly all right when I went to bed, but I was woken before dawn by this awful pain in my right ear.'

'Let me have a look.' He took out some kind of instrument and looked through it inside my ear. 'Mmm,' he muttered. Then he took some tweezers and starting probing about. The agony increased and I couldn't sit still. It was all I could do to stay on my seat.

Suddenly, a few seconds of such pain that I thought my head would explode with it, and then it abruptly eased, as the medic gently pulled something out of my ear canal.

'There's your trouble, Sergeant Sherwood,' he said in triumph as he laid the offending article on the palm of his hand. It was a dead insect, about the size of a wasp.

'This little beast ate through the dirt and wax in your ear while you were asleep, and died inside. That's where your pain came from.'

Of course, having no soap, we all suffered from this build-up of grime and wax, which caused a lot of our lads to suffer troubles with their ears, but I hadn't heard of anyone with a dead insect inside one of them.

'So how did that little blighter manage to crawl its way through all that in the first place?' asked the lad who had looked in my ear earlier.

'I'm amazed anything could get in there!' laughed Reg.

'Maybe it had to fight so hard to get in,' grinned Geordie, 'that the wee thing was all worn out and couldn't escape.' He made a sad face.

'It was as big as a hornet!' I protested, with slight exaggeration. 'Are you telling me you feel more sorry for that cruel insect than for me?' I tried to look offended, but couldn't help laughing with the lads. It was such a great relief to get rid of the worst of the pain, and to know there was nothing seriously wrong with me. Another lucky escape.

Over the next few days, the ear was still quite sore, but that soon wore off and I hoped I would never have to go through such an ordeal again.

Now that we were nearing the end of work on our stage of the railway, some of our so-called 'fit' men, including me, were gathered together by a lieutenant and given new orders.

'The Japs need more men to go and work up-river at the next camp, and you are the strongest men we have left.'

'Call this strong?' asked one of the other sergeants.

'Well, at least you're still standing,' replied the lieutenant.

'Do you mean Kanu 2 camp, sir?' I asked.

'No, you'll be going further than that, to Kinsaiyok. The cholera played havoc up there and they lost a lot of men.'

'Isn't that why it's called the worst death camp?' asked Reg.

'Yes, probably,' nodded the lieutenant. 'But the cholera is over now.' He paused and turned to a Jap standing next to him. 'Now, I've asked the interpreter to tell you more about your role when you get there.' He stood back.

'You go finish railway,' began the interpreter. 'Men behind with work. We need speedo-speedo at Kinsaiyok.'

I groaned. Just when we thought life might get a little easier . . .

As Geordie and Reg walked back to their huts, I strolled dejectedly back to mine. The misery I felt to be going up-river to more 'speedo-speedo', just when we'd thought all that might be over, was only lightened by the fact that at least I would still have some of my pals with me. As long as we stuck together, I knew we could keep each other going, and buoy up some of the younger lads too.

I was mentally preparing myself to leave Kanu for the dreaded Kinsaiyok camp the next day, when I had a surprise visit. You remember the Japanese interpreter with near-perfect English who befriended me at Tarso, and probably saved my life there? Well, this Jap interpreter had just been moved to Kanu and he immediately came to find me. Strange as it may seem, I think we were both genuinely pleased to see each other.

'I am sorry you are leaving,' he said with a smile. 'I wanted to say goodbye, and also to say sorry about the way many of you have been treated by the guards.'

'Thank you,' I nodded. 'But it wasn't your fault.'

'No. But I am sorry too about the many men who have died in Kanu camp.' He bowed his head in sadness. Then met my gaze again.

'I appreciate that,' I said, as we shook hands. 'I won't forget your kind words.'

'Good luck and God bless you,' he said. 'I will pray for you and your men.' He bowed and turned to go.

As I watched him leave my hut, I recalled that although this Jap often found himself in the thick of trouble, I had never once seen him raise his fists or lose his temper. He had always apologised for his companions and been courteous to our lads. I can honestly say that throughout my experience as a POW, this interpreter and the knitting *gunso* who saved my life a few months earlier were the only two Japs I encountered that showed any kindness or humanity at all. If only one or two others had been like them, we might have lost fewer men.

15

Football Tricks at Kinsaiyok

January 1944

On a scorching hot morning about a hundred of us were marched about twenty-five kilometres up-country to Kinsai-yok camp. We had heard the stories of how the cholera epidemic had blasted through the whole camp and only a few had survived. We dreaded what we might find there.

It was a surprise and great relief when we arrived and saw that the whole place looked fairly clean and tidy. And, considering how much they had suffered, the survivors seemed remarkably cheerful as they greeted us.

'Hello lads, welcome to Kinsaiyok hotel,' grinned one of them.

They showed us to a couple of empty huts, which had been scrubbed and swept out.

'I can smell disinfectant!' gasped one of the young lads in my group. 'I haven't smelt that for ages.'

'No, we got one issue of it after the cholera epidemic,' explained a corporal who had been with us at Tarso.

'So, has it gone, the cholera?' I asked.

'Yes, nobody's died of cholera here for weeks now, thank God.'

As we talked with the lads that evening, they told us about the camp and how they had got it ship-shape again.

'You've done a good job,' I said. 'Everything looks well organised.'

'Yes, since your Colonel Lilley arrived, we've really cleaned up and everything has improved,' said an Aussie POW. 'Now there's a man for you.'

'He's quite fearless,' agreed Geordie.

'Yes,' I chipped in. 'I remember him from when he was with us at Changi and Ban Pong camps.'

'He stood up to the Japs all right,' added Reg.

'That's what he's done here too, mate. He never stops requesting more food and medical supplies.'

'The guards hate his guts.'

'But he gets things done. The hospital has some new equipment and the chaps in our cookhouse do their best to stretch our rations.'

'We have activities for the men on our afternoons off, and there's even a camp barber.'

'Really?' I put my hand up to feel my matted thatch of hair, straggling on to my shoulders. I'd only been able to hack at it before. 'I'm first in the queue for a haircut,' I grinned. 'And a good, clean shave.'

'And I'm your man for a concert or two,' added Reg, getting his ukulele out of his haversack and strumming an impromptu tune.

'Hey, mate,' grinned the Aussie POW. 'You're good . . . for a pommie!'

At that, Reg added a few choice lyrics about the Kanu guards . . . and we all laughed together.

'George Formby, eat your heart out!'

As we toured the camp before lights out, I noticed a tidy cemetery near the river. It was immaculately kept, with not a weed out of place, and dozens of little graves with home-made bamboo crosses stuck neatly into the ground. About twenty of us entered this sacred little spot in the jungle, and we all paid our respects to these fallen comrades in our own ways. I knelt down by one of the graves, stroked the cross and bowed my head. Others strolled between the crosses, but all of us were lost in our silent thoughts, mourning so many lost lives. I later discovered that a lot of the cholera victims' bodies had been burnt in a crematorium the men had built, well away from the huts at the far end of the camp.

Australian POWs beside the graves of comrades who died during
the construction of the Burma-Thailand railway, c. 1943.

Although we had been told we would have to labour hard here
on the railway, we soon found out that most of the work had been
completed on this section of the line too. Our job was just to help
the engineers lay the sleepers and fix the tracks, which was curious since we had been kept away from these important finishing-off
tasks at Kanu. We took what chances we could to split the wood
or loosen the rivets without being found out, laughing to ourselves
as we imagined the havoc our finishing touches would cause. I
expect some of the engineers noticed later, when they inspected
the line, but hopefully they didn't spot everything.

Strange though it seemed, we were beginning to build ourselves
up quite well with less onerous work and longer periods of rest. We
even began to do some exercise and we felt things were looking up.

'Hey, Sarge.' A young soldier ran over towards me one evening.
'Some of the guards are kicking around a football. Come and
see,' he grinned, as if he knew me.

125

I tried desperately to think where I'd seen him before. Then I remembered.

'It's Ray, isn't it?'

'That's right, Sarge.'

'It's great to see you.' I shook him by the hand. 'How are you? Weren't we still at Singapore, the last time we met?'

'No, Ban Pong, Sarge,' he corrected me. 'Your group were marched off first, so we went to different camps, and I wasn't well for a while. But I'm not bad now.' He looked over his shoulder, then back at me. 'Let's go and take a look.'

As we walked across, I thought back to those matches we had in the early days. 'You were always keen on your football, weren't you? And good at it too. Remember those matches we played at Havelock Road camp?'

'Yes, Sarge. I'm going to try and get fit again when we get home and see if I can try out for one of the clubs.'

'Give me your address, Ray, if you can find something to write it on, and I'll see if I can organise a trial for you.'

'Oh, would you, Sarge? That would be amazing!'

We had now reached the Japanese compound where, sure enough, a group of guards were kicking around a proper, leather football on a large patch of open ground.

'Did you know?' he asked them loudly, pointing at me. 'This man was a professional footballer in England.'

They looked puzzled.

'Footballer,' repeated Geordie, who had come to join us, and mimed a goal kick. One of the guards came over to me.

'You football?' he asked.

'Yes, my work was football,' I said, slowly.

The following evening, a couple of the guards brought their interpreter over to see me.

'You are a footballer?' he asked.

'Yes, I was a professional footballer. It was my job in England.'

'You want play football?'

'Yes, I'd love to play football.'

'Where we play?' I thought it was odd that he asked me this, but I had an idea.

'We can clear the ground in the middle to make a small football pitch.'

'We give you tools,' he said. 'You get men to make team. Guards play prisoners.'

So that is what we did. Ray gathered together some of the younger, fitter men and all my pals came to join us too. We cleared a piece of spare land between the cemetery and the gate, next to the guardhouse, and we agreed to meet to have a kick-around together. Not many of us had any footwear left by this stage, so I was a bit worried about my feet.

But the Japs must have thought of that too. They gave us a few pairs of simple plimsoll-type shoes to put on. From then on, we often played a sort of football with them in the evenings, with some 'friendly' matches. It seemed very strange that these devils, who were so cruel to us in the daytimes at work, could smile and kick around with us in the evenings. We were glad of the chance, but we couldn't trust them, so we tried not to be too good.

One evening though, without thinking, I started to juggle about with this football, like I used to do in those days when we were training at Reading. The guard who owned the ball watched me for a while, then walked across and asked me to teach him some tricks.

'I give food,' he said, motioning at me and the lads who were with me. I thought this would be another empty lie, but I went along with it all the same and taught him to do a few fancy things with the ball. He was full of smiles and, for the first time I could remember, a Jap kept his promise.

We continued to play in the evenings and, with these guards being much shorter than we were, it was hard for us not to beat them sometimes, but strangely enough they took it all in good part. This was certainly a treat for us, after all our previous, awful experiences. And as long as we kept playing football, which we loved, we kept getting extra food, so that was a great deal for us and our friends.

Life was getting better now. Work on the railway was lighter, and being alongside the Japanese engineers, the guards didn't dare chastise us too much. We were getting more food rations into camp, together with some medical supplies, and of course the extra eggs and vegetables we gained by playing football with the guards, so we did all right.

On the evenings when we weren't playing football, or putting on concerts, I sometimes ran a general knowledge quiz between the Brits and the Aussies. The officers had a few well-worn books and magazines, so I got the questions out of those and mixed them up. That way, both sides would be able to answer some. These quizzes were quite popular and great fun, bantering as we played, and there was a fair bit of cheating, so we passed some pleasant evenings. It was good to hear the men laughing again.

Of course, as always happened when things were looking up, our food rations were suddenly cut right down and we were all suffering again. In desperation, two Aussies and I planned a robbery. At this time we were getting no sugar to put on our rice or in our tea.

'I know where there's a go-down, mate,' said one of them. 'Where the Japs store their sugar in huge sacks. About 240 pounds weight, I guess.'

'But surely they keep this go-down locked?' I asked.

'Too right,' said the other lad. 'But I saw one of the guards come out of there today, shut the door, and what do you know? He forgot to lock it up.'

'Blimey!' I was amazed. 'This is our chance.'

'But it's got to be tonight.'

We planned this escapade as best we could, realising the consequences if we were caught. At the very least, a bad beating up, or perhaps something much worse. We tried not to think about it too much.

'I know where I can get some smaller sacks,' I suggested.

'That should make it easier to move.'

'Yes,' agreed the second Aussie. 'And whatever sugar we can get back into camp, we'll have to split it up straightaway between the huts, while it's still dark, to reduce the risk of being found out.'

At exactly one o'clock in the morning, the three of us waited until the duty-guards had passed by, then we crawled through the barbed wire of the perimeter fence with my six empty rice sacks. Still keeping low and dodging the guards, we made our way through the jungle until we came to the rear of the go-down. We had to stay still and remain silent now, until they stopped patrolling and fell asleep, which we knew they always did.

Finally, an hour later, we crept round to the side of the store and unlatched the door with as little sound as possible. One of the Australians remained outside to keep watch, just in case, while we slowly opened the bamboo door and moved in. As our eyes accustomed to the gloom, we saw what we had come for – giant sacks marked 'sato': lovely sugar! I nearly whispered something, but realised even that sound could carry in the night air. We poured as much sugar as we could into our six rice sacks, lifted them out of the hut and pushed the door to.

Covering our tracks as best we could, we now began our back-breaking journey, lifting and dragging by turns. We would each take one sack about twenty yards, then go back for the other three, eating handfuls of sugar as we went. We thought it would give us energy, but by the time we got it all back into camp, we felt very sick.

While it was still dark, we split up most of the sugar and delivered it around the camp, from one hut to the next. By now the dawn was breaking and it was almost time to get up.

For the next two days, men were stuffing themselves with sugar all over Kinsaiyok camp. We enjoyed sweet rice and sweet tea, and we ate it on its own as well. We were doing quite well, keeping it all hidden away. But on the third day our luck ran out. After our night raid on the go-down, the guards in camp discovered they were short of sugar. Somehow, one of our lads heard and the word got around that at seven o'clock that evening the guards planned to search the whole of the camp.

So it was panic stations. We knew that if they found any of this sugar in our huts or among our things, not only would it mean the three of us would have to own up to our crime, and that would probably be the end of us, but all the POWs would be made to suffer too for not having reported us.

Well, you can imagine, everyone was rushing around, getting rid of what sugar they had left. Men were eating it by the fistful until they couldn't take any more, then burying what remained, or throwing it into the latrines as a treat for the millions of maggots that lived there. Finally, just in time, we were ready for the search.

At seven o'clock, half a dozen Korean guards, led by a Japanese sergeant, turned everything upside down, determined to find the evidence. But, fortunately, they found no signs of the sugar. What a relief for us all! The following day an officer told us he thought the Thai labourers, based in the nearby camp which was closer to the go-down, must have stolen it. I don't know if that's what the Japs assumed too. God help those natives. I hope they didn't suffer for what we did.

16

Talk About Bananas!

March 1944

As the last section of the railway through Kinsaiyok was completed, so more medical supplies began to reach us. It was too late of course for the many thousands of POWs and native workers who had already died in this wretched slavery. I'm damn sure that three-quarters of those who were slowly and painfully murdered by the Japanese could have been saved with proper medical provision and more food.

Late as they were, the medicines and equipment were a godsend and transformed the camp hospital. At last the medics could do their work and there was a real sense of optimism throughout the camp.

By now, you will know that the only thing any of us had to wear were ragged loincloths. So can you imagine how astonished we were one day when we were given an assortment of clothing to share out between us?

'It's not Harrods, Sarge,' quipped Ray.

'No, more like a stall down the market,' I said. 'But who cares? They're clothes aren't they? Let's try them on.'

Well, you should have seen us as we pulled on this job-lot of colourful garments. We looked at each other and laughed.

'Now I really can call you "short-arse",' said Reg with a raucous laugh. 'Those shorts don't leave much to the imagination.'

Of course, we were taller than the Japanese, so everything was too short and we looked like we were dressed in hand-me-downs we'd grown out of.

I smiled at the thought. As a young lad, with so many of us to clothe, I had never worn anything of my own. Everything was hand-me-downs from someone or other. My mother always made sure we had clean clothes to wear, but they were darned and patched, often scratchy and with the colour boiled out of them.

It was not until I was spotted kicking a ball around the park and signed up to Reading Football Club that my parents took me to a shoe-shop to buy me my first pair of proper new football boots. You should have seen how proud I was!

We were now doing better than at any time since the surrender at Singapore, more than two years before, and the death toll dropped to no more than two or three a week.

Morale was high and, though our rations remained the same, the Japs now paid us a few yen and allowed some local Thais into camp so that we could buy a bit of extra food from them, mostly bananas, duck-eggs and greens.

I could see the change in us all within a week or two. Just fancy, we went from near starvation and slavery on the jungle railway to nutritious food and rest, with nothing more to strain us than a few fatigues in camp and a programme of concerts, quizzes and other activities.

'Why-aye man, this is the life,' said Geordie, patting his tummy after we had consumed a bowl of rice with a couple of eggs and some fruit stirred in.

'It's not bad is it?' I agreed. 'The best food I've eaten in years. I reckon the Ritz couldn't do a better rice pudding than that.'

'And this one was a lot cheaper than the Ritz.'

Having more leisure time, as well as having built up the strength and energy to play, meant we could play more football, which was a joy. I tried to coach Ray a bit whenever I could. He was coming on well.

Life by the river Kwai certainly took on new meaning for us all . . . until one morning when we realised what we feared, that this was too good to last.

We were just sitting and eating our breakfast rice with banana and some sugary tea, when along strutted a guard.

'*Kiotsi*,' he barked out. So we all had to stand up to attention.

'All men on parade,' he ordered. 'Speedo-speedo.'

We hadn't thought we would hear that phrase again.

'Not some new slave-labour project?' groaned Reg.

'God save us!' swore Geordie.

'I wouldn't put it past them,' muttered Ray, sunk in gloom.

'You never know, it could be something good,' I grinned, knowing the reaction I would get as we strolled over to the patch of land we used as a parade ground. And I was right.

'Stop being so bloody positive!'

'Speedo-speedo!' shrieked the guard, prodding us with his bamboo stick.

So we lined up on the parade ground in front of a man I recognised as a railway engineer. He started to speak in Japanese, and the interpreter translated for us.

'In two hours, a train will pass through camp,' he told us, looking very pleased with himself. 'You men line up by railway to see train.'

Right on time, as we waited along the embankment two hours later, we heard the whistle of a steam train approaching. Suddenly, I thought back to those tricks of ours – the split wood and the loosened rivets. I had never imagined that we would have to watch the first train travel on this bit of track. What if it all fell apart and derailed the train? They'd be sure to know it was our fault and punish us brutally. I was torn between wanting to upset their proud jubilation, and crossing my fingers that our efforts at sabotage didn't work . . . yet.

As the train chugged slowly through, Nippon flags waving, we could see the carriages packed with Japanese soldiers, all armed to the teeth. At its rear, this train pulled a tail of open wagons carrying field guns. We were ordered to wave as the train passed by, but we did so with heavy hearts.

I suppose I was relieved that it hadn't been derailed this time, but I hated the knowledge that we had been forced to build this railway, lined with blood, agony and death. None of us survivors will ever forget the hell we went through to enable that train to pass through our camp, and all the other death camps along the Kwai – the great price we had paid for it with the lives of our friends. I will carry their memories for the rest of my life.

A few days later, we were ordered on parade again. This time the news brought mixed feelings.

'You return to base camp, where you rest to end of war,' translated the interpreter. 'You will have plenty food and medical supplies.'

'It's bound to be a lie,' said one of the lads as we returned to our hut. 'Why can't we stay here and rest?'

'Yes,' added Reg. 'We can't trust them.'

'The bastards,' spluttered Geordie.

'You're right, lads. But we have to hope for the best.' I tried to keep up morale as we prepared to leave Kinsaiyok for the unknown. 'Please God, the war will end soon.'

Well, perhaps the Japanese hadn't lied this time. As we arrived at our rest camp after a long trek down-river, we couldn't believe our eyes.

'It's only a bloody banana plantation,' grinned Taffy Miles in his Welsh sing-song accent.

'Talk about bananas, man!' exclaimed Geordie. 'There's got to be millions of the ruddy things!'

'And they're all ripening just in time,' beamed Reg. 'Champion!'

We were in heaven – it was nothing for us to eat between fifty and a hundred of these small bananas in a day. They were everywhere, all around the edge of the camp, and we gorged ourselves on them.

Local natives brought duck-eggs by the thousands to sell us

for almost nothing, so we were in clover with all this healthy food. Geordie, Reg and I used to make a fire and, with a little palm oil which we also bought from the Thai pedlars and a frying pan made by flattening a piece of waste metal we had found, we cooked duck-egg omelettes. Can you imagine? We cracked about twenty or twenty-five duck-eggs into the pan. We loved our omelettes.

Mind you, this over-eating of rich duck-eggs was not doing us much good as we suffered from diarrhoea and constipation by turns. My weight shot up, though some of it was probably the beriberi fluid retention under my skin. I didn't care, as long as I had food to eat after almost starving to death for so long. Who could blame us for making pigs of ourselves? The only downside was that there were a few of our men who overate to such an extent that their weak bodies couldn't cope. It cost them their lives, poor souls.

But, on the whole, this rest camp was just the job. We were doing nothing, just lounging about. All we did all day was eat and rest, and even the guards left us alone. The Japanese were keeping their word and our days of hell seemed to be over . . . for now anyway.

Our hospital huts here were fairly well equipped and everything was kept spotlessly clean. We still had several sick men, of course, suffering from all the usual complaints, but at least the medics could treat them and feed them up, a bit at a time. They did a grand job.

The Japs now gave us a regular supply of quinine to combat our malaria, but almost everyone in the camp, including me, still suffered from beriberi. We realised it would take a long time for our vitamin and mineral deficiencies to be put right, and we still weren't eating a sufficiently varied diet.

While in this rest camp, I met up with a man from my hometown, Reading. Ben Russell was a big strong man, well able to take care of himself, and the finest POW scrounger I ever met.

Even now, when life was getting better, he continued to take terrible risks, like stealing from the Jap cookhouse. Yes, Ben was fearless.

We talked about our Reading haunts a lot, and our loved ones too. For a while Ben helped me to forget things, terrible things, that had happened to us in the death camps. And I'm sure his good humour helped me to recover from a bout of dysentery I'd been suffering from for a while. We found him a space and he moved into our hut.

One day, I had a dreadful toothache that drove me mad.

'You need that tooth out,' grinned Ben with a twinkle in his eye.

'Maybe,' I agreed, not sure I could trust his wicked tricks.

'Don't worry, mate. I'll get it sorted for you.' He took a length of cotton thread that he unravelled from the hem of his bright orange Japanese shorts and tied one end round my throbbing tooth.

'Turn round,' he ordered.

As I did so, I immediately felt a yank on the thread and out came my tooth. What a relief. It was such a good extraction that I hardly felt it, so I was lucky. I had seen many POWs having their rotten teeth pulled out and having to put up with threads that slipped off teeth, over and over again, with painful pulls every time. Indeed, some of them ended up having to endure bad toothache for months until someone could make a successful job of it.

One of the problems, of course, was that we had no toothbrushes, and the diet we ate was all soft, so there was nothing to help our teeth stay clean and strong. The way I used to try and clean my teeth was to get a piece of bamboo, cut it almost to a point, then keep rubbing it up and down each tooth. I used to lie on my lousy bunk, rubbing my teeth for ages, using charcoal as toothpaste. You wouldn't think that black charcoal would make your teeth whiter, would you? But it worked. The other thing I did every day was to chew on a piece of bamboo till it was pulp. I believe that's the reason I managed to save my teeth, all except two, while other men were losing most of theirs.

It was now spring 1944 and we were beginning to feel better than at any time since we left Singapore. That seemed like a lifetime away already. POWs from camps all along the Kwai were being brought to join us, so we renewed a few old friendships and enjoyed many raucous sing-songs together. We were all in good spirits.

'This ain't so bad,' laughed Ben at one of our concerts.

'You're right,' I agreed. 'Perhaps we're going to survive the war after all.'

Everyone paraded for a lecture, or so we thought. The Japanese interpreter stepped forward and looked along the ranks of men, the Aussies and the Brits, some recently arrived and still frail from the railway, others like ourselves now a little fitter and well rested.

'All you fit men,' he began. 'We take you back to Singapore.' I remember the gasp of surprise that rose up all around me. I was as shocked as everyone else – Singapore, where we first became captives of these wily people. They weren't all sadists then, but perhaps the war had turned them that way.

'Back to square one,' muttered someone behind me.

'You rest in Singapore. Then we take you on Imperial Japanese ships to good camps in Japan.' The interpreter paused while we took that in. 'In Japan you all have easy time, till end of war.'

'If you believe that . . .' murmured one of my lads, as sceptical of these promises as I was.

'Too right mate,' added one of the Aussies, a little too loudly, so that one of the guards came over, swishing his bamboo stick.

So, I thought, we are going to Japan. Yes, that bit is probably right, but I bet that's all that's right.

We soon found out their plan for us once we reached Japan.

'The CO asked the Jap commandant point-blank,' said the lieutenant to me as we were drinking our black tea on the steps to my hut. 'He said we needed to know what we had to prepare for when we got there.'

'Did he get an answer, sir?'

'He certainly did, Sergeant. The little Jap commandant showed him on a map where we were headed.'

'So, will it be a rest camp?'

'What do you think?' He put his head on one side and puffed on his jungle-leaf roll-up as if it were a cigar, trying to blow a smoke ring.

'I think we'll be slaving for the Japs.'

'Spot on, Sherwood. Our chaps will be detailed to work on the docks, down the mines or in the carbide factories.'

'Well sir, it might not be so bad – nothing can be as wretched as working on the railway.'

'That's what I like about you, Sergeant. You always look on the bright side.'

'Not always, sir.'

Well, now we knew. I broke the news to the lads in my hut.

'They'll work us to death in the end,' moaned Ray.

'Not if we do all we can to survive,' I said. 'We've got this far in one piece—'

'Only just!' interrupted Geordie.

'We'll show those Japs what we're made of,' added Ben, flexing his impressive muscles. Despite the slavery and malnutrition, he had never lost all his strength.

It was a crushing blow, of course, after everything we had endured in the past two and a half years, to know we had more hard labour to come, under the watch of the cruel Japs.

The following morning, every man capable of standing was ordered out on parade on the centre ground of this easy-going rest camp, in its beautiful semi-tropical setting.

The guards sorted us out and counted us into groups.

'You be ready six o'clock tomorrow morning for train to Singapore.'

So this was to be the first part of our journey to Japan.

17

Back To Square One – Singapore

May 1944

I think it was about 20th May 1944 that we left our base camp in Thailand for the first part of our journey, all the way back through Malaya and into Singapore, and no looking at scenery out of the train. It was sweltering steel trucks again for us, truly back to square one.

The journey was as long and the conditions as harsh as the first time, two years before, but this time our numbers had been so depleted that, even with fewer wagons, we had a little more space inside to move about or sit down on the dirty floor, and one corner could be used as a toilet for those caught short. It took about a week and several of the men needed medical attention in the claustrophobic heat and squalor.

Though desperately thirsty, we dared not drink any water without first boiling it at each stop to kill the germs. We had all had too many bad experiences during our captivity to take any risks with this, so it was a miserable and exhausting journey.

When we finally arrived, most of us in a woeful state and many unable to stand, we were unloaded in a shambles from the trucks, sucking in mouthfuls of fresh air as we clambered out into the open. I was astonished to see that they had supplied special transport for the sick, while the rest of us were gathered for a short march, about a mile from the station to our camp.

On passing through the gates, the guards directed us to various billets to sort ourselves out and get some rest.

Somebody let out a long whistle, and we all stood and stared.

'Look at that, Sarge,' grinned Ray with astonishment.

'Proper buildings!' Ben rubbed his hands together.

'About bloody time!' added Reg.

It was true. After two years of appalling squalor, crammed together in flimsy huts that gave little shelter and let in the torrential rains, not to mention the wildlife, we would have solid walls and roofs at last in this former army barracks. And a proper lavatory in each building.

We settled in all right over the next few days and organised routines to keep the camp clean and get everything done.

After about a week, we were ordered on to the parade ground and addressed by an English-speaking Japanese officer.

'Men now work,' he told us. 'Men go to docks, unload boats. If men work hard, get letters.'

That was a clear enough message, and gave us plenty to talk about as we collected our breakfast rations. There was excitement in the air. Letters – could that really be true?

'So we've got to work again,' said one of my lads, exhausted by the train journey. 'I don't feel strong enough for all that lifting we'll have to do on the docks.'

'Howay man,' Geordie chivvied him. 'It canna be as bad as working on the railway.'

'And it will be worth it, lads,' I added. 'If we get letters from home, at last.'

'Do you think they will keep their word, Sarge?' asked one of the youngest. 'I haven't had a letter since we first came to Singapore.'

'No, none of us has,' I agreed. 'But all we can do is wait and see . . . and hope.'

So that's what we did, and we were rewarded a few days later when, true to their word for once, they allowed a fleet of Red Cross lorries to deliver more than a hundred sacks containing thousands of letters to the centre of our camp. While the fittest of us were working at the docks, a detail of sick men sat down to sort the mail, some of which was more than two years old.

All day on the dockside I felt like a kid going to a party, or waiting for Father Christmas to come. I tried to stay calm, but my insides bubbled up with increasing excitement as the long hours dragged on.

I'm sure you can imagine the elation, the jumping for joy there was when we returned from work.

'Hey, Sarge.' One of the light-sick lads came running towards me. 'There's a bundle of letters for you. Quite a lot of them by the look of it.'

'Thanks, Charlie.' I could have hugged him. I can't tell you the excitement of getting my hands on the first letters from my loved ones, the thought of opening and reading them, hearing all their news, finding out about the new baby who was now a two-year-old child. There was so much I wanted to know, but most of all that they had not forgotten me. A feeling of enormous relief flooded through my body as I rushed across to collect my precious bundle of mail. I felt more excited than I'd ever been in my life.

That first time, untying the bundle, spreading out the thirteen envelopes, recognising the different handwriting, looking at the postmark dates, I trembled with anticipation.

I didn't know where to start, but of course it had to be with my darling wife Christine. There were several from her, all with old postmarks, going back to early 1942. I soon discovered that I had a lovely baby girl, a daughter she had called Sandra. I whispered it to myself several times, trying to get used to my daughter's name. I liked it. Christine said she was a bonny baby. Of course, she was bound to be, I smiled, with the two of us as her parents.

I read through all of Christine's loving letters and learnt that my father had bought Philip a new little football, which he tried to kick around in our garden. I couldn't wait to get home to have a kick-about with him. There was so much I wanted to teach him. Sandra too. I wanted to meet her and get to know her. I hoped she

The first page of Johnny's scrapbook.

would like to have me as her father. Christine's letters said she often spoke to both of them about their Daddy and showed them my photo, which brought tears to my eyes.

I read letters from the rest of the family too, my beloved mother, father, brothers and sisters. I felt as if I was the happiest man in the world. I probably was at that moment, along with all my pals reading their letters. It was a wonderful feeling to read how much I was loved and missed, and to know that we finally had a link with home, even if these letters were so old. Perhaps we would receive newer ones soon . . .

Well, I read my letters over and over again that evening, then hid them away to read the next night, and every day after that, full of joy.

But there was a sad moment in all that rejoicing for me, when I realised that probably half of these letters must be addressed to men who had given their all and perished on the railway of death. I'm not sure, but I think all unclaimed letters were handed back to the Japs. Maybe POWs in hospitals or scattered in other camps would eventually claim a few of these, but what happened to those never received? And did their families even know?

A few days later, the Japs had another surprise lined up.

'You get Red Cross parcels,' announced the interpreter.

And we did . . . one parcel between every thirty men. This of course meant that we got almost nothing. We found out later that our Japanese and Korean guards had been using the food parcels for themselves since we arrived back in Singapore. We saw them smoking American cigarettes – Chesterfield and Camel brands, and I think Lucky Strike as well. They must surely have known how our POWs were missing decent cigarettes . . . and they smoked them all in front of us.

One of their favourite tricks was to light up an American cigarette, take one puff on it, then crush it under their foot and say 'demi-demi', which meant 'no good'. Then they moved away and watched with amusement as our boys rushed in to try and retrieve the prize. It reminded me of those desperate scrabbles on the railway. The winning POW would pick up the flattened fag and wrap it in a piece of discarded Japanese newspaper or leaves to tease out, roll and smoke later.

The Japs continued to try and undermine our morale, and they weren't doing badly at it. Our rations were nothing special, with very little protein, fat or greens, so we now had to rely on what we could steal at the docks to augment our diet.

We unloaded ships bringing stolen loot in from the conquered southeast Asian islands. Sometimes it was sugar, which of course we filled ourselves up with whenever we could. Or maybe it was a boat-load of cigarettes, which pleased our smokers, or palm oil to give us a little fat.

We were under constant supervision by our Korean guards, but if ever they turned away for a moment, we were into everything. Oh boy, oh boy, some of the antics we got up to. Those of us who still had water-bottles used to share around the water to empty them and then fill them up with palm oil, or dry them out and fill them with cigarettes. It took our guards quite a while to discover this little escapade.

Two POWs were caught out pulling this trick. They were taken back to camp and given a good going over. The next morning, when we were marched off to work, these two men were each made to carry a heavy block of wood at arms' stretch above their head. No matter how hard they tried to hold it there, at risk of further punishment, it was inevitable that their arms would sag, and when this happened, the guards gave them a beating and made them hold it up all over again. This went on, with the men getting weaker until they collapsed. At this point the Japs put their boots in, with a vengeance. As soon as the men regained consciousness, they were dragged up again and so it continued, day after day, morning and night.

A lot of the lads were afraid to take any chances after that, for fear of the same treatment. Most of our men weren't strong enough to stand up to the guards' cruelty, but there were a few daredevils who still managed to find ways to smuggle food and cigarettes into camp.

The guards started lining us all up before we left the docks. They would get us to form five or six lines of about twenty men in each. So what we did was to make sure the front line of POWs never carried any loot, then we would quickly switch places with a pal in front, and now the men who had something would be in the front line, which had already been searched. Then the same with the second row, and so on, until they had finished. It was dangerous, we knew, but the guards were so busy searching our water-bottles that they never noticed us changing around. I suppose we all looked the same to them.

Fortunately, my smuggling ring was never detected, so each night we could make our camp food more palatable with sugar or whatever. All in all, we managed pretty well.

At this time we were joined by some POWs from Java who were adept at catching cats, which they said made a good stew. But that didn't appeal to me or my pals, though we did have some occasionally, for our health's sake.

This life seemed to be full of surprises. When we lined up on the parade ground one morning, the Japanese interpreter made another of his shock announcements.

'You very soon go on Imperial Japanese convoy to Nippon.' This was their word for Japan. 'It is beautiful land of rising sun, where you rest to end of war.'

'What's a convoy, Sarge?' asked a young soldier as we returned to our hut.

'Don't you know anything?' said Reg.

'It's a group of ships all moving along together,' I explained. 'It's supposed to keep them all safe.'

'Do you think it will be better there?'

'Well, it might be, if we can rest till the end of the war.'

'Believe that and you'll believe owt!' spluttered Geordie.

'Yes, I know. You're probably right, but we can hope, can't we?'

'Aye. Maybe it will be good for us,' agreed Reg.

But something that happened down at the Singapore docks a few days later disturbed me. It was when I got into conversation with one of the English-speaking Chinese civilians working for the Japanese. Somehow the conversation got around to football, which of course is always one of my favourite topics.

'I played football here once,' I said.

'In Singapore?'

'Yes, before the war. I was a footballer and I played on the Islington Corinthians world football tour.'

For a moment he looked surprised, then suddenly his face broke into a beaming smile. 'I went all games at Anson Road Stadium,' he said. 'What your name?'

'Johnny Sherwood. I was the centre forward,' I explained.

He looked astonished and shook my hand most enthusiastically – I thought he would never let it go!

'You won all games in Singapore,' he grinned with admiration. 'You made many goals.'

'Yes, I was one of the goal-scorers.'

'I saw you make all goals in one game – five goals. Yes? And you make six goals of nine in game with Malaya at Anson Road?'

'Yes,' I laughed. Fancy him remembering all that.

'You stay, I go get friends.' He ran into a nearby go-down, disappeared for less than a minute, and came out again with about a dozen Chinamen, all wanting to shake my hand.

'Where you been?' asked one of them.

'Just now, in the war?' I asked. They all nodded. 'I was in Siam for two years, building a Japanese railway.' In those days, everyone called Thailand Siam.

'Where you go next?'

'We've just been told we are going to go in a convoy of ships to Japan.'

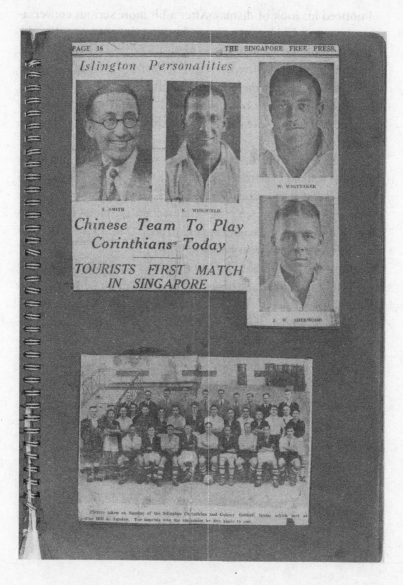

Cuttings from Johnny's scrapbook about the Islington
Corinthians matches in Singapore, January 1938.

I noticed his look of dismay. After a bit more serious conversation, the other Chinese men went back to the go-down, but the first man took me aside, with an anxious expression on his face. It certainly had me worried.

'You will never get there, sir,' he said in a wavering voice that instilled fear into every bone in my body. 'The American submarines,' he continued, 'are sinking every ship going from Singapore to Japan.'

'Thank you,' I said gravely, trying to take in this shocking news.

But as I walked back to camp that evening, I had already started to think about it more rationally. Surely there was no need to be worried? After all, weren't we going to travel under Red Cross flags? The Americans would never torpedo a Red Cross ship, so there was nothing to worry about.

Usually, I was glad that I had a positive attitude – I'm sure it got me through all those dark times on the death railway. But perhaps I should have taken that Chinaman's warning a little more seriously.

18

The Kachidoki Maru

August 1944

Each of those last few days, as I worked in the docks, I saw several ships limping in with damage to their sides.

'Why are so many ships damaged?' I asked a Japanese guard who could speak a little English.

'Many fogs,' he said. 'Ships bang together in fogs.'

I saw a Malay worker standing nearby, shaking his head, so I went over to him to ask what he thought.

'America boom-boom,' he replied.

The Chinaman's words came back to haunt me. I didn't want to frighten the lads, but I needed to see if anyone else knew anything, so I mentioned it quietly to Geordie after we'd eaten our half a cup of rice that evening. I knew he wouldn't want to spread alarm any more than I did.

'I met a Chinaman on the docks the other day and he told me the Americans are torpedoing ships on the way to Japan.'

'I've heard some rumours too,' he nodded. 'The native workers on the docks say that only one in ten ships reaches Japan.'

'How can they know that? They're just trying to frighten us.'

'Maybe.' Geordie stroked his chin in thought. 'But there must be some truth in it. We see a lot of damaged boats coming into the docks, so something is happening.'

'Yes, but they're Japanese boats. I'm sure we'll be going under the Red Cross flag, and the Yanks wouldn't attack that.'

'That's what you think, but I don't trust these Japs. Anyway, what if it's foggy, and they can't see our flag?'

'The captain might light up our ship.'

'And pigs might fly! Come off it Johnny. Can't you see what danger we could be in? The submarines wouldna even surface – they'd just launch their torpedoes on any ship, assuming it's Japanese.' He paused. 'Man, the lads are saying we're going to be fish-food. Shark-food more like, I reckon. The bloody Japs don't give a damn about us.'

'You're bang on there. I'd be very surprised if we're being taken to Japan to rest. I reckon we'll have to work our guts out for them yet again.'

'If we get there . . .'

As I tried to get off to sleep that night, I tossed and turned, battling this new dread. In the end, I came to the conclusion it would all turn on whether we were under the protection of the Red Cross – surely the Yanks would check through their periscopes first. And that would benefit the Japanese guards and crew as much as it would us, so I just hoped the odds would be in our favour. I'd been lucky all these years. Surely it couldn't stop now . . . but another part of me knew it probably had to stop sometime . . .

September 4th 1944, the day after my birthday, dawned to shouts of 'All men go Nippon. All men go Nippon', as the guards strode round the camp, ordering us to get up.

So the day had arrived and we packed our meagre possessions into our tattered haversacks and lined up, ready to depart.

'We're going to be sunk,' said a young lad in the line near me. 'A man in our hut had a nightmare about it. We're going to be torpedoed and sunk and we'll all die.'

There was a flurry of fear and panic all around him.

'That's right,' added his mate. 'Any survivors will drown or be food for sharks.'

'Look lads,' I butted in. 'You know as well as I do that night-mares rarely come true in real life. So it's not worth worrying about. Let's try and be positive about this move. Surely anywhere we go will be better than this hell-hole of a camp and our starvation rations?'

'Well, maybe . . .'

'I'm not stupid, I know the Japs will make us work darned hard, if and when we get there, but the war can't go on for ever, and if the Yanks are around—'

At that point, I was rudely interrupted by a guard's rifle butt in my ribs.

'No talk,' he screeched.

Medical officers were ordered to separate those who were 'riding sick' from those who were 'walking sick', though of course the very sick men had not been able to leave their beds, and would not be coming with us.

Next, the guards divided us into two random groups, often separating pals from each other, which caused quite a stir. Especially for me, as Geordie and Reg were made to join other groups. We then had to count ourselves off in Japanese.

'*Itchi* . . . *nee* . . . *san* . . . *shee* . . .' This took quite a while and had to be done by every group in turn, with a hefty wallop if we dared to get it wrong.

Finally, we were ready to go. There was no ceremony about it; we just marched in a subdued line out of camp. I say marched, but for many it was more of a ramble as most of us were suffering from one disease or another, from being on such low rations while in Singapore. And none of us could keep up the pace the guards demanded, which meant a lot of bamboo sticks at our backs. It was three miles to the docks and we'd had no breakfast, so we were in quite a bad state, suffering from hunger and thirst when we arrived.

It was a rude awakening for me – a blow to my hopes, when we reached the dock where two grey cargo ships were waiting for us. One was the *Kachidoki Maru* and the other was the *Rakuyo Maru*. I was alarmed to see on each ship the Japanese flag of the rising sun, and no Red Cross markings at all. How would the Yanks know they were carrying prisoners of war? I turned cold, despite the searing heat, and felt heavy, as if I had a slab of granite in my chest. Thank God each ship had a dozen lifeboats, but would they be enough for all of us? I shuddered to think what might happen if not.

We had to sit down on the hot concrete of the dock and wait while the cargoes of rubber, cigarettes and scrap-metal were loaded. Next came a large group of Japanese wounded and sick soldiers, along with several of their women nurses, in blouses and baggy trousers, tied at the ankles. The Jap invalids were all carefully carried or guided into the passenger cabins amidships on the *Kachidoki Maru*.

'Look,' said one of the other sergeants in our party. 'It's that bastard, Lieutenant Tanaka.'

I followed his gaze, up to the bridge, and there he stood, the most notorious sadist of the death camps we'd been through, the worst possible commander for such a perilous journey, with our lives in his hands. Now I was really worried.

Finally we were herded on to this forbidding grey ship, the *Kachidoki Maru*. Herding was the word – treated no better than neglected animals. We were just cattle to our guards. Nine hundred British POWs were pushed and shoved along the deck to two hatches, where we were forced down into the dark and dirty holds, shoulder to shoulder. The heat enveloped us like a steaming wet blanket and there was nothing down there but a rudimentary scattering of straw, reinforcing our animal status as far as the Japanese were concerned.

As our eyes adjusted to the gloom, we could see that each hold had been divided into two by a kind of shelf of wooden planks, the whole of their length. This meant that twice as many men could be loaded down there, but none of us could stand in the four-foot headroom. As we each did our best to find a space for ourselves, more and more men were being pushed down, the sick as well as the half-fit. They just kept coming, and we were unable to move or breathe properly by the time everyone was in place. I tried to look out for my pals, but it was no good. I couldn't make anyone out in the gloom, unless they were up close.

I was running with sweat in the bottom part of the hold, with more men's sweat pouring on to me through the gaps between the boards of the upper level. The whole place was a dark, foetid dungeon, an airless furnace. The sick were crying out, and the rest of us were horrified at our fate. The feeling of claustrophobia and impending doom hung heavy. I knew we would have no chance if we were attacked and sunk.

'Where's the toilet?' yelled somebody.

'There ain't no toilet down here, mate.'

'Bloody hell! I've messed myself.'

Within minutes the whole place stank as the poor souls with dysentery were unable to hold themselves in and everywhere was fouled. The stench was abominable.

Men were passing out around me, so I picked up one of them and carried him as best I could, trying not to trample on too many people as I manhandled him up the single ladder, through the hatch and on to the deck, where I laid him out in the hot but breathable air. Several more of those who had fainted were passed up the ladder and a few of us laid them down to recover.

A sudden stream of Japanese assaulted us from the bridge as Lieutenant Tanaka lost his rag, with a storm of abuse. The guards started prodding and poking people back down into the holds, hitting us with sticks, so we couldn't rescue any more. But I felt a huge relief to be able to suck in some deep breaths of fresh air for those few moments, after the hell of the dungeon below.

Minutes later, I was forced down the ladder again, but this time managed to get a space nearer the hatch. The complaining now turned into cries for food and water. We had received none so far that day, and in this inferno, we were losing any fluid we had left in our bodies, so we were desperate. A few of us, including me, still had nearly full water-bottles and passed them around among the sickest men we could reach.

I gazed with a sense of foreboding at the hot steel walls and how deep we were in the bowels of the ship. How long could we live like this, in these conditions, without water? Would we really be torpedoed and drowned down here, after all we had gone through? Would this hell-hole become our grave?

Just then, to increase our terror, the engines started up with resounding rumbles and clanks that deafened us all, and the guards on deck prepared to batten down the hatches.

The few British officers we had with us now began to make their views heard to the Japanese officers on deck, where they met to protest against our intolerable conditions. Of course, we could hear nothing of their discussions, but it seems that the tyrant Tanaka perhaps realised our numbers could technically over-power his few men, even though we were unarmed, and heeded the clamour.

The first we knew of it was when I and the other sergeants were called up on deck.

'Gentlemen,' our commanding officer addressed us all. 'We have complained that our conditions are inhumane and the Japanese have agreed some concessions for us.'

'Not much, I bet,' whispered the man next to me.

'First, both hatches will remain open throughout the voyage to Japan, to allow our men to come out and spend some time on the deck each day, as long as we stay within the area at the front of the ship.'

'All of us, sir?' I asked.

'Yes, Sergeant Sherwood. During the hot daylight hours only. And the men may use the latrine only by permission, one at a time.' There was only the one '*benjo*', an open wooden toilet construction, jutting out from the side of the ship, over the sea, with just one seat. This was the only facility for nine hundred men, many of whom had dire need of the toilet at all times.

'What about at night?' asked someone.

'Everyone must go below into the holds before dark and stay there till daybreak.'

'But it will still be possible to use the toilet at night,' added a lieutenant. 'You sergeants will take turns to be on night duty on deck and only let the men through one at a time. We must not let there be a queue, or the Japanese may ban our use of it altogether.'

'Yes sir.'

'We must ensure everyone adheres strictly to these rules,' explained the CO. 'Or we will have to spend all twenty-four hours below deck.'

As we dispersed, the CO called me back.

'Sergeant Sherwood, I am putting you in charge of number one hold.'

'Yes sir,' I saluted, then went down the ladder into the hold to pass the word round. There was a sense of relief as this news of concessions became known and once the ship was on its way we organised the men to come up on deck again, in orderly fashion. Those who were sick and unable to come up had to remain below, but at least they had more space to lie down and more air to breathe.

Standing at the deck-rail, I could see a large number of Japanese ships in the dockyard as we chugged slowly out, perhaps forty of them, many with damage. My heart sank. Out of the dock area, we stopped and dropped anchor. I supposed we were waiting to get into convoy formation with other ships.

Still we had no food or water, and many of my mates were in a bad way. At sundown, I reluctantly made sure everybody went down again into the holds.

Finally, desperately hungry and thirsty, I was allotted the role of mess sergeant.

'You will select four men to bring with you to collect the rations for all the men in your hold.' It was now dark and at last we would have our first meal of the day and our first fresh water to drink.

What we didn't know was that the tanks of drinking water were far too small for so many passengers, so it would have to be severely rationed from the start – just one pint per man per day. This ship had never carried such a large human cargo before, but at least it was able to carry huge quantities of sacks of rice. The only problem there was the limited space for cooking.

Right from the start, every time I went to the galley to collect food, I took with me four canteens and filled them with fresh water every journey, to pass around among the men, in addition to their ration.

The food ration that first evening was half a cup of rice with a finger-sized piece of dried fish. It was the only food we had eaten all day and not much better than nothing for our desperately weakened bodies. Being one of the sergeants on latrine duties, I was lucky enough to be allowed to stay out on deck each night, to sleep in the clear air, tucked up against one of the bulkheads on the foredeck. And when it was my turn, I would stand by the hatch to number one hold and let up no more than six men at a time, but not in an obvious queue, to use the single-seat *benjo*.

Although the holds were less hot at night than during the day, the air was still stifling and the men's thirst too great for them to bear. They needed more than a pint of water a day – more like twelve pints to counter the amount of sweating down there. They cried out pitifully for water, and I spent as much time as I could procuring extra, illicit canteenfuls to pass around.

One of the guards at the galley who could speak a bit of English got into conversation with me on the second morning. His English was not very good, but we managed to make ourselves understood.

'Japan number one country in world,' I would say to him each time.

He loved it, grinning broadly as he gave me some cigarettes. I wasn't a bit interested in smoking, but I used to pass them around some of the men who were desperate for a puff, so it was worth the pretence.

We sat at anchor for several days, with our men getting weaker and weaker and the conditions below absolutely abominable. I was responsible for them, and went down there with more water whenever I could, but it barely kept them alive. Whenever I thought about their terrible plight, I felt sick with worry.

God, how lucky I was not to have to stay in that stinking furnace. Gradually, night after night, I smuggled more of the men out of the hold and up on deck, hiding them wherever I could around the place. I was anxious and fearful about taking such a big risk, but I couldn't leave them to die. If the guards ever realised, they didn't let on.

Some of those left down there were unable to stand and too ill to move so I tried to help them, but it was hopeless. I would have needed many gallons of water to give all nine hundred men even two or three drops each. However, in the daytime, with only the sick in the hold, I did usually manage to get water to each of them. But their cries for more water still rang in my ears for hours after I had climbed up on deck again.

Early on the morning of 6th September, I watched from the deck-rail as the Japanese crew raised our anchor and moved the ship forward to form a convoy with the *Rakuyo Maru*, full of British and Australian POWs, including many of my friends, two more passenger ships and two large tankers. Finally, four escort ships joined us as we began our journey out to sea. Later, some other cruisers and destroyers would tag on, to make a convoy of about twenty-five in all. We had two planes flying over us most of the time in those first few days at sea. I suppose they were checking for submarines.

The weather was clear, torrid and windless to begin with as our convoy sailed northwards, the harsh sunlight burning our skins and parching our lips. But on the fifth afternoon at sea, clouds appeared and broke open, dropping glorious, torrential rain on us. All the POWs on deck stood with their mouths open, drinking in the cool nectar and letting the rain wash the grime away from their sore bodies. It was a great relief and raised our morale no end. Then we gathered all the containers we could, our water-bottles and the few mess tins we had, and started to collect it for our sick comrades below, and to store some for the next day. This certainly was a gift from the gods, just in time. The rain lightened to a steady drizzle, so for this day at least, the first since leaving Singapore, nobody needed to suffer from thirst.

19

Sitting Ducks

September 1944

On 11th September, we were joined by more ships and our convoy re-formed. This was the end of the aeroplane protection, now that we were so far from land. So the Japanese put more guards on lookout duties, which raised the tension among them and spread to all of us too.

About one o'clock in the morning of 12th September, as we were moving along quite peacefully, there was a sudden flurry of activity among the lookout guards and there were more Japanese officers on the bridge. We were in trouble. Our convoy had run into an American submarine nest and we were being attacked from both sides.

First, a destroyer was hit and blew up right next to us, shooting shrapnel in all directions.

By God, this shook me rigid. Would we be next? My first thought was for all those poor men in the holds if that happened, and my whole body began to shake. My stomach heaved, but I tried to stay calm.

We stood at the rails in shocked silence, watching the destroyer on fire. It sank in minutes. Then another volley of torpedoes struck a couple of ships, setting fires and exploding ammunition magazines, lighting up the night sky.

All hell was let loose on deck, as Japanese guards charged about in utter panic, shouting and cursing wildly, completely out of control. By contrast, our lads were quiet and cool. Of course, this was partly because we were too weak or ill to do anything energetic, but mainly it was due to bloody British guts.

Our CO stood on a capstan, amid all this mayhem, and beckoned those of us on deck to gather round him. He raised his voice as much as he could above the noise.

'It is apparent that we are being attacked by American submarines who are unaware of our presence in this convoy,' he explained, with the coolness of an officer on any English parade ground in peacetime.

'Stating the bleeding obvious,' said one of the youngest lads.

'Sshh,' said those nearest him.

'Now, I want you all to stay calm and keep your heads about you. We haven't been hit yet, and may escape this attack, so there is no need to panic. Remember your British courage and we will all get through this.'

'That's the courage those bloody Japs will never understand,' I said to the man next to me.

'Spot on!' he replied with pride.

The worst of the Japs' panic seemed to ease and we settled down again.

Then a shout went up. 'There's a ship coming straight for us!'

Pandemonium followed as our ship's officers gave a series of short blasts of our siren and tried to turn away. Now we could see it was a large tanker, coming closer and closer, until finally it struck the bow and scraped down the side of the *Kachidoki Maru* with a thunderous sound. I felt the whole ship shudder as it listed to starboard, sending showers of metal sparks across the deck, missing each of us by inches.

'Have we been holed?' somebody yelled, and we all ran to look over the side. But we couldn't see enough to be sure.

'What's going on?' The shouts of hysteria came up from the holds. 'Have we been torpedoed? . . . Can we come up on deck?'

I ran over to the hatch of my hold. 'It's not a torpedo. But we've been scraped by a tanker. We can't see what the damage is.'

Meanwhile, the deck was slanting at a more acute angle and I feared the worst. Then we seemed to rock from side to side. We were too busy trying to hold on to think what to do next. But before long, miraculously, the ship stopped rocking and righted itself. Phew!

Now, suddenly, a new volley of torpedoes attacked ships all around us. The air burst with noise and the sky lit up as the subs attacked. All the men on deck, including me, stood at the rails in shocked silence, as we watched in horror. The sea was alive with exploding torpedoes and the night aflame with blazing ships and the booms of depth charges.

Even with the night illuminated, it was difficult to see which ships were hit, and only later did we discover that our sister ship, the *Rakuyo Maru*, full of POWs, had received a direct hit and was sinking. What a terrible shock! We all knew men who were on that ship. Geordie Ashbridge must have been on there, I assumed . . . and Reg, and the others. I hadn't seen any of them since we'd been separated on the quay. I prayed they'd got off before it sank, and were safe in the lifeboats.

POW survivors from the torpedoed Rakuyo Maru rescued by the USS Sealion.

161

After the Yankee subs had sunk almost half the convoy, or that's how it looked to me, the remainder of us were scattered about all over the place, across the darkening sea. Thank God that, despite the damage, our ship and all of us in it were spared. A complete miracle, I thought. How lucky we had been.

In the early hours through to dawn, what was left of our convoy licked its wounds and re-formed, then proceeded on its way. Maybe that was it, and now we could continue our journey in peace.

I thought back to that Chinaman on the dock at Singapore, and his words to me that day: 'You will never get there, sir. The American submarines are sinking every ship.'

Well, I thought, *you were wrong this time, mate.*

The following morning, when I took my party of four to the galley to collect the men's breakfast rations, the friendly Jap strode up to me.

'Americans demi-demi,' he shrieked at me in a filthy temper. 'They no good. Sink Japanese ships.'

'Americans number one,' I answered indignantly, before I realised what I was saying.

That did it. He gave me such a clout with his fist that it sent me sprawling across the deck on my backside. I immediately jumped to my feet. As ever, it always paid with our guards to take the punishments and get up at once.

I turned to walk back to the galley with my men, when he called me over. Though my head was spinning from his punch, I walked back towards him.

He put his hand in his pocket and I wondered whether he was getting out a revolver . . . but no. Unbelievably, he took out a full packet of Japanese cigarettes and gave it to me.

'Tonight, all ships sink,' he said with a cocky smile.

'Yes, I know,' I replied with a smile. It was bravado I suppose. I didn't want him to see my fear.

As we carried on collecting rations and taking them down to

the men, I managed to fill five extra water-bottles without anyone noticing. I took four of them down to the lads in the hold, who were by now in a terrible state, many of them hardly strong enough to drink.

The fifth water-bottle I kept with me at all times, tied round my waist, in case of emergencies. Throughout that day, the old routines returned and it was as if nothing had happened. Some of the crew pasted a thick, grainy mixture on to the damaged side of the ship to strengthen it, and we all realised we had been extraordinarily lucky that the tanker had not pierced the metal.

The majority of our men were now so sick that they couldn't move from the holds, where they lay all day, too weak to do anything for themselves. When it was time for the lads on deck to go back down to the holds again at dusk, I felt so uneasy that I went and found the Jap with the cigarettes.

'Very bad in hold,' I began. 'Can some men stay on deck tonight?'

Surprise, surprise, he nodded. 'Yes, Johnny. Few men stay on deck for little time.'

I went back down to the hold to see if I could help any of the light-sick men up to the deck, but I was absolutely flabbergasted to find that hardly any of them could manage to climb the ladder. They couldn't even stand up any more. Those few extra men that could get up on deck with my help, now made the most of the cool, fresh air and hid themselves in all the nooks and crannies they could find in the area near the bow of the ship.

It was a still, dark, night with a pale moon shining as the ship zigzagged every few minutes, to try and evade detection. Of course, we didn't know about radar or sonar in those days – we'd never heard of them, so we had no idea that, lurking beneath the ocean, American sub crews were tracking our every movement.

Seeing quite a few of our men now settling for the night up here, I was relieved to think that at least they would have a better chance now, if the Yanks attacked us again that night. But there were still hundreds of poor, sick men in the holds, barely hanging on to life. What chance would they have?

That night, 13th September, tragedy struck and our luck deserted us. Suddenly, at about ten to eleven, the first torpedoes hit their target. As we watched the dark sky light up behind us with two terrible explosions, I could see we were now sitting ducks. The tears ran down my cheeks as I wept with fear, and I silently prayed, *Please, God, spare us*.

There was a momentary lull, only seconds, and I wiped away my tears, daring to hope. Bombardier Stuart Merritt, from Aldershot, stood next to me at the rail.

'Maybe we've been lucky after all, and escaped for a second night,' I said to him. But I spoke too soon.

The deafening sound and smell of tremendous explosions filled the air as the *Kachidoki Maru* took two direct hits at once. The whole ship shuddered beneath my feet. Immediately there were terrified shouts all across the deck. The bloody Japs ran every-where, shrieking and wailing, panicking and falling over each other, trying to lower the lifeboats for themselves to scramble into. It was complete pandemonium.

In the holds they heard only muffled sounds at first and were unaware we had been hit. But the engines stopped and the ship began to tilt.

There were shouts from below: 'What's happened? . . . Did we get hit? . . . Can we come out on deck?' But there was no panic down there, yet.

Suddenly, the ship tilted further. We were now cocked up at an angle of about thirty or forty degrees and a lot of the boys, at least eight hundred of them down there, were shouting and screaming as they tried to climb out of the holds, but the opening was only one man wide and the ladder was leaning backwards at an impossible angle. It was a heartbreaking scene.

At least, out on the deck, we could see what was happening,

whereas the men in the holds were now even more petrified than we were. They knew they hadn't a chance unless they could get out somehow, which seemed almost hopeless at such an angle, though the fittest might have made it. They must have realised they would drown – a slow suffocating death. I wanted to go down to see if I could help them, but an officer stopped me as he went over to the hatch and shouted to the men below.

'We have been torpedoed,' he explained. 'But we must all keep calm. The ship is at an angle, but it has settled down and it doesn't appear as if we will be at risk of sinking. So I want you all to stay calm down there and don't worry.'

The cries of fear stopped and the poor blighters below took that officer's word for fact. I was horrified. Surely this tub was already past saving?

Only seconds later, suddenly and without warning, our whole ship started to tip right up. We were sinking fast and there was no time to lose.

'We're sinking!' the officer screamed down to the men in the hold. 'Every man for himself!'

The next few minutes were the most terrifying of my life.

I looked down the hatch and my heart lurched at the sight of those thin faces, contorted with anguish and terror as the few most able men, their arms outstretched, desperately tried in vain to scale the ladder, against the pull of gravity, and I could do nothing now to help them. I shall never forget that moment. I see it in my nightmares.

All around me there were men scrambling up the steep slant of the deck amid fearful shouts and wails.

'Help me . . . I can't swim . . . I'm slipping . . . We're all going to die!'

The ship itself creaked and clanked as it shifted in the sea.

I could hear revolver shots somewhere, among the chaos. Then a shout from one of our men.

'There are two Jap officers shooting their wounded men – the bastards!'

'I saw the captain shoot himself just after the torpedoes struck,' said one of my lads.

We had no time to think about that, as we hurriedly inflated some life-rafts and threw them overboard for our men to climb into from the sea, along with anything else that might float.

Our end of the ship was now sticking right up in the air, with the stern already submerged, and men were jumping wildly into the dark waters below. Stuart Merritt and I fought our way to the rails, which were now like a vertical ladder.

In the midst of all the panic around us, he screamed at me. 'Jump well out, Sarge, or you'll be sucked under.'

As I prepared to jump, I looked down to see heads and debris bobbing up and down everywhere. I was conscious of the continuing cries for help from those still clinging on to the deck, those who couldn't swim or didn't dare jump. But there was nothing I could do for them now. I could only save myself. I was counting down to jump. 'Please God, let me make it,' I said under my breath. Would this be it? Would Johnny Sherwood's luck run out at last?

20

Shark-Infested Waters

September 1944

I took a deep breath and jumped as far out as I could, landing in the water with a terrible pain in my backside. As I dropped below the surface I realised I must have landed on someone, and probably killed him, poor soul. At the time I had to focus on survival, but later I felt dreadful about that and wondered who it was.

It seemed an age, sinking ever lower into the depths, my lungs bursting, until suddenly I shot back up again, gasping for air. I remembered what Stuart Merritt had said about the danger of being sucked in as the ship sank, so I swam away from her as fast as I could, with the base of my spine still hurting like mad. Finally, when I thought I was far enough away, I turned around. Floating on my back and treading water, I watched the *Kachidoki Maru* slide gracefully out of sight, down to her peaceful resting place on the seabed, taking with her about eight hundred young British POWs, men who had no chance at all of survival in the holds which became their tomb.

In the moonlight I could see and hear men struggling to stay afloat, screaming for help, and bodies drifting by. We had jumped empty-handed and what clothes we'd had on had been mostly torn off us when we hit the water. I took in the scene as best I could, terrified at the prospect of sharks and other dangers lurking beneath.

I could see a number of lifeboats, only half full of Japs and pulling safely away. What hope could there be for us? I looked around to see if I could find my pal who'd jumped with me.

'Stuart,' I yelled as loud as I could. 'Bombardier Merritt!' But it was no good, I couldn't locate him. Perhaps he had already swum away in a different direction and couldn't hear me. But deep down I knew it was possible he had been less lucky than me and had drowned. Would I ever find out?

I floated and swam, floated and swam, for what seemed like hours in the darkness, until my luck turned again and I found a drifting hatchboard – a piece of wood about six feet long, two feet wide and four inches thick. 'Thank God,' I said out loud. 'This is just the job.' Then, in my head, *I can cling on to this and rest all right. Then maybe someone, or maybe a ship, will come along and pick me up.* How naive I was!

Thankfully, it was a beautiful night and, apart from a heavy swell, the sea was not too bad and not too cold. I could see heads bobbing up and down on the waves all around me. And in between them were lifeboats. As far as I could see, they only contained Japanese and Korean soldiers, and one or two female Jap nurses.

I wondered at first whether to go and climb on to one of these, but I was soon put off when I witnessed one POW attempting to board a half-empty lifeboat. As he clambered aboard, a Jap slashed him with a sword and tipped his body back into the sea. So I kept my distance after that.

In the next two or three hours, I collected six more POWs around my hatchboard. I was glad to be helping them stay alive, but it was going to make things difficult for so many of us, with such a light piece of wood. Only two men, one at each end, could hang on to it at any one time and remain afloat. With a third man it started to sink. So I organised us into a rota, with two men resting at the board, while the other five swam or floated around, without losing anyone. But we found it very hard to keep everyone together, and one of these boys had swallowed a lot of thick oil when he landed in the sea, where it was leaking out of our ship. His body and face were covered in the stuff.

It must have been about three in the morning when I suddenly realised that I still had an improvised string belt round my waist and my full water-bottle attached. What a godsend that turned out to be. It gave us all that little bit greater chance of survival.

One of the lads was a Scottish sergeant. For some reason, I had never met him before. He must have been in the other hold. Anyway, between us we made sure that everyone had a fair go at resting at the board. This way, we might all survive long enough to be picked up by God knows who.

However, as time wore on, the sick lad who had swallowed so much oil grew weaker and weaker, frequently being sick and losing the strength even to cling on. He seemed to be losing his mind, barely conscious, and it became increasingly difficult for us to look after him as we struggled to keep ourselves going.

Covered in oil, he was too slippery to hold properly, so we had to hold him on to the hatchboard now, treading water furiously and using up what little energy we had left. As soon as we let go of him, he slipped off. He was in a very bad way.

'We can't look after him much longer,' said the Scottish sergeant.

'No,' I agreed. 'The other boys are very tired too and they need a rest.'

'I don't think he's going to make it, do you?'

'No, I reckon you're right.' I didn't like to admit it, but I knew we were both thinking the same thing.

'We can't let him pull us all down,' added the Scot. 'I think we should let him go in peace.'

Reluctantly, I nodded.

'We can look the other way, and if he loses his hold, we let him go?'

'Yes.'

And that's what we did. We felt terrible about it, but what other option did we have? It was survive or die, and this man was beyond saving. We had to think of the others now. But I've been haunted by it ever since, plagued by guilt. How could I have let a man die like that? I don't think I'll ever forgive myself.

As the morning approached, the swell grew higher and the remaining six of us drifted aimlessly on the peaks and troughs of gigantic waves. At one point, we came close to another lifeboat, filled with Japanese guards, singing their bloody heads off. Whenever any of our boys drifted too close to them, these sadistic guards stood up and waved their swords and knives at them. It was obvious they had no intention whatsoever of permitting any of us on board their lifeboat, even though there was room for a few more; some of the other lifeboats we saw were actually nearly empty. No, these Japs seemed to prefer to watch our lads drown than help them in any way.

The hours wore on and I noticed fewer and fewer bobbing heads, as they vanished beneath the waves. I felt sick for them, and the families they left behind, and of course frightened for us too. I may sound soft-headed, going on about all this, but you will understand if you've ever been through a similar experience.

Any time now I was expecting to see sharks. I knew these were shark-infested waters, and I'd heard some gruesome stories about killer sharks in the South China Sea. I didn't think we had a hope of survival once we spotted those black fins approaching us. But the strange thing was, we hadn't yet seen any sign of them. Where were they all? Perhaps they were lurking beneath us, waiting for the daylight? Surely it could only be a matter of time before they attacked?

In the early hours of the morning, in shock, dog-tired, thirsty and hungry, I felt very low and my mind was all mixed up. I desperately needed to sleep, but I didn't dare, even when it was my turn to hold the hatchboard. But I do remember thinking over and over again, *Well, Johnny, this is it, my boy.*

The sky began to lighten with the coming of dawn, and our little party of men were still fighting on. But we were full of anxieties, and what worried us most now, apart from sharks, was how we could cope with the blinding heat of the day, the burning sun on our bare skin and the raging thirst that would overcome us all as soon as the sun was up.

We six battled on in the same old routine, two by two changing places at the board at regular intervals, surviving one minute at a time, one hour to the next. This small piece of wood was now all that stood between us and certain death.

My water-bottle of liquid life-saver kept us going a little longer as we passed it round for just one sip each, only enough to keep our throats moist to make sure we didn't choke to death. If we'd drunk it all overnight, I knew we couldn't have lived out the day. We all agreed on this, with great British restraint, but I know how hard the lads struggled to keep to it.

'Time for another sip,' I would say, lifting everyone's spirits again.

'Thanks, Sarge,' said the youngest. 'Thank God your water-bottle was full when you jumped!'

'It's a bloody miracle,' grinned the Scottish sergeant. 'Mine came off with my kilt!'

We all managed a smile, knowing his kilt must have gone a long time before, but it was a comical image. He was quite a card this Scot. It was fantastic how he could be cheerful when all the odds were on us perishing. I wish I could remember his name. I hope he survived the war.

We drifted on through the morning hours, the sun burning our skin to blisters and cracking our lips to painful sores, aggravated by the stinging salt-water. As we tossed on the ocean, we passed more Japs and Koreans in lifeboats and kept as far away from them as we could.

We took more sips of the water, just warm now as the sea heated up in the scorching sunlight. If we hadn't had this fresh water to share, we would have had to resort to drinking sea-water. We later learnt that many of our lads did just that in their desperation, the salty water sending them mad, which sometimes threatened their pals' safety as well as their own.

'Why don't I feel hungry, Sarge?' asked one of the lads, mid-morning. It was strange, considering that normally we were constantly conscious of our ravenous hunger. 'I don't know. I'm just the same. Perhaps other things have taken over that space in our minds. Maybe fear?'

'Aye,' agreed the Scot. 'A haggis would make me sick right now.'

'It would make me sick any time,' said another lad, trying to smile through his cracked and swollen lips.

'When we get picked up,' said our Scottish friend, 'and you get asked what you'd like to eat, what will you say?'

We went round the board with this game, two clinging on and four of us treading water.

'Sausage and mash for me.'

'Roast beef and Yorkshire pudding,' I said. 'And a pint.'

We carried on discussing our favourite foods and drinks for a while, which passed the time, before we sank back into a weary silence, and into our own fears. Despite the food fantasies, we were becoming a very depressed little party now, as the day wore slowly on.

I kept a furtive lookout for black fins above the water at all times, without letting on to the others, not wanting to stir their fears in this direction. I tried to appear calm, but inside I was a maelstrom of fear. I didn't see any sharks, but I felt sure I would do soon, and wondered what if anything I could do about them when I did.

I decided to start another conversation. I had to do something to keep my mind off the fear of sharks, and I knew we all needed a way to occupy our thoughts and stay sane in the middle of this hostile sea.

'You know, I think I must have crossed the South China Sea on my football tour before the war,' I said. 'Though I don't really remember it.'

'Were you a proper footballer then, Sarge?'

'Yes, a professional footballer – that was my job.'

172

'Cor, I wouldn't mind that job!'

'Yes, I was lucky.'

'Not half.'

'I'd never even been abroad till then . . . unless you count Scotland!'

That raised a smile from the Scot.

'Did you really go round the world?'

'To a lot of countries, yes,' I nodded. 'We even played in Singapore and Japan.'

The lads looked surprised.

'Well, they weren't our enemies then.'

'What was the best country you went to?' asked the Scot. Anything to keep our minds occupied.

I thought about it for a moment, while we changed turns on the hatchboard.

'Egypt,' I said, and started to tell them about the highlights of our visit there. 'The pyramids were marvellous, but the thing that stood out was when King Farouk invited us to his palace for coffee.'

'Crikey! Did you meet him?'

'Yes, but we didn't just meet him, he came and sat next to me, with his interpreter, and we had quite a chat. He seemed like a good bloke.'

'What did you talk about?'

'About the game we'd played the day before, and all the fire-crackers going off in the crowd. Luckily it didn't stop us winning the match. But the best bit of that day was when the king played a joke on us. He handed round a box of cigars and we all took one. He got one of his people to light them for us and we took a few puffs . . . then came the surprise.'

'What?'

'The cigars all went off with loud bangs, one after another! It took us completely by surprise, and the king thought it was hilarious. We all had a jolly good laugh about it.'

Cuttings from Johnny's scrapbook - King Farouk, and the Islington
Corinthians team on arrival in Egypt, October 1937.

My throat was so dry now that I knew I had to stop speaking. We had so little water between us, and no idea how many hours lay ahead.

As the waves increased in size again, and we drifted up and down with them, we were finding it very difficult to keep ourselves together. One of the party would be carried away by a freak wave, and as soon as he had struggled back to us, another was swept away. Our Scottish sergeant showed terrific strength and courage in helping to keep our group together.

Around one in the afternoon, judging by the sun, we realised we had been in the water for about fourteen hours and we all felt a great fatigue coming over us, together with a deeper depression. We had so little strength left and could barely stay awake. To be honest, I think we all knew our time was nearly up and that we were doomed to drown, but nobody said so.

'We'll soon see a ship,' I began, as cheerfully as I could. 'I'm sure the Yanks will come and rescue us.'

'Aye,' agreed the Scot. 'We have to keep our eyes peeled.'

'Yes, it's not like buses. If we miss one, there won't be another along in a few minutes,' I added as I grabbed the arm of one of our lads, who was beginning to drift away with his eyes closed. I gave him a gentle shake.

'Sorry, Sarge,' he muttered hoarsely. 'I must have fallen asleep.'

'We have to keep together,' I said. 'Here, have my turn on the board.'

It really sickened me to think of what these good young soldiers had been through the past few years on the death railway, and that they had survived, only to be faced with almost certain death in the depths of the South China Sea, many miles from any hope of rescue or escape.

Suddenly, I realised something.

'Do you realise, lads?'

'What, Sarge?'

175

'We're free! Out here, we're nobody's prisoners. For the first time in three and a half years, we're bloody free. If we can be picked up or find our way to neutral land, we could go home free men.'

'I hadn't thought of that. I wish I wasn't so tired, Sarge. Then I could feel happy about it.'

This thought of freedom, no matter how impossible it was in our predicament, started me off thinking again about my lovely Christine, as I so often did. I thought back to the days when we were courting, the first time I took her to a football match, her great pride and her sparkling smile whenever she saw me score a goal for Reading. I remembered the day she first told me she was pregnant, and our excitement in sharing this news with our families. So many memories of Christine crowded my mind and made me feel even more alone out there in the vast, enemy seas.

How much longer could we last? Surely we would drown, one by one, or be eaten by sharks? Where were they? I couldn't understand why we hadn't seen any of those menacing fins. Then it suddenly struck me: maybe they had been frightened off by the noise of the explosions, or by the danger of swallowing the film of oil that now covered much of the sea around us.

My memories of Christine faded into a distant haze that I could no longer hold on to. I was desperately tired and weak.

I shook myself up somehow and passed around the water-bottle for another sip each. That seemed to refresh us a little, enough to gather round the gutsy Scot when he broke into a rousing chorus.

'I belong to Glasgow, dear old Glasgow town . . .' He ran out of words at that point, and with a strained grin he hummed the rest rather out of tune. But it had the desired effect and we all burst into crackly laughter.

It was fantastic. What courage that man had, to sing and force a smile at a time like that, when all the odds were on us drowning before the sun set.

That started us off, and next we sang 'Rule Britannia', then 'Land of Hope and Glory'. By now our voices were too hoarse to sing any more, and we settled back into our depression again.

It was late afternoon, we had been in the sea for seventeen hours and we had little hope left. We had stopped talking to each other now, and were just concentrating on trying to keep surviving a little longer.

Suddenly, out of the distance, loomed a large warship. It was like I imagine a mirage to be, and for two or three seconds I couldn't believe it. None of us could. But then we let rip. We screamed and shouted with delight.

'Yippee!'

'It must be an American ship.'

'Do you think they've seen us?'

'Let's wave to make sure,' I suggested. I tore off the rag from around my waist and waved it wildly in the breeze above my head.

'Where's your kilt, Jimmy?' joked the man next to the Scot. 'They couldn't miss us if you waved that!'

'Aye, the Yanks love a kilt,' he replied.

Just at that moment, as the ship drew nearer, our mood suddenly changed. This was a Japanese cruiser, full of little Jap sailors manning the guns, pointing them straight at us.

'The bastards are going to shoot us,' yelled the youngest, in terror.

'If they are going to, why the bloody hell haven't they?' asked the Scot.

I strained my eyes to see what else was going on on-board and around that ship. I could see men and life-rafts peppered all over the sea, swimming or rowing towards the vessel, but many of the bobbing heads were far distant and I wondered whether they would be able to make it. We were now only about twenty-five yards from this cruiser, close enough to see that they were only picking up Japanese and Korean survivors from the lifeboats.

Lucky Johnny

Once they were all on board, they made no move towards us and I felt sure this was it. Our last and only chance of rescue gone. I can't tell you what depths of misery I felt at that moment of realisation, looking away in despair.

178

21

The Struggle for Safety

September 1944

'Look Johnny,' said the Scot. I was surprised he knew my name, then realised it was probably his name for any Englishman, just as we'd called him Jimmy. 'Look!' he repeated.

I turned round to follow his gaze back to the ship, where there seemed to be a heated argument going on. A crowd of sailors and Japanese survivors were loudly exchanging their opinions, all the while keeping their eyes trained on us and the few other Brits who were approaching them. An officer was also arguing fiercely with the ship's captain on the bridge.

'I reckon they're trying to decide what to do,' I said, with a sudden flicker of hope in my voice again.

'Do you think they'll let us on?' asked one of the lads.

'They better had!' exclaimed the Scot.

'They've still got the guns trained on us. Maybe they're arguing about whether to shoot us.'

'I don't think they'd waste the ammo,' I said. 'They only have to leave us here and that would be as good as shooting us.'

'Maybe the bastards want to recapture us,' suggested the youngest. 'So they can take us to Japan to do their dirtiest work, as usual.'

'Well that would be better than drowning here,' I said. 'At least we'd have food and water and somewhere to sleep.'

'You hope!'

Just then, the arguing stopped and one of the officers on the bridge came out to the deck, picked up a loudspeaker and lifted it to his mouth.

179

'Look, maybe he's going to talk to us.'

Sure enough, he turned to face us and a few others now gathering nearby.

'Look, it's Tanaka,' I said in disbelief. That fiend got everywhere.

Speaking in excellent English, he shouted to us as loud as he could. 'You will have fifteen minutes to get on board. Anyone not on board in time will be left behind.'

Well, you never saw such a sight in your life, as everyone fought and struggled to get to safety. All we survivors found just enough strength from somewhere and wasted no time in swimming over there. Four of the crew shinned down a rope ladder on the side of the ship and two went off to gather exhausted POWs into their life-raft, while the other two stood in another life-raft at the bottom of the ladder and helped pull us all on board and pushed us up the ladder towards the deck. As weak as we were, we each doggedly climbed, one rung at a time, determined to reach safety in time. How we made it I don't know, but all six of us reached that deck before the fifteen minutes were up.

I was just about to collapse in a heap on the deck when I heard my name.

'Johnny!'

I turned to the sound of a familiar voice.

'I was hoping I'd see you again.'

'Stuart! Thank God you made it!'

'And your luck held good too. I knew it would.'

'If it hadn't been for you, it probably wouldn't have.' I tried to smile. 'Thanks pal.'

'Come on, let's find a space to rest.'

Suddenly, the siren sounded and that was it. They pulled up the ladder and we were away. There was panic among the Brits aboard when we realised that a few of the stragglers hadn't made it, but the sailors left them the life-raft, and there were now empty lifeboats floating nearby, so we thought they had a chance of survival for longer, till another ship found them.

'Why did that devil, Tanaka, take us on board?' asked Stuart, as we lay flat out and breathing heavily on the deck.

'I'm as amazed as you.'

'It makes no sense.'

'Unless . . . Perhaps he sees us as his slaves, to do his work for the Emperor.'

The Japanese cruiser set off, full-steam ahead. We had no idea where to, but at this point we really didn't care. We were completely done in and immediately fell asleep where we lay, all of us strewn across the open deck. Two or three hours later, they woke us up to give us our first meal for nearly twenty-four hours – a ball of sugared rice each, and a few containers of water between the lot of us. It wasn't enough to slake our raging thirst, but it was better than nothing.

We gobbled down the rice, took some sips of water and fell back into a deep sleep, all huddled together now in a corner of the cruiser's deck, with the night drawing in. Like on the *Kachidoki Maru*, we were only allowed the use of one improvised *benjo* – a wooden lavatory built over the side of the ship, but at least there were fewer of us now to share it, and our stomachs had been empty for so long that we survivors wouldn't need to go till morning.

In the early hours, we were woken again to be landed on an island. I think it was called Hainan. We were taken off the ship and led into some rotten old sheds.

'You rest here,' said one of the guards. 'One day or two, ship come. Take you to Nippon.'

For once, we were happy to obey orders. We did nothing but rest and sleep, on the floor of course, with no bedding or covering at all, and most of us with no clothing left on us.

The few officers who had survived with us did their best to keep us cheerful.

'The war will soon be over, chaps,' said the sole lieutenant, with a grin. 'Then we can all go home for tea!'

'What I wouldn't give for a cup of proper English tea,' said a young lad.

'Nice and strong, with milk and sugar.'

'Maybe a nip of something in it?' suggested Stuart.

'What are we going to eat, Captain?'

Our most senior officer got up and walked over to the corner of the main shed, where there were a couple of sacks and a small barrel. 'They've left us a bag of dried fish, and a container of water,' he replied as he came back to sit with us. 'We'll have to ration that out into two meals, breakfast and dinner.'

'Hopefully they'll collect us again tomorrow,' added the lieutenant.

'What if they don't?' asked a chap behind me.

'What if they never come?' asked another.

'Come on lads,' I interrupted. 'Let's look on the bright side. We're alive aren't we, and relatively safe here, with no work to do and no guards to bother us for a day or two.'

'Well said, Sergeant,' smiled the captain.

It was true. The only guards we had were two Koreans who had been abandoned on the island with us. They watched us from outside during the day and from a nearby shack at night.

Several of the boys with us were very sick and we all helped to look after them as best we could. Most of them had swallowed too much of the oil that had leaked from our torpedoed ship, or been blinded by it, while others had the usual diseases, or injuries from the torpedoing or the jump to contend with. A few of the men suffered terribly from broken limbs and we had nothing to splint them with, except their own bodies. We all had painful sunburn blisters, and many had heatstroke. Every one of us was in a poor condition, stick thin and starving, so we were a sorry sight.

The two worst cases were a Londoner, Tommy Taylor – who, by some miracle, had managed to keep with his twin brother Walter, who looked after him – and Corporal Frank, a smashing chap from Liverpool, who I'd met right at the beginning, in

Singapore, though we'd spent most of the time since in different camps. Frank was a man who had always been full of life and kept cheerful, even in the direst situations. I stayed with Frank and looked after him as well as I could. I sat and talked with him, telling him all sorts of things to give him hope.

'When we get to Japan, we'll have some medical supplies,' I said. 'Then you'll soon mend and be up on your feet again, back to your old rascal self.' He gave me a half-smile, but I could see he was in a pretty bad way and I had my doubts.

The next day, the guards ordered us on a shambling parade, apart from those too sick to walk.

'Transport will come for sick,' said a Japanese officer who had just arrived. 'You march to quay.' He waved in the general direction.

So we marched, or rather staggered, Stuart and I carrying Frank between us, along the beach and round the head to the open bay, where my heart sank. What a shock. The only vessel in sight was a large oil-tanker.

'Is that how we are expected to travel the rest of the way to Japan?' I groaned.

'It couldn't be any worse than the holds of the *Kachidoki Maru*,' said Stuart.

'But what if we're torpedoed again?' I shuddered to think about it, with all that fuel-oil on the ship.

We boarded the tanker in our straggly line of wretched souls and found some shaded corners of the bare, metal deck, close to the bridge.

A large group of POW survivors from the *Rakuyo Maru*, all Brits and Aussies, joined us on the deck. I searched them for the friends I knew had been on that ship. It was a great relief every time I saw a familiar face, but I felt a hollow ache of sadness when I tallied the ones who were missing. Perhaps they'd been rescued by another ship, I reasoned in hope. We'd probably meet up again in Japan, or at the end of the war. That turned out to be true of two or three of them – though I didn't know it at the time, of course – but many other friends and colleagues were lost on both ships, drowned in the holds, or in the open sea.

One of the Aussies cast his eyes around the tanker and turned to me. 'We're just waiting here for another ship to pick us up, right?'

'No,' I said. 'They told us they're taking us to Japan on this one.'

'But that's impossible! We can't survive for more than a few hours in this cauldron.'

It was true, there was hardly any shade, so most of the steel deck was burning hot. We had no bedding, no clothes and too little water.

'Yes, and you know we'd be gonners if this tub got torpedoed,' added his mate. 'With the tanks full of oil, we'd be a giant fireball!'

'We've got to make a stand,' insisted the first Aussie. 'We must demand to go on a proper ship, a safer one.'

He got some of his pals together and they started shouting, louder and louder.

'No go to Japan on tanker!' they yelled in unison three or four times. The sailors looked shocked, and they came and hit some of the protesters with their sticks and rifle butts. But it didn't stop the Aussies. More and more POWs joined in the chant.

The tanker's captain came out to face them. 'You must go Nippon,' he insisted. 'Men no shout. Rest. We go Nippon tomorrow.'

'Oh no we won't,' bellowed the ringleader. 'We only go on another ship.'

'No other ship,' said the captain.

'Then we swim back to Hainan island.'

'No swim. We shoot you if swim.'

'Shoot us, then. We'd rather die swimming than burn to death or be torpedoed.'

'You swim, we shoot,' repeated the captain.

'You get new ship or we swim!'

'We no go till tomorrow.'

'Then tomorrow we swim.'

Boy, these Aussies were brave. I saw the look of fury on the captain's face as he turned and marched away. I didn't fancy our chances either way.

'What if the Japs set off while we're asleep, Sarge?' asked one of the lads near me. One of the Aussies must have overheard him.

'Don't you worry mate, we'll take turns to keep watch through the night.'

Things settled down a bit after that, as the *Rakuyo Maru* POWs found spaces to sit across the deck. There were more of them than us, and most of them were in a much better condition than we were.

I was relieved to find out they had a medical officer with them, but I saw the horror in his face when he looked at the terrible state of some of our men. He couldn't hide his dismay and seemed unsure where to start, but gradually he made his way round all of us.

'I'm sorry I have nothing to give you, lads,' he said several times. 'But I'll do my best to make you as comfortable as I can.'

'Sir, please could you come and look at Corporal Frank,' I called out as he approached our corner of the deck.

The medical officer checked him over, took his pulse and assessed his condition, then took me aside. 'I'm afraid your pal is in a bad way, Sergeant. All you can do is try and make sure he has as much water as he needs, and keep his spirits up. I'm sure you'll do all you can.'

'Yes sir.' I nodded gravely. 'He's a good man. One of the best.'

'If we can get him to a camp hospital with some supplies in Japan, then we might be able to save him.' He paused. 'If we can keep him going long enough.'

'What about food, sir? He says he can't eat anything.'

'No, I think he may be right about that. Water is the most important thing.'

My heart sank. Where and how was I going to find any water? We were all desperately thirsty, but we would have no water till after sundown, and then not enough.

The medical officer moved on to his next patient, and I sat down again by Frank.

'The doc says they can put you right when we get to Japan,' I reassured him. 'So you just have to keep going till then. It can't be far.'

When he had finished his round, the MO got some of the fittest men to fill buckets with sea-water from the sluice the sailors used to scrub down the decks and throw it over us all to cool us down and wash away the worst of the oil. This met with screams of agony from those with open sores or wounds, but it was the closest thing we had to antiseptic.

The oil-tanker was hard to endure, all of us crammed into whatever shade we could find to avoid the burning metal of the deck. It was another living hell, with very little food and such a small ration of water that the men were dying of thirst, and we could do nothing about it. Far from getting Corporal Frank enough water to drink, I could do little better than wet his lips.

When I had jumped from the *Kachidoki Maru*, I lost my precious letter from Christine, the one I'd kept from the Red Cross bundle we had received in Singapore; the one that was over two years late, that told me about the birth of my daughter Sandra, and that told me how much she loved me. Now it was gone. We had all lost what few treasured possessions we had.

The only things I had left in this world now were an old rag slip that was tied around my loins, my water-bottle, a ring on my finger that my beloved Christine had given me before I left England, and an old Rolls razor I found in the shed on Hainan island. I spent hours cleaning the wretched thing with my bit of rag, and eventually restored it. But possessions meant very little out there unless they helped us stay alive. I learnt that the will to live is very strong in man. It was certainly strong in me.

As the hot day wore slowly on, the lack of water was even more punishing than the heat of the sun. *Please God, may we have water soon*, I prayed silently. The survivors from the *Rakuyo Maru* seemed better able to cope than we were, with our men having been deprived for so long. Every minute felt like an hour or more. Our throats were so parched they were swelling up and our lips were so cracked and encrusted with salt that we could hardly speak.

Just as I neared the end of my tether, curled up by a bulkhead, I felt something. I didn't believe it at first, but it quickly became more insistent. I looked up.

'RAIN!' I shouted and leapt awkwardly to my feet. 'It's bloody raining!' I yelled through the sudden torrent of water from the sky. Everyone that could, joined me out in the middle of the deck, almost running about in excitement, our mouths open wide to catch this cool elixir of life. This was no shower – it was a proper storm, a torrent of treasure. Just in the nick of time.

Suddenly, this day had turned from despair to joy. We scoured the deck for any containers we could find to catch rainwater in. Men were collecting it in their hands and drinking it, then catching more to take to our invalids. We stored water in buckets, a few abandoned tins, cups we made out of thrown-away cardboard, and even the few items of clothing we had left.

I found a couple of empty cans and swilled them out. Then I filled them up for our sick to drink from and to wash them down with. I truly believe that storm-water helped some of our sick men to survive, when they were nearly lost.

At last I could give Frank a drink to revive him a little. I lifted his head to help him and tried to force some of it into his mouth, but his lips were so very dry and painful, and his mouth still lined with oil, that he was unable to take in more than a few drops at a time. Sadly, it wasn't much, and I knew it might be too late, but I prayed it would help him keep going. When Frank could take no more, I bathed him all over with the cool water to comfort him.

* * *

After the storm, it was time for me and three of the lads to go to the galley to collect our rations. While I fetched this food for the boys, I had to leave my pal Frank lying, very lonely, in a corner of the deck.

'I'll be back soon,' I assured him.

I knew he could no longer speak, but he slowly raised his hand onto my arm.

'Don't you want me to leave?' I asked gently. 'I wish I could stay with you, pal. But I have to go. The men are all waiting for their food. I'll be as quick as I can,' I continued, as I left his side.

When I got to the galley it was the same predicable diet as always – rice and dried fish. But there was one big problem – nothing to eat out of. We had to take bucketfuls of rice out on to the deck and pile it there for the men to make it into balls to eat. Of course, this meant that, if it were to be a free-for-all, those who were first could have more than those who were last, and there would be virtually nothing left for the large number who were too sick to come and help themselves.

So the lads and I had to organise small groups to come up at a time, and we tried to make sure there was enough to go round. This took much longer than we expected, having to watch the men carefully as they came and went. And it was quite comical to watch each other juggling these boiling hot balls of rice from hand to hand.

However, the good thing about being on the rations detail was that it gave me the opportunity to steal extra food from the galley to share with my boys, so it worked out quite well.

Finally I returned to Frank's side . . . but it was too late. He had passed away. When he'd tried to hold me back, perhaps he'd known it was his time. I felt sick. I took one final look at him, his face now composed at rest, and held his cooling hand in mine for a few seconds while I said my own little prayer for him. Then Stuart and I wrapped his body in an empty rice sack I got from the galley.

In the fading light we placed Corporal Frank's shrouded corpse on a length of wood and carried him to the side-rail. There were four of us, and our lieutenant came with us to say a prayer aloud for his soul. Then we slid him gracefully down, into the dark sea.

I watched the waves for a while, with a hollow feeling inside. I had lost yet another good friend in this cruel war and now I felt an overwhelming need to find some small space on the crowded tanker where I could be alone with my thoughts.

22

False Alarms and False Hopes

September 1944

Whether it was anything to do with the previous day's protests, or part of the plan, I will never know, but on the morning of 16th September 1944, as we prepared for another hellish day on the tanker's searing deck, a Japanese whaler drew alongside. It was a huge whale-factory ship called the *Kibibi Maru*.

'You go on whale ship,' shouted the captain, through his loud hailer. 'You go now.'

'Speedo-speedo.' The guards prodded us into straggly groups. 'You go, speedo.'

They herded us on to the whaler, carrying our sick and wounded men between us, which gave them all a lot of pain and distress, but at least we would be in a better ship for the journey. Well, that was what I thought. The whaler had in fact been converted to hold fuel-oil in its hold, under the whale deck, so we would still have gone up in a ball of fire if we'd been torpedoed again. But fortunately we didn't know that.

Once on board, we were pushed down a ladder.

'Sick men go,' ordered one of the guards, pointing at a corner of the lower deck.

We put the sick men down gently to lie where the guard had indicated, and the rest of us had to sit or lie on the bare metal in any other space.

There were a few dim lights, so I looked around and saw that this deck ran the whole length and breadth of the ship, with a

190

vast, hinged ramp at one end, and winches to pull in the whales from the sea. There were various machines and boilers for rendering the whale-blubber, though they looked as if they hadn't been used for a while.

Suddenly I saw something – the shape of a head, with its back to me, but I immediately knew who it was, across the sea of men.

I scrambled upright to get a better look, to be sure.

'Reg!' I yelled with a momentary surge of energy.

He turned right round to face me and his face lit up.

'Johnny Sherwood! Is that really you?' He got up and came over to join Stuart and me. 'Where have you been?' We hugged like children, we were so relieved to see each other.

'It's good to see you, Reg. I thought you were a gonner.'

'Me too.'

'Which ship were you on?'

'The *Rakuyo Maru*.'

'So you sank before we did.'

We sat in silent joy for a moment, the joy of finding each other.

'But what about the others?' I hardly dared to ask, but I had to know. 'Geordie?' I asked him tentatively.

'I don't know, Johnny,' said Reg, both our faces serious again now. 'I never saw him on our ship.'

'And I didn't see him on mine, but there were nearly a thousand of us. Maybe . . .' I dared to hope. 'Maybe he was in the other hold and I just never saw him.' But then my heart lurched again. What if he had been in the holds when the *Kachidoki Maru* sank? He wouldn't have had a chance. Surely if he'd survived, he would be here? I didn't dare voice my thoughts to Reg, and he probably felt the same. I feared that, by saying something, we might make it real. We lay down side by side on the deck to rest. At least we had both survived. I couldn't really expect more . . .

It wasn't just our invalids who were in a bad way. We were all suffering from sores and other uncomfortable ailments, such as dysentery and scabies, both highly infectious, and boy did they spread. As we tried to settle in to yet another kind of hell, many of our lads were confused and we were all drowning in despair. There seemed no end to all this neglect and abuse. We had nothing – not even enough energy to pass the endless time.

'How long is it till the next food, Sarge?' asked a lad I'd met on the *Kachidoki*.

'Too long,' I replied.

'Tell us a story about your world tour, Johnny,' suggested one of the boys who had survived from my unit.

'Later,' I said. 'I'm too tired now.' I had always been happy to tell football stories, but today I hadn't the heart for it.

'Go on Johnny,' goaded Reg. 'Look at us, we're tired and depressed. The lads need something to think about, something to cheer us all up.'

I knew Reg was right.

'All right then.' I sat up and pulled myself together.

'Tell us about the time you scored nine goals,' he prompted me.

'That was in Manila,' I began. 'But I didn't score them all,' I laughed.

A lot of the boys had turned towards me now to listen.

'It was our opening game in the Philippines and there was a British ship in port. All our games in Manila were in the Rizal Stadium, the Wembley of Southeast Asia. But because of the intense heat during daytimes, we always played our matches in the evenings, under the floodlights.

'On this particular night, we played against a Chinese team and one whole section of the stands was packed full of these British sailors, all shouting loudly for our team from the minute we came out. Boy, did those lads support us! You've never heard so much noise.'

'Tell us about the goals, Sarge.'

'Well, with all that tremendous support, it was no surprise that we started off with a flourish. We scored five goals in the first

Cuttings from Johnny's scrapbook – the Islington Corinthians
win 9–0 in Manila, March 1938.

half, and I was lucky enough to score all five of them. If I remember rightly, four of them were headers. I was always being ragged for scoring better with my head than my feet!'

'They're always the best goals,' yelled a voice from the back.

'After half-time, the other team rallied a bit, but not enough. We had such great teamwork on our side, you see. We'd been playing together halfway round the world by then and I couldn't have scored any goals at all without my team-mates.'

'Like who?' asked Stuart.

'Well, there was Sonny Avery, a very fine cricketer and a great friend of mine. He was a brilliant inside-forward on our tour for the first three months, then they flew him back home to play opening bat for Essex. Our captain was Pat Clark, and our vice-captain was my room-mate on the tour, Bill Whittaker. He was a talented stopper-centre-half, probably the best in England.

'The key player as far as I was concerned was Bert Read. He had a wonderful tour as our regular outside-right. Whenever he played, I was almost always on the score-sheet. I couldn't have done it without him.'

'Tell us more about the match, Sarge.'

'Well, a few minutes into the second half, Bert got possession and did a bit of ducking and diving to get it all the way down the field, then across to my head, so he made it another easy goal for me. After that, my team-mates came up trumps with three more in the net, so we won 9-0. I think that might have been our best win on the tour.'

'How many games did you play altogether?'

'I think the team played either ninety-five or ninety-six matches all told, but I only played in seventy of them.'

'Why was that Johnny?'

'Well, our manager didn't put me in the team until we'd played quite a few games across Europe, but when he did, I was lucky and scored the winning goal, so he made me the permanent centre forward after that. But when we got to India, I had to miss a few games because of an ankle injury. Fortunately it soon got better.'

'Do you know how many goals you scored altogether?' asked a voice at the back of the listening group.

'Yes. I never kept count, but we had a journalist from *The Times* with us throughout the trip and he told me it was seventy goals.

'Blimey, that's an average of a goal in every match!'

'Yes, but lots of my team-mates scored goals too. It was all teamwork.'

Everybody seemed in a lighter mood for a while after that. Reg had been right and I was glad I had taken his advice. But now I slumped down for a rest. I felt so tired all the time, and everyone else was the same. We were just too weak, too depressed and many of us too ill to do anything. Would this bloody war ever end?

Although we were below the main deck, at least we had plenty of headroom this time and it was quite airy – not as claustrophobic as the holds of the *Kachidoki Maru*. But it was just as unbearably hot and we sweated like pigs, so severe thirst and dehydration were a constant problem.

'Water . . . I need water,' came a faint cry from the corner.

'Please can somebody get me some water to drink,' echoed another.

'I'm so parched.'

'I don't want to die of thirst.'

The men's piteous cries made me feel so helpless it hurt to the pit of my stomach. I was angry that there was nothing I could do to help them. Damn the bloody Japs. This was a terrible torment for every one of us, and it is something I have never been able to forget.

The guards were stationed at the top of the ladder, and we were only allowed up on to the deck to use the *benjo*, one at a time. But most of the sick and wounded couldn't make it, so excrement went everywhere. The stench became unbearable.

The sweltering day dragged on as the ship set off on the next leg of our journey. We had no idea how long it would take, and we all feared that Yankee subs might come and plague us again.

'*Mishi*,' shouted a guard down the hatch later that day, when it was finally time for food. 'Two men *mishi*.'

That meant two of us had to go up to the galley and collect rations for all the POWs. As before, we had nothing to eat the rice with, so we had to roll it into balls with our fingers off the metal deck. It was far too little food and hardly any water – barely a few sips each out of the communal bucket to last us from early evening to the next morning, if we were lucky. Sometimes we had no water at all. It's no wonder that we lost at least one or two men every day, dying quietly in a corner and their bodies buried at sea.

You know, it's a terrible feeling when you're almost dying of thirst; your throat is burning and all your joints tremble with weakness. I cannot express how awful I felt. We were desperate.

God, I wonder just how much more we can take, I thought to myself. But take more we did.

That night as I lay down to sleep, coverless, with my bare skin on the metal deck, I couldn't stop thinking about Corporal Frank. There must have been some way I could have helped him survive. Had I not had to go and get the rations, I wondered, could I have kept him alive? I was so miserable for his family, for him . . . and for me.

But we were all in the same situation. Our troubles kept piling up, one torment on top of another. My only hope – a faint one but it was all I had – was that when we reached Japan our captors might treat us more like human beings.

In the meantime, we had to linger on, endure and somehow survive. And every time we thought it couldn't get worse, it did.

Out in the open sea, over the next few days, the whaler lurched from side to side in the typhoon storms that were building up. Fear was our constant torment.

Every wave that slapped the hull made us jump and every clank of the ladders against the sides of the ship sounded like a torpedo hitting us, sending every able man rushing headlong for the ladder. The booms of the depth charges at night were so loud that we felt we were going mad with terror. What was happening? Had we been hit? Was the ship sinking? Would it be our grave?

To make matters even worse, the typhoon reached its full force, tossing the whaler so ferociously on the sea that we were all struck with acute seasickness, making our dire conditions even worse and increasing the stench.

When the storm had subsided and I was finally able to go up to the *benjo* again at around midnight, I saw that we were now in a small convoy of boats. Sat on the seat slung over the side of the deck, I was nearly deafened by a sudden explosion that split the night air and lit up the sky. A nearby ship blew up in a ball of flame. More explosions followed as the Yankee torpedoes homed in on their targets.

'Not again!' I yelled out through the blazing sky and the black smoke across the sea. 'Please God, not again!'

The Japanese crew were in chaos, running everywhere in fear and panic.

Nobody bothered about me, so I stayed where I was and tried to stay as calm as I could, just in case we should be torpedoed. I knew I'd be safer if I was ready to jump from the *benjo* than risk going back and drowning on the lower deck.

As the crew launched depth charges, booming through the dark waters, I prayed like mad.

I think maybe God heard my prayer, as there were no more torpedoes that night. I can't tell you the relief I felt when the violence stilled to the quiet lapping of water and I finally returned to my comrades below.

'What happened up there Johnny?' several of them wanted to know.

'What was all that noise?'

'Did you see anything, Sarge?'

'Yes, the first torpedo struck a ship and blew it to pieces. Then more torpedoes struck their targets.'

'How many ships are with us?' asked Stuart.

'I'm not sure. It all started up before I could count, but I would say maybe a dozen.'

'And how many sunk?'

'At least two or three I reckon, though I couldn't tell for all the smoke.'

'Do you think they were all full of Jap bastards, and not our lads?'

'I bloody well hope so.'

'Did anything hit us, Sarge?'

'No, not this time, thank God.'

'But if the Yanks are about, they'll probably come back,' suggested one of the older men, saying out loud what we were all privately dreading.

'Get praying, lads,' I said. 'And hope we're past the worst of it now.'

Over the following days and nights, there were so many false alarms that we all turned into jibbering, nervous wrecks, trampling over each other to get to the ladder at the slightest noise. Once it was just a tin mug dropped on the upper deck that caused our panic. Gradually, as we sailed towards their beloved homeland, some of the guards became more lackadaisical and allowed a few of us up on deck at a time. As often as I could, I would find a hidey hole and stay there all night, in the fresh cool air, where I could see what was going on and be ready to act.

There were a few more near misses, when the sea teemed with American subs and smaller boats in our group were hit and sunk. On one of those nights, a torpedo caught an escort craft and blew it up in a flash.

'Bloody hell! That torpedo had our name on it,' said Reg. 'It was definitely coming straight for us, but that escort got in the way.'

'Thank God!' I nodded.

'It's that luck of yours Johnny, like you told us about what your mother used to say.'

'I ruddy well hope I get back in one piece to thank her for it,' I said.

I didn't imagine I could ever rejoice at reaching Japan, but at least I knew we were safe from torpedoes when we got there. It was 28th September 1944 when we approached the harbour and all the Japs on the whaler cheered loudly, '*Banzai, Banzai.*'

Later that day, after they had all left the whaler, we were allowed to struggle ashore, helping or carrying our sick men.

'Bloody terra ferma!' yelled one of our lads with relief, as soon as his feet touched the ground.

The guards herded us impatiently into groups and 'marched' us in straggly lines to the town square, our walking sick staggering as best they could with our help, those with dysentery – unable to control their bodies – emitting excreta as they went. All this was watched with astonished curiosity and probably disgust by the locals. Few of us had any clothing left, none of us had been able to wash for weeks, all of us were painfully thin, most of us were ill and several were still covered in black oil. I'm sure they had never seen human beings in such a state before.

'You sit,' ordered a Japanese sergeant. 'You rest.'

'Not more sitting!' groaned one of the boys.

'Never mind rest,' added another. 'It's food and water we need.'

'Yes, we're bloody starving.'

'And desperate for a drink.'

'Mine's a pint,' called out Reg, which caused a few weary laughs.

But the guards didn't like that, and made it clear with their rifle butts that we were to stop talking. So there we all sat and waited . . . and waited . . .

Finally, darkness fell and brought with it a new problem – the cold night air. After all the unbearable heat of the journey, the cold of that first night in Japan hit us damned hard. With no clothes to protect us, no food in our bellies and our bodies just bags of bones, we all began to shiver. Soon my whole body shuddered with cold and I couldn't make it stop.

Luckily, a guard arrived with news and the sergeant turned to face us.

'You go hall, *mishi* and sleep.'

'Did he say food?'

'Yes, and inside, out of the cold.'

'Speedo-speedo,' shouted a guard as they tried to get us all up and into a line again. But we were too weak to hurry. Desperate for warmth and food we tried our best to march off, but I have to admit it was not much more than an untidy ramble, carrying or helping our invalids along with us.

We were taken to a large hall, where all the sickest men had to go to one side of the hall and the rest of us to the other. Then the guards handed out small bowls of rice, half-portions for the sick and full ones for the rest of us, with pieces of salt fish and mugs of water. At last we could quench the worst of our thirst and put something in our stomachs.

'Now we need some decent medical supplies for our sick men,' I said.

'Do you think we'll get them, Sarge?'

'By God, I hope so.'

Now came a great surprise. The guards issued each of us with a blanket, a whole big, clean blanket for every man to wrap around himself and lie down with. This gave us not only some physical warmth, but also a small hope that maybe we were going to be looked after here in Japan, the land of cherry blossom. Sleep came quickly that night, the best sleep we had had in weeks.

The next morning, new guards arrived to take over.

'Men go out,' the one in charge shouted to us.

We all stood up, holding tightly on to our rolled-up blankets, and got ourselves into lines. Then the guards came along and, without a word, separated us into two separate parties, with transport for our sick. What a bloody relief that was, watching the new guards lifting the sick men carefully into the trucks. I and my party were marched to another big hall.

'All men take off clothes,' ordered the young Japanese sergeant.

Of course, this didn't take long as hardly any of us had any clothes left, other than perhaps a bit of lousy rag around our waist to cover our loins. We had to put any belongings we had in a pile with the few discarded clothes. This was the moment I nearly broke down. I had to throw my precious, life-saving water-bottle on to the pile, the bottle that had survived with me throughout the tortures of the past three years, from one death camp to another, through every horror of our war. It was a bottle that had saved my life, and the lives of many others, but now it had to go.

I tossed it on to the heap and turned my back, with a big lump in my throat, struggling to hold back the tears. Isn't it strange how a man can endure every physical and psychological hardship, every torment and fear, and yet in one small moment such as this, he is closest to breaking?

I strode over with as much determination as I could muster to join the others as we were taken into another part of the building. What we saw there astonished us.

'Bloody hell!' shouted one of the lads.

'Bloody marvellous, more like,' grinned Stuart.

'I don't believe it!'

'Champion!' shouted Reg.

'When did you last have a bath, Sarge?'

'Back in the Ice Age!' I laughed.

This was the best surprise we'd had for years, and the first hot bath since before our surrender in Singapore.

Taking up most of the room was a huge communal bath.

'Men get in,' said one of the guards as the others came around giving out bars of soap – which were better than gold bars to us that morning.

'Yes, sir,' replied one of the men with a mock salute, as we all jumped into the glorious hot water. This was an order we were all happy to obey. We wallowed in the wonderful luxury for about an hour, the warmth soothing our aching bones as we washed three years' grime out of every crevice of our bodies and lathered ourselves clean.

Apart from my hair, which was so long it was down to my shoulders and a terrible mess, I felt I was almost back to normal again.

But our surprises weren't over with. Back in the first room again, our rags and belongings had been cleared away and in their place was what looked like a very colourful jumble sale stall. Shorts and shirts of all styles and sizes, in bright reds, oranges, pinks, greens, purples and every lurid colour you can imagine, many of them in wild floral patterns. We could hardly believe it. Next to the clothes was a pile of soft shoes like the Japanese wear. There were plenty enough for us all to have a pair, but of course most of them were too small for our big British feet.

It was quite a scrum, trying to find something I wouldn't be too embarrassed to wear. We were all in the same boat.

'Get you!' shrieked one of the POWs, laughing his head off. 'You look like a tart!'

'You can talk! Who let in the hula-hula girls?'

'Hey, Sarge. This one is perfect for you,' grinned one of my lads, holding up a particularly fetching, bright pink shirt with a frill round the neck.

'Yes,' I said. 'I'll take that. It will be just the job . . . as a cleaning cloth.'

'Ouch!' cried the biggest man in the room, trying to fit his foot into a small Japanese rubber plimsoll.

'Who do you think you are? Cinderella?' laughed Stuart.

'One of the ugly sisters, more like!' added Reg.

'Try this pair, mate. They look like a clown's shoes they're so big.'

'That's probably just what they are.'

We finally managed to get everyone kitted out in something that vaguely fitted them. Luckily, most of the shoes were mules, without backs to them, so our heels stuck out, but at least we had something to cushion the soles of our feet.

'Why do you think they've done all this for us, Sarge?'

'I don't know,' I replied, as puzzled as everyone else. 'Maybe they've decided at last to treat us like human beings again.'

'No, there must be some reason for it.'

'I don't trust the bastards,' muttered Reg. 'They're up to something, I'll bet.'

'Maybe they've seen the red light,' I wondered out loud.

'How do you mean, Sarge?' asked one of the younger boys.

'Well, we know the Americans are sinking a lot of ships . . .'

'You can say that again!'

'The Japs probably realise they're losing the war,' I continued. 'And they know they'll be slaughtered if they don't start treating us better.'

'Are you sure they're losing the war?'

'No,' I shrugged. Of course I couldn't be certain, but I told them I didn't think the Yanks would let the Japs off the hook after what they did at Pearl Harbor, remembering back to our foreign posting in 1941/2, when we were diverted to Singapore because of the catastrophic Japanese attack on the American navy.

'So you think it will all be over soon, Sarge?' By now a lot of the men were listening in to our conversation.

'I reckon it will,' I nodded, and I could almost see the mood lift right across the room.

Just then we heard the sound of transport outside and we moved to the windows to see a number of Japanese army lorries pulling up.

'You go trucks,' ordered one of the guards in a shrill voice, and we lined up to leave the hall, taking our blankets, along with any spare clothes and shoes we could tuck inside them to smuggle into our new destination. Our minds always on food, we might need something to barter with.

As we filed out of the hall, we were split into groups and funnelled into various of the lorries, according to where we were supposed to be going. Most of the POWs were told they would be going to somewhere called Honshu, and a few of the Aussies were off to Yokohama.

'You go Kyushu,' said one of the guards accompanying my group of Brits.

After a short lorry-ride, we were loaded on to a train – not cattle-trucks this time, thank God, but proper carriages. As the train chugged through the countryside, we looked out of the windows at the picturesque Japanese villages we passed, the flat landscape and whole families in sampans along the river, selling their goods to passing boats. How far was it to Kyushu? What would it be like?

23

Fukuoka – Yankee Air-Raids

September 1944

Finally, on 30th September 1944, we arrived at our destination and were marched from the railway station to our new residence – Fukuoka camp, number 25. As we later found out, this POW camp was on the southern tip of Japan, near Nagasaki.

'Hey look, Johnny. Proper barracks!' grinned Reg as we walked into the camp itself, to see a group of large, two-storey, wooden buildings.

'Have we died and gone to heaven?' said Stuart.

'Steady on,' I said. 'It may look solid, but a prison camp is definitely not heaven!'

'Well, it will do me for now.'

'Do you think this was a Japanese army camp, Sarge?' asked a corporal.

'It looks like it.'

As we stood out there in the yard, looking around us, a miracle happened. Striding up towards me with a grin almost as wide as his shoulders, was a man I had thought I would never see again.

'Hey, canny lad. You're still with us then!'

'Geordie! I can't believe it's you. I thought you had drowned.' We shook hands, then fell into each other's arms and I couldn't stop the tears coming to my eyes.

Neither of us spoke for several seconds, just glad to have found each other alive.

Finally, I wiped my cheeks with my hand and stood back a little. 'It's wonderful to see you again, old pal.'

'Champion!' added Reg as he came over to join us. 'Where have you been?'

'I was on the *Kachidoki Maru*,' he said, as we walked slowly towards where the men were all gathering.

'But I never saw you . . . Which hold were you in?'

'Number two.'

'I was in number one hold, but then I got lucky and stayed on deck most nights.' I paused. 'I can't understand why I never saw you.'

'I had a bout of dysentery for the first three or four days, so I was too weak to climb up on deck. But I just got better in time, before the torpedoes hit. I managed to scramble up our ladder before the ship tipped too far, and I just made it.'

'So you jumped off?'

'Aye, and I got lucky, just like you usually do,' he grinned. 'I managed to swim away and eventually, a few hours later, I found a life-raft. Fortunately, the Japs had just abandoned it to climb on to a big, half-empty lifeboat with their mates, so a few of us swam towards it and helped each other to clamber aboard.'

'You were luckier than me, then. All I had to cling to was a hatchboard, taking turns with a few other survivors, but at least it kept us afloat—'

'Come on boys,' interrupted Reg. 'The officers are calling us together.'

We were split up into groups of about thirty men, each under the care of an NCO, a non-commissioned officer like me. I must say, I had a lot of good men under me, including my old pals, and we all got on well together during our time there.

It was a clean and tidy place, this camp, much to our relief. There must have been about twenty-five to thirty dormitory rooms inside each building and all the POW groups were led to their own allocation of rooms. We were about five to a room. Our room was light and airy, with two rubber and rush mattresses to share on the floor, about three foot by six – the first thing like a proper bed we had slept in since Changi camp in Singapore. We were given two padded covers each for bedding, which was going to be bliss, though we would certainly need them in the cold winter climate of Japan.

'Howay, Johnny – come and see this!' Geordie called me into a room at the end. 'It's the first bathroom I've seen since 1941.'

'And look, a proper basin with taps that work,' I added, excitedly turning them on and off, on and off. It seemed like pure luxury.

'And a toilet too!' Geordie grinned as he pulled the chain and a satisfying gush of water completed our joy.

'Come and see this, boys.' I called to our three room-mates to come and share the fun.

'Bloody hell,' said Reg, flushing the toilet. 'This certainly beats those jungle latrines!'

'And we don't have to share it with maggots either!' laughed Stuart.

The five of us spent a happy ten minutes, playing like children. We couldn't believe our luck – what a bonus. We settled in a treat, very encouraged at this new start.

We had a medical officer with us in camp – Captain Mathieson. And the British officer in charge, our CO, was Captain Wilkie who, before the war, had worked as a civilian in Singapore. They gathered all our fit men on parade to tell us how the camp would run.

'I have been informed,' announced Captain Wilkie, 'that all of you will have to work hard and behave yourselves, now that you are in Japan.' He paused and surveyed our straggly and highly colourful ranks. 'Under no circumstances whatsoever,' he stressed, 'are you to do anything wrong. In particular, NO stealing. The Japanese commandant has made it very clear to me that if anyone is caught stealing, they will make the whole camp suffer.'

'He said "caught",' whispered Geordie with a devilish twinkle in his eyes. 'It's not if we steal, but if we are caught stealing,' he said.

'And you NCOs,' continued Captain Wilkie. 'You will be held personally responsible for anything that goes wrong in your section.'

'I have inspected the hospital,' added Captain Mathieson as he stepped forward. 'And you'll all be pleased to hear our hosts have given us a small assortment of medicines, so the first sick parade will be tomorrow morning.'

'Champion!' said Reg, echoed by many others.

The two British captains stood down, and up stepped a Japanese officer and his interpreter, flanked by twelve of our new guards. The officer gave us a long and strident lecture, his high-pitched, jerky voice giving us a clear idea of what he was talking about. Finally, the interpreter took over.

'When you see a Japanese guard, you must always salute him if his head is covered, or bow if not. You must always do this. You will get big bashing if you do not.'

'Not likely,' snarled a man behind me. 'You won't catch me bowing to any Jap.'

'Well,' some wit replied, 'watch out for that Big Bashing – he sounds like a nasty piece of work to me.' There were a few sniggers from the lads.

As we very soon found out, they meant what they said and some of our lads did indeed get a big bashing for not obeying that order. It all became a bit of a farce, and we couldn't help laughing to ourselves as we and our comrades kept bobbing our heads up and down every time another guard came into view.

'It's like a cartoon film, this,' said Stuart. 'Like one of those Charlie Chaplin scenes.'

Later that day, two guards came and issued us with more new clothes, American-style this time. We wondered where they'd got them from – perhaps they'd intercepted the Yanks' supplies.

'You look after clothes,' said the senior guard. 'This work

clothes,' he held up some hard-wearing, dark shirts and trousers for us to see. 'This best clothes.' He showed us some sweaters and lighter trousers, then gave them all out to us. 'You keep best clothes clean.'

On the first day, we were allowed to rest, and we were given the best rations since we had been captured in early 1942 – plain and still mainly rice, but more of it, with plenty enough water. And our Japanese captors also provided us with a fair amount of medical supplies. But sadly they came too late for Tommy, one of the Taylor twins.

Our medical officer, Captain Mathieson, did everything in his power to help this ill-fated boy, and to make him as comfortable as he could. But the poor blighter had swallowed so much oil while fighting for his life in the South China Sea that survival became impossible for him. It had been painful to watch him struggling desperately to breathe for so long, so it was a relief when he died and was finally at peace. I felt guilty at being pleased for him, but consoled myself with the thought that even his family back home would surely have agreed with us.

His twin brother, Walter – who had looked after him so faithfully throughout our journey to Japan – had somehow managed to stay with him. He was a Londoner, and a very good pal of mine. Having stood up to traumatic conditions throughout his twin's illness, he now collapsed into grief.

He came to see me that evening and poured out his heartbreak at losing his brother and not having been able to do anything to help him recover.

'Johnny,' he sobbed. 'How could Tommy have survived all those hard months of disease and starvation in Singapore, those terrible two years on the railway of death, the sinking of our ship and all those hours in the oily sea, only to die like this?'

'I know, Walter,' I consoled him, my arm round his shoulders. 'It's a terrible war, and so unfair. We've lost a great many good men, and your brother was one of them. But we have to go on, to

209

think of the people at home. Your folks will grieve for their son, but they still have you and they will be overjoyed to see you back with them again, so you have to concentrate on yourself now.'

'But if only I could have kept him going.'

'You did your best. In fact, you did an amazing job, without any medical supplies or help, you did keep him going. Probably much longer than anyone could have expected. He was a very sick man.'

'Yes, I know, Johnny.'

We talked on for most of the evening, crying together and sharing the good memories we had of his twin. Finally, this sad young man seemed to brighten up a little. He got up to go, turned and put his arm around my shoulder.

'I'll be all right now, Johnny,' he said with a faint smile, and walked away. What a brave man.

The guards formed us into working parties and my party was detailed to work in a carbide and chemical factory, about a mile from the camp.

'Right lads,' I explained to my men. 'We have to split into two twelve-hour shifts, six in the morning to six in the evening, and then the other way around.'

'So they want blood out of us again?' groaned Geordie.

'I don't think I can take it any more, Sarge,' moaned one of the boys.

'However hard we have to work,' I said, 'it surely can't be as hard as on the railway, so I'm certain we'll cope. It can't be for long now, lads. The Yanks will end the war soon, you'll see.'

'I bloody well hope you're right, Sarge.'

'I've met our foreman. I have to call him the '*hancho*'. He looks about sixty-five and seems all right. He told me that if we do our work well, he will be happy with us.'

'I've never heard of a happy Jappy, yet,' joked Reg, and we all laughed.

'Well,' I said, 'we'll soon find out, when we start work tomorrow.'

Sure enough, he seemed to be a fair man, despite being Japanese. Perhaps it was his age. He watched us working with interest and some slight amusement, I thought. Then one evening he called me aside.

'*Hancho*,' he said in a stern voice. I looked around, but he obviously meant me. 'You no work. You make men work hard.'

So, after that, I arranged with my lads that I would stand around, shouting and bawling at them whenever he was there, but as soon as he went they could rest as much as they liked. In between times, I worked alongside the men, as long as he didn't see me doing it.

This ruse seemed to work so well that the foreman gained confidence in me as his co-leader. On the night shifts, as long as the men worked really hard to get their quota of work done, we could all have a couple of hours' sleep. That made a big difference, I can tell you.

It was now nearly Christmas 1944. The work was very heavy, making carbides for the Japanese navy's ships. Of course, this meant we were once again being forced to help our enemy's war-effort, but what could we do? We had no choice. If we had refused, we would have starved to death. The weather was getting colder and the rations reduced almost daily now.

A funny thing happened one morning, when I arrived at work. The Japanese *hancho* came up to me and said 'Hancho presento.' Then he put his hand into his pocket and pulled out a small potato. '*Emo*,' he said. I assumed this was Japanese for potato. I tried to keep a poker face.

'I bring you *emo* every morning,' he said, with a serious expression.

I didn't really know how to respond, so I just thanked him and bowed. He seemed happy enough with that. It quite amused me how he used to slip this little potato to me each day. Anyone would think he was doing me a favour. I suppose he thought he was, but it wouldn't go far. I had heard that the local Japs were really short of food themselves now, and I assumed this was partly the weather, the season, and partly, I hoped, the Americans tightening the screw.

I went back that first time and told my boys about it, cutting this small potato into twenty-nine tiny pieces to soak in our stew.

Out of the blue one evening, when we returned from the day-shift at about a quarter to seven and were going into the mess room for our rations, the interpreter issued a most peculiar order.

'You eat food with chopsticks. In Japan, all people eat with chopsticks. You in Japan. You eat with chopsticks.' The guards gave out pairs of Japanese chopsticks to all our men.

Up till that point, we had been using our own, home-made spoons and forks, and our fingers of course. But they took all our forks and spoons away to make us use the chopsticks.

It wasn't a laughing matter, for none of us knew how to use these things and we just couldn't get the hang of them. Some of us couldn't even pick up one grain of rice, let alone eat our way through a bowl of it. And fishing for morsels of food in our stew with the guards looking on to enforce the rule was a complete farce. Just imagine coming home after a twelve-hour shift at the carbon factory, starving hungry, and having to cope with that. As soon as the guards turned away, of course, we picked up as much as we could with our fingers and gobbled it down.

Eventually, the Japs complained because our meals were taking too long to finish and our officers explained.

'These men have never used chopsticks before,' said Captain Wilkie.

'Yes, it's impossible for them to eat their food with them,' agreed Captain Mathieson.

The next day the Japanese commandant himself, together with his interpreter, came to scrutinise us at mealtimes. Finally, it was agreed that we could have our spoons and forks back.

* * *

Well, we survived Christmas and it was now early 1945. The American Air Force were beginning to worry the Japs, as we could tell by their reactions. They ordered a working party of POWs to dig a huge air-raid shelter in the camp. Then, every time the sirens went off, the guards drove everyone in camp into the shelter. After a few weeks, we were spending more time in the shelter than out of it. And as the Yanks were now coming over in their B29s several times each day, and once or twice every night, this meant we were getting very little sleep.

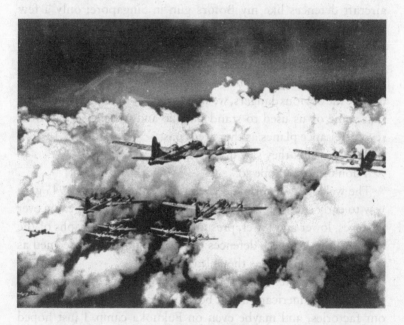

B29 Superfortresses on their way to bomb targets in Japan.

Whenever the sirens sounded, the bloody guards would rush around the barracks, in and out of our rooms, shrieking at us.

'Speedo-speedo. America Sikorski *demi-demi*.' I knew that *demi-demi* meant no-good, no-good, so we had to leave the comfort of our beds and rush down to the shelter, to be driven inside by the frightened Japs. On the rare occasions when they were panicking so much they forgot to collect us, we simply took no notice of the warning, watched the fortress-planes going across the camp, then turned over and went back to sleep.

At the factory it was just the same, spending two or three hours of each night-shift in the shelter, and much of the day, as the air-raids increased and we noticed the reconnaissance planes flying very low over the factories and docks. We were delighted that there was so little opposition to them. No large-scale anti-aircraft defences like my Bofors gun in Singapore; only a few small arms being fired spasmodically and the odd Japanese plane intercepting.

When B29s flew over the factories, the Japs used to make a run straight for the shelters, not caring about us at all. But by now, despite the obvious dangers, we were so happy to see the Americans that some of us used to stand outside and wave cheerily at the reconnaissance planes as they went past.

'Do you think they saw us, Sarge?'

'I don't know. I hope so.'

The welcome warmth and cherry blossom of spring 1945 gave way to early summer, as each day the American planes came over in waves, lower and lower, presumably taking photographs of the area. All the Japanese defences were silent now and it seemed as if the Yanks could do as they pleased.

Our spirits were rising fast, but there was always that niggling fear that the Americans might be planning new bombing raids on our factories, and maybe even on Fukuoka camp. I just hoped they knew we were here.

24

Piling on the Pressure

July 1945

It was now late July 1945, and with almost monotonous regularity the Yanks flew over our camp in the middle of the night, on their way to the factories and the docks, where they dropped hundreds of incendiary bombs, setting light to the wooden buildings.

'Man, look at those factories burning,' said Geordie, as we sat up and watched them from our billet in camp.

'Yes, they're so flimsy they're burning like matchwood,' I agreed with a smile, but with an uneasy feeling in case any of our men were inside them.

If they came when we were on the night-shift at work we would wait for the all-clear to sound and come up out of the shelter to fight the fires. As fast as we got one beaten out, there would be three more to extinguish, and we had very little to fight the flames with as they consumed the wooden buildings and threatened the chemical stores.

Some nights there would be dramatic explosions that lit up the whole sky, as munitions factories were hit, or oil-tankers in the docks. And still the B29s kept coming. How none of our men were killed, to my knowledge, and so few injured when they were at work, I'll never know. Thank God the Americans never used any explosive bombs in this industrial area, or many of us POWs would have been killed, and I might not be here to tell the tale.

Our rations had gradually reduced through the first half of 1945 and we were now on a starvation diet once again. I don't think the

Japs had much to eat themselves either, with the Americans effectively blockading the movement of food. Fortunately, by this time they were paying us a few yen now and then for our work at the factory, and they started to let some local traders into the camp so that we could obtain more desperately needed food they had grown. Of course, only the workers had any money, so we had to share all our extras with the lads in the camp hospital, and the men who worked there.

Some of these traders brought in basketfuls of delicious satsuma oranges twice a week for us to buy. They were such a treat that we ate them by the dozen to begin with. I still remember the sweet taste and the juicy flesh of those satsumas. We toasted the peel to eat as well – we were so hungry, we would have eaten anything.

Our meat supply was almost nil, but we did manage to buy some vegetables from the traders, and when our yen ran out, we had a collection of colourful clothes to barter with. They seemed to appeal to the locals more than to us, and they certainly fitted them better. Although we were all painfully thin, this fresh produce gave us much needed nourishment which helped us to feel healthier than for a long time.

Meanwhile, for the sick men, and anyone who became ill, Captain Mathieson had a few medicines he could give us, so we were not too badly off. And our morale was high.

Although we could not get news of how the war was going anywhere else in the world, we felt sure the guards knew they were losing the war in Japan. Many of them would flare up and they became increasingly short-tempered, looking for any opportunity to chastise us. Our interpreter lost every shred of his former mildness and started to bash our men up, just for the fun of it.

For instance, he would examine our 'best' clothes that we wore in camp when we weren't working. We had been warned to keep them clean, but now he started looking for anything to shout about. If anyone had lost a button, or torn a sleeve, he went berserk. Here, I thought, was a lunatic if ever I saw one.

I remember one particular morning, as I walked past him without bowing to him, he screamed at me. '*Curra-bugere.*' That was Japanese for 'You bugger.'

He collared me.

'Leave him alone,' I heard Geordie yelling across the yard as I was pushed along to the guardroom, where this bastard ordered me down on my knees. Now for the first time towering over me like some raving lunatic, this animal smacked my face so hard, with the flat of his hand, that he knocked me sprawling on the floor.

My temper boiled up inside me, but I had to keep it from showing. Whatever punishment he meted out to me, I had to take it all without flinching, as always, to avoid something worse. So I got back on my knees, and what did this devil do next? He started to flick me with his forefinger and thumb, underneath my nose in an upward movement.

This was surprisingly painful and he gleefully carried on so that I feared that my nose was tearing off. He continued this treatment to screams of laughter from the Jap guards. It was only after he had split my nose open and blood splashed out all over the place, that this brute – and that was what he was – allowed me to go. My nose was in a mess, and very sore for days afterwards.

I'm sure you can understand how much we all hated our captors, and this man was one of the worst at Fukuoka. Most of our men couldn't wait for the war to end so that they could string up the bastard.

By now, the Yanks were putting on the pressure big time, much to our delight. We were therefore all the more surprised one day to learn that we would be receiving a Red Cross parcel each. We knew these parcels were getting through, but of course ours were all stolen by the Japs. A few of our light-sick men had to act as servants to the camp commandant, and they'd seen a cupboard full of tins of our Red Cross food in his kitchen. And we'd seen the Jap guards smoking 'our' Chesterfield cigarettes too.

At this stage, they were allowing us a small allocation of Japanese cigarettes each. I always gave mine to the lads who craved a smoke.

'Cor, these are real chokers,' said Reg, the first time we were given them. 'You're lucky you're not a smoker, Johnny. They're bloody awful.'

We had all given up hope of ever receiving one of the Red Cross parcels to share, let alone one each. As usual, they were stringing us along and we didn't know when, or even if, they would arrive.

Fortunately, we didn't have to wait for long and the parcels arrived as promised, one for each of us.

'Marvellous!' said Walter, opening his up.

'Will you just look at all this food?'

'It's like Christmas,' I said with a big grin that lasted for hours.

There was something of everything in these parcels. We pigged out straightaway on the chocolate bars and biscuits, saving the tinned foods for later, when we followed up our starvation rations with several feasts of sardines or corned beef, followed by Spotted Dick and condensed milk. It was bliss.

If only our Red Cross parcels had got through to us in Thailand, as intended during those years on the railway of death, just think how many lives would have been saved.

At work every day, it amused us to watch the Japanese *hancho* trying to get the carbon factory going again after each incendiary raid. Almost every night now, the B29s would hit some part of the factory and set it ablaze. As soon as we'd put out the fire, there would be another one, and another. It was chaos, and we thoroughly enjoyed it, as long as it was only incendiaries. Of course, there was always the fear that one night the proper bombing might start, but I am as certain as I can be that, by now, the Americans knew we were there.

'Where are all the planes coming from, Sarge?' asked one of the lads.

'They must be based on an aircraft carrier, or maybe they've taken an island somewhere.'

'But there are so many of them.'

'Well, maybe there are two carriers,' suggested the corporal.

'Or islands,' some wit added.

'But it feels as if they're not far away now.'

'I know what you mean. Watching them pass over every night, it feels like they're almost with us, doesn't it?'

'It can't be long now, Johnny.'

'I bet you're right. It looks like the B29s can do just what they like.'

'Except that the Japs have brought over lots of ack-ack guns now.'

'Yes, but they don't seem to trouble the Yanks. They come over whenever they want to.'

'I wish they'd get on with it and win the war.'

'I'm with you there, son. We all are.'

'It could be just days away,' I added, desperate to be right.

On the night-shift one night, at about 1.30 in the morning, the air-raid sirens went off and the guards drove us down into the shelter again. I remember this particular night very clearly.

As usual, across came the B29s, flying even lower over our factory. The Yanks always made a dummy run above the target first, without dropping anything. We crossed our fingers and prayed like mad that it wouldn't be bombs this time. As they passed over the second time we held our breath until they had gone.

'Phew!'

'Thank God it was only another incendiary raid.'

The all-clear sounded and out we came, the guards at the front, running about forty yards to our factory workshop, which was fully ablaze. As they ran, we looked around to see what the damage was this time.

What a shock! The whole area was on fire, with burning

incendiaries all over the place. I removed eight of them myself from the tin roof of our shelter. We wouldn't have had a chance if the roof had been wood, like all the buildings around us. And how lucky we were that our friends didn't drop bombs. If even one of those incendiaries had been a bomb, we'd all have been gonners in a moment. I was struck by the irony that our biggest worry now was not the Japs, but our allies the Americans. I only hoped I was right that they knew we POWs were here.

Back at the camp that breakfast time, we had a surprise.

'You lads missed all the excitement last night,' began the POW kitchen worker with a grin.

'Why, what happened?' I asked.

'You'd have heard the noise if you'd been here, Sarge,' said one of the lads.

'Yes, the commandant's big Alsatian went mad in the Jap chicken house, and killed nearly all their chickens.'

'What did the commandant do?'

'Somebody shot the ruddy thing and brought it to our cook-house, with orders to put dog on the menu for tonight.'

'Something German for dinner – just what we need!' joked Reg.

'Is it all right to eat dog-meat?' asked Walter.

'It will be the first fresh meat for ages,' I said. 'We've killed and eaten most other kinds of protein in the jungle, so why not the commandant's dog? It's got to be better than rat.'

'I'm going to skin it straightaway and cut it up for tonight's stew.'

'Good man.' I nodded.

So, that evening, a rest day, we all sat down and tucked into our bowls of dog stew.

'Where's the dog?' asked Reg. 'I didn't get any!'

'Me neither.'

'You won't have any chunks of it,' said the kitchen worker. 'The meat's boiled away in the stew, but it's there all right.'

'Mmm, it's quite tasty,' I said, in surprise. 'It's definitely got a different flavour.'

'I got a bit of soggy meat in mine,' cheered Walter. 'It must have been the dog. It's an improvement on plain, watery stew.'

'Does the commandant have any more Alsatians?' asked Geordie, an evil gleam in his eye.

Later that night, talking with my room-mates, I finally broached the subject that had been on my mind ever since we arrived at Fukuoka. 'I wonder what happened to Ben Russell.'

'That lad from your home-town?' asked Reg.

'Yes.'

'I saw him on the deck of the *Rakuyo Maru*,' said Walter. 'So he must have had a chance. But we all swallowed a lot of oil in the sea, like my brother Tommy did. A lot of men drowned in it. I don't know about your friend Ben, but . . .'

We sat in silence for probably a minute or two, probably longer, thinking of all those of our friends we had lost. There was another question I desperately wanted to ask, but found it difficult to mention. As I was plucking up the courage, Geordie came to my aid.

'Do you remember that young lad, Ray? The footballer?'

'Yes, I was wondering about him,' I said.

'He was in my hold on the *Kachidoki*. He was ill too, much worse than me. I don't know what it was – probably malaria as well as dysentery.'

I went cold. This was the news I had been dreading. I had such high hopes for that boy. 'So he . . .'

'Aye, Johnny. I'm afraid he didn't make it. He died just two or three days out from Singapore.'

I often thought of Ray, and what could have been. I still do sometimes. I had intended to introduce him to a few people in football when we got home again, after the war. He had talent. I could have helped him go far. What a waste it all was. But I

221

knew we had to focus on the ones who were left, so that's what I would try to do. I was determined not to lose anyone else if I could help it.

The guards got it into their heads that we should all be made to do physical exercises when we got up or came back from work each morning. So they brought a cumbersome, old gramophone player out on to the parade ground each morning, wound it up and played records for us to move to.

The Japs themselves were very serious about this, showing us their moves and putting everything they had into it. They demonstrated the actions and we had to copy. Of course, our boys were not very strong or fit, so they used as little energy as they could, and only when the guards were looking in their direction.

Emaciated POWs after liberation from a Japanese camp, 1945.

You should have seen all us thin, gangly men trying to make these expressive, cavorting movements in time to the weird strains and rhythms of Japanese music. It sounded out of tune to our ears. Everyone looked so funny, and I knew *I* must look a right charlie as well. It gave us a laugh or two, believe me. In fact, we couldn't stop laughing and the guards grew very angry with us. But we just couldn't do it like they did.

They gave up trying to get us to do it in the end, but it's a pity they didn't give our fitness and health a little more consideration during our previous three and a half years of slavery.

223

25

Death-Ray

August 1945

It was 9th August 1945 and I was on the day-shift at work. As usual, the air-raid sirens sounded not long after our shift began and our guards scrambled like rats into the shelter – still just a dugout with a corrugated tin roof and no door. By now, we were so used to this routine that we took our time, ambling across the yard so that we could see what was going on.

Sure enough, along came the first wave of Yankee planes. What a beautiful sight that was. Over they came, unscathed by the furious Japanese ack-ack banging away at them.

'Go on, you beauties!' shouted one of the lads. 'Let 'em have it!'

As I watched them flying on through the sky, I was horrified to see one plane shot down. I was transfixed, watching what happened as it broke up into pieces, hurtling down to earth. Among the debris falling out of the sky, I suddenly spotted a badly twisted parachute, hardly open at all, with a Yank dangling from it, poor chap. My insides turned over as I watched him plummet down and disappear behind the buildings. I knew how it must have ended.

'Get down, Johnny,' shouted Geordie, who hadn't seen this.

I ducked down part of the way into the shelter before the next wave of B29s came over. I was filled with a turmoil of fear and foreboding for that poor man and his loved ones in America. All I could do was to lie flat out on the earth floor of that shelter's doorway in a daze, unable to put that horrific image out of my mind.

I don't know how long we waited – it must have been quite a

while. Finally the all-clear sounded and the guards pushed us out of the shelter, but straightaway there was another warning and down we went again.

The air-raids kept going, so we had to spend hours in the shelter that morning. Some of us, including me, edged our way out a bit to watch the action. I looked up at the planes as they passed over, thinking it was strange that none of this lot had dropped incendiaries. I remember wondering what their mission was as I watched them fly into the distance, across Nagasaki Bay.

I cannot remember what the time was, but I do very clearly remember the great rumble we heard. It was so loud that I instinctively ducked my head down for a few seconds. When I opened my eyes and looked across towards the city of Nagasaki, just visible in the distance, I saw a fast-growing black cloud that spiralled upwards, then outwards at the top in the shape of a white-capped mushroom. I watched the black turn grey as it rose ever higher, then among the grey I saw multicoloured sparkles, like beautiful jewels in the sky.

'Bloody hell!' I gasped out loud, thinking this bomb must have landed on a chemical factory to make such an enormous and colourful cloud. 'Some poor blighters have copped it.' I was shocked, thinking it might have killed a few workers in that factory. Little did I know.

After a while, the all-clear sounded. But this time, instead of being sent back to work, we were paraded, checked and counted, then marched straight 'home' to our billet at Fukuoka camp 25. This was a very strange turn of events.

'What do you think's happening, Sarge?' asked Harry, as we walked along the road.

'I've no idea. All I can think is it's something to do with the Yankee air-raid on Nagasaki, but I don't know why it made them stop work and send us back to camp.'

'Bloody peculiar if you ask me,' said Bill Pask, rubbing his eyes.

'What kind of bomb do you think it was?' asked a lad behind me.

The mushroom cloud over Nagasaki after the atomic
bomb was dropped, 9th August 1945.

'Not like one I've ever seen before,' I replied. 'But I reckon it might have hit a chemical factory to make that ruddy great cloud.'

'Yes, it must have gone up miles into the sky.'

'It made such a bright flash,' said Bill. 'It damn well blinded me at first.'

'I ducked my head down as soon as I heard the sound,' I said.

'Me too,' nodded Reg.

'It's a good job you did,' said Bill. 'My eyes are really hurting me now.'

When we got back to camp, we started telling the others what we'd seen.

'Yes, we saw it from here as well,' said one of the light-sick men who was outside at the time. 'I wondered what kind of a bomb could have caused such a giant cloud.'

'How many planes did you see?'

'I think there were four or five that went over before the bomb went off.'

Just then, all the working POWs were ordered out into the camp yard.

'At ease men,' began Captain Wilkie. 'I have just been informed by our interpreter that you will not be going back to work for a few days. But the camp commandant wants you all out on parade here tomorrow morning at 0900 hours.'

'Do you know what it's about sir?' asked one of the other NCOs.

'No, I'm in the dark as much as you are, Sergeant. We'll have to wait till tomorrow morning to find out.'

Well, full of curiosity, we got ourselves on parade the following morning as ordered, with all the guards in attendance.

'What the hell's going on, Sarge?' whispered Harry, next to me.

'It must be something important with all the guards on parade at the same time.'

The camp commandant and the interpreter both stepped on to the platform in front of us.

'They don't look very happy,' muttered Stuart, next to me.

'No, they're in a filthy temper, all right, by the look on their faces.'

The commandant shouted and bawled at us in his shrill voice for all he was worth, gesticulating like a raving lunatic. This went on for several minutes until, with foam coming from his mouth, he finally shut up, and the interpreter took over.

'Your friends the Americans,' he began in a belligerent manner. 'They have done terrible thing. They have dropped DEATH-RAY BOMB on our sacred land. They have killed many thousands Japanese people. They have killed women and children.' He had worked himself up into such a state that he had to pause and take a deep breath.

Looking daggers at all of us he continued. 'The Americans will be made to pay for deaths. If Americans step on Japanese land of rising sun, all prisoners will be SHOT.' He stopped there and, to make sure we had understood it, he repeated his final threat. 'If Americans come on Japanese land, YOU WILL ALL BE SHOT.'

For a few seconds there was a stunned silence, as we tried to take in all this astounding information. The commandant and the interpreter stepped down, barked a few orders at the guards and stalked off.

My first thought was: *Oh God, please don't let this happen to us, after all the horrors we've been through*. But I knew from past experience that, with these sadistic people, anything could and probably would happen.

Captain Wilkie, our senior officer, walked over to the platform and stepped up.

'Gather round chaps,' he said, as he looked over his shoulder to make sure the interpreter was out of range.

'I want to reassure you that, whatever happens in the next few days or so, I will do everything in my power to keep you all safe. I want you to ignore that evil threat. If the Americans do arrive on land, we will be all right. They will make sure we have nothing to fear from those Japanese tyrants. So don't worry yourselves about it. Let's just hope that their days are numbered.'

As we walked back to our barracks, we were all rather subdued and most of us were in a state of mental confusion. Should we be happy or sad that so many ordinary Japanese people had been killed? Could the idea of Americans coming to save us be a real prospect now? Could we believe Captain Wilkie's reassurances, or should we fear for our lives? As soon as we were back in our billet, the lads started firing questions at me, with almost the speed of an ack-ack gun.

'A death-ray bomb, what could that be, Sarge?'

'How could it have killed so many people?'

'Surely no bomb ever invented could do that?'

'What do you think it all means, Johnny?'

'Do you think the Yanks will land in Japan?'

'Will they come here?'

'Could the bloody Japs really shoot us all?'

The questions came thick and fast and my mind was racing. 'Hey, whoa lads. I can only answer one question at a time . . . except that I don't know the answers any more than you do.'

The next hour or two was spent in continuing discussion.

'We're all going round in circles, boys. But I think the real message here is that the Yanks must be on their way, and they've rattled the Japs to pieces.'

'Three cheers for the Yanks,' yelled Reg. 'Hip, hip . . .'

'Hooray . . .' We gave three of the loudest cheers you've ever heard.

We knew now that the Americans were getting closer, but we lived in a strange limbo for a few days, locked up in camp with no work to do and the same old routines, just talking endlessly about what might happen next, punctuated by the air-raid sirens throughout the day and night, with the guards making us go down to the shelter every time.

Otherwise, the camp guards were unusually quiet, just maintaining a watch and keeping their distance. They left us alone to do whatever we wanted, as long as we kept well away from the camp perimeter.

I was walking out in the yard to try and build up my fitness, when Captain Wilkie came over to me.

'Have you got a few minutes, Sergeant?'

'Yes of course, sir.' We stopped to talk in a corner of the yard.

'Sergeant Sherwood, I think this is it.'

'Really sir? What do you mean?'

'Something very important is going on, and it's clearly bugging the Japs.'

'Yes, sir.'

'I've been talking to some of the other sergeants too. It's my opinion that the Americans are about to invade the mainland, or perhaps they have already invaded.'

'But if they have, sir, surely we'd have been shot? Or else the Japs would have all scarpered?'

'Yes . . . you have a point there, Sergeant. But I believe the Yanks are preparing to invade.'

'How soon do you think it might be, sir?'

'Well, that's impossible to say. And we can't be sure of anything of course, but I have a gut feeling about all of this. What do you think, Sherwood?'

I paused to consider what I should say. 'I think you may well be right, sir, and I very much hope you are. I know the men would go wild. But I think it's all very difficult to piece together. We just don't know enough. I mean, is the war still going on everywhere, or just here? And the Japs are such a bloody proud race, or pig-headed more likely, that I can't see them ever agreeing to surrender.'

'All of that is quite true. But I think that death-ray bomb, as they call it, has changed everything.'

'It's hard to be patient, isn't it sir?'

'You're damned right there, Sergeant. If only we had some news.'

* * *

230

Later that day it was much the same – all the lads sitting about in groups all over the camp, whispering together. Some looked worried or afraid, others were pretty cheerful, but I didn't know what to think, knowing the distorted way these cunning devils' minds worked. One thing I knew for sure: if only I could get my hands on that bastard interpreter, after the war was over . . .

26

Free at Last!

August 1945

The following morning we got our answers . . . and a whole lot of new questions. I woke very early and looked out of our window to find, to my utter amazement, all the Japs had disappeared. I couldn't see a single one, across the yard to the guardhouse and up to the gun-towers – they were all empty. Nobody was guarding us at all. I was completely baffled and felt the first stirrings of excitement that maybe . . .

'Get up you lot!' I went around shaking the lads in my room. 'You've got to come and see this – the Japs have scarpered!'

Everyone shot out of their beds and came to the window.

'Champion!' shouted Reg, the Yorkshireman, punching his fist in the air.

'Bloody hell!' yelled Stuart, at the top of his voice. 'Am I still dreaming?'

'Is this a trick?' wondered Walter. 'Maybe they're hiding.'

'No, they've scarpered all reet,' said Geordie in a gleeful voice. 'Hoo-bloody-ray.'

'Help me get the others up,' I said. 'They have to see this.' We went down the corridor, banging on doors to rouse the lads.

'Up and out boys – it's a wonderful day. Come and see for yourselves.'

We gathered down in the yard, with men from all the other billets, but no Japs to be seen. We explored the whole site, and it looked as if they'd left in a hurry. We were now alone – just the Brits, nearly two hundred of us, with nobody to tell us what to do. What an incredible day!

'It looks like we're free lads. After three and a half years of hell, we're really free!'

'Free at last! Yippee!'

You should have seen us prancing about the parade ground in our excitement, cheering and whooping for all we were worth. It was pandemonium – marvellous mayhem.

Finally, we calmed down enough to rustle up some breakfast and we sat around the yard on that beautiful August morning discussing our astonishing situation, still not really sure what was happening.

'Why do you think they left, Sarge?' asked Walter.

'Or maybe they didn't go, not really,' suggested Reg. 'The devils could be lying in wait nearby to shoot us if we try to leave the camp. Remember what they said about shooting us all if the Americans landed?'

'Then we'd better not leave just yet,' I suggested. 'Until we're absolutely sure. But something must have happened.'

'Do you think the war has ended?'

'There haven't been any air-raid warnings since yesterday.'

'Yes, that's true.'

'Could the Yanks have landed?'

'Or maybe the Japs know something we don't.'

'They know a lot we don't, like whether the war is over, and whether they're going to shoot us all dead.'

'Or whether the Yanks are going to drop another death-ray bomb, over all the Fukuoka camps, or—'

'Steady on, lads,' I interrupted. 'I don't know about you, but I've had the gut feeling for a while now that the Americans know we're here. In fact I'm sure they know.'

'I bloody well hope so,' said my old friend Geordie. 'If they don't, we could all be gonners.'

'If it was up to me,' I added, 'I'd say we should stand our ground and see what happens. Somebody will surely let us know if we've won the war.'

'So who is it up to, Sarge?' asked Walter.

'The officers,' I said.

'Well, I bloody well hope they make the right decision,' muttered Reg.

'Whatever they decide, that's what we'll do.'

While this discussion continued, inside the barracks our two captains were apparently having a similar conversation, and they soon passed round word to us sergeants, which we passed on to our men.

'Righto, lads. I've got our orders here from Captain Wilkie. He says we must sit tight in the camp and make the best we can of our situation until we receive news.'

We chatted on, in high spirits, all the way through till about eleven o'clock.

Suddenly, from out of the south, came the unmistakable drone of approaching B29s. As they drew closer, we had the thrill of our lives. The Yanks flew two planes very low over our camp, so low we could see the airmen waving to us. We shot to our feet in delight, everyone jumping for pure joy. It was quite a sight, to see all us feeble skeletons, suddenly energised and full of vigour for one short blast of exultation.

One of the planes flew on, perhaps to another POW camp, while the other turned a semi-circle and flew back over us, lower than ever before, dropping leaflets like billowing snowflakes, before a final exchange of waved greetings, a dip of each wing, and the pilot took his 'baby' back to base.

We all scrabbled about, picking up these flimsy bits of paper with the most robust words on them.

'The Imperial Japanese Army has unconditionally surrendered.'

So there it was, in black and white. This wicked war was over at last. Boy oh boy, how we celebrated.

'We're FREE . . . FREE . . . FREE . . . !'

We all went absolutely crazy with joy, kissing and hugging each other, shouting and leaping about like children. It's impossible for me to describe our feelings on that memorable morning, but I'm sure none of us will ever forget our exhilaration at such marvellous news.

Minutes later, another B29 approached and dropped more leaflets. I thought perhaps the pilot didn't realise one of his pals had already dropped some on our camp. But when we picked them up, we realised they brought more wonderful news.

'Mark your camp very clearly. Between 4pm and 5pm today we will return with food, medical supplies and clothing.'

Grown men, and hardened as we were by our years of torture at the hands of the cruel Japanese, we all cried tears of excitement and delight. We sang and we danced in celebration – who could blame us? Now at last we could live like free human beings again and recover our dignity.

After about an hour or so of this, when we had almost exhausted every ounce of energy and emotion, Captain Wilkie sent round word to gather our units on parade.

The two captains stood together, facing us.

'I know how thrilled we all feel at this morning's events, but you must keep calm. Your first job is to follow the Americans' instructions. I will detail some of you to go outside the camp to find a nice open space and mark it very clearly, so that the Yanks can see it when they come over later on with our promised supplies.'

'Why not here inside the camp, sir?' somebody asked.

'Because we don't want anyone killed by stray crates,' he explained.

After he had dismissed us, he took me aside. 'Sergeant Sherwood, I'd like you to pick out five of your men and take all the white sheets you can find from the guards' quarters. Tear them into strips about six inches wide, take them out of the camp

Allied POWs wave at American aircraft from their
prison camp, clearly marked 'PW'.

gates to the nearest, large open space and mark out "Number 25 POW Camp, Fukuoka" on the open ground, where you are sure they will be able to see them. Do you understand?'

'Yes, sir.' I saluted him with renewed enthusiasm.

He saluted back, with a smile. 'I know I can count on you, Sergeant,' he said, and I felt quite proud.

I chose my best men, my pals, and we followed Captain Wilkie's instructions to the T, laying out the letters as large as we could and weighting down the strips of sheeting with heavy stones, before returning to camp.

Now all we had to do was to await the arrival of our American friends and their life-saving supplies.

We had our lunch, the usual rice and vegetable stew, almost enjoying it in the knowledge that our next meal would be a free-dom feast. After lunch, we settled down to rest while we waited to hear the familiar drone of B29s approaching. The time moved very slowly, so slowly that, to be honest, I thought they weren't coming. Had we dreamt it all? No, we had the leaflets to prove this was real. Four o'clock went by, and every minute seemed like an hour as we counted its passing. It got to about half past four . . .

Suddenly, there was that longed-for sound, coming closer and closer. In our excitement, we all climbed up on to the roofs of our billets, waving and shouting like crazy.

As they approached, one plane broke away from the other two and circled round our camp a couple of times, flying lower and lower until we could clearly see the grinning faces of those Yankee airmen waving to us in solidarity.

The pilot then flew up to join his mates in the other two planes. They all flew higher above us, keeping us in their sights, and made a couple of dummy runs. Then, on the third pass, they began to drop parachutes, all in different colours, with crates of food and other supplies underneath.

'One, two, three' – together we counted them as they fell through the air. 'Ten, eleven . . . sixteen, seventeen.' It was a very accurate drop, and all seventeen crates fell within fifty yards of their target.

As we waved the planes goodbye and climbed down from our rooftop vantage points, Captain Wilkie again asked me to go, this time with our ten fittest men, to the dropping area, to bring back these precious treasure-chests into our camp.

'But make sure that neither you nor your men open any of these crates until they are safely inside the camp, where I can have them all checked, sorted and distributed. That's a strict order, Sergeant.'

'Yes, sir,' I saluted, slightly disappointed that we couldn't take a dekko inside some of the crates as we carried them in.

When we reached the drop, the first thing was to make sure we had all of the seventeen crates in sight. They were all intact except one – a drum of American chocolate that had burst open, shedding its contents all over the drop area. Fancy anyone expecting these men who were half starved to just collect all the bars of chocolate and carry each one unopened back to camp!

I was no better than any of the others, and I have to admit I was one of the first to give in to temptation. Well, we all started to tuck into this chocolate, gobbling it down as fast as we could, the beautiful brown chocolate melting in our mouths and slowly oozing down our throats. We were in heaven. Nobody would know how many bars of chocolate there had been in this drum, so we were sure we wouldn't be found out and we kept on eating it until we felt sick. Of course, had we realised it, that was just what our medical officer, Captain Mathieson, was trying to avoid, so now we would have to try and hide our overindulgence.

We managed to carry or drag all the drums and crates into camp, where everything was taken to the mess hall, to be opened and sorted.

First they opened the clothing and that was distributed straightaway. It was a wonderful feeling to be able to wear proper, Western clothes again – trousers that were long enough to fit us and proper leather boots with thick soles and laces.

Most of the food was tinned meats, fruits and vegetables, together with puddings, condensed milk, and of course chocolate. Fortunately there was still a lot of that left to be shared. The other commodity that came with the foods was a crate of American cigarettes – a wonderful gift for the smokers among us who had never stopped craving a good smoke. The foods were stored, to be allocated to us a little at a time. Captain Mathieson was very clear about that.

'You mustn't upset your digestive systems by eating too much at once,' he said. 'After all these years on starvation rations, your stomachs have shrunk and you could kill yourselves by gorging on rich foods, so we have to ration them to build you up in a sustainable way.'

That didn't sound like much fun to us, having to be sensible after so long, but of course we knew he was right. And those of us who had overdone it with the chocolate had only ourselves to blame when our tummies rebelled. We really had to pay for that secret pleasure by spending most of the next two or three days in the latrines.

The following morning, just as we were wondering whether, now that we were free, we could stroll out of the camp and explore our surroundings, Captain Wilkie again gathered us together on the parade ground.

'I know some of you men would like the chance to get out of the camp and see some different surroundings, but I am afraid I must order you all to stay here until we have confirmation that we really are free, and what our next move will be.'

Once again disappointed, we sat in groups around the camp, discussing our fate.

'Do you think the Americans will have landed by now?' asked Harry.

'Or maybe we will see them parachute in,' said Reg.

'No, I reckon they'll come to the port in ships,' suggested Stuart Merritt.

'I'll bet you a packet of fags they're already here and organising our evacuation,' laughed Geordie. 'Those canny Yanks don't waste any time to get things done.'

'However they come, I bloody well hope it's today!' I said. 'It can't be a minute too soon.'

'Anyone would think you had a plane to catch, Johnny,' joked Reg.

'I wish I had!'

'Where would you go, Sarge?'

'Home of course!'

'Not me,' said Harry. 'I'd go to . . . Honolulu.'

'Why-aye,' said Geordie with a wicked grin. 'It's those girls in grass skirts with their bare breasts you're after, isn't it, bonnie laddie?'

'He'll have to fatten himself up first to catch one of them,' added Reg. 'They like their men with a bit of meat on them.'

'I'll have to see if I can steal an extra can of corned beef, then,' said the boy, unfazed by all the teasing.

'Did you go to Hawaii on your football tour, Johnny?' asked Geordie.

'Yes, that was marvellous,' I said with a smile, remembering the wonderful welcome we had received there. 'Boy oh boy, it was out of this world. We played two games in Honolulu, against rather moderate opposition, and won them both quite easily. Then we were taken on a sightseeing tour and met a lot of lovely people. Then a group of beautiful girls escorted us to the wonderful Waikiki Beach.'

'Oh yes?' sniggered Reg. 'Did you have a good time?'

'We had a ball!' I laughed. 'They just couldn't do enough for us.'

'Oh, ho, ho! We all know what that means, don't we lads?'

'You can think what you like,' I smiled, unwilling to admit anything straight out. 'It was the kindness and consideration of those warm people and the welcome they gave us that will stay with me all my life. We were treated like heroes.'

'Spill the beans, man,' said Geordie. 'Go on. A canny lad like you – I bet you had a few love affairs?'

'I can't deny I had my moments,' I admitted with a grin. 'But they were mostly in other places we visited. In Hawaii we went everywhere together in a group, so the only romance there, apart from the odd innocent embrace between dances or as the girls sat on our knees, was in the beautiful, lilting music they played on the quay as we boarded our ship to leave them. All the girls, with flowers in their hair, placed garlands around our necks and there were plenty of kisses as we said our goodbyes. Sorry to disappoint you lads,' I said. 'But, sad to say, we didn't have time for any love affairs in Hawaii.'

'Don't believe him, boys,' laughed Geordie.

'Pigs might fly,' agreed Stuart.

There was a pause in the conversation as we all waited for something to happen.

'If only the Yanks would come and set us properly free.'

'Don't they know how long we've been prisoners?'

'It will probably take them a day or two to get organised,' I said. 'After all, we don't know how many other POW camps there might be around here. The Yanks have probably got a lot to do, if they really have landed.'

'I suppose so,' sighed Walter. 'But I wish they'd bloody well hurry up and get here.'

'Tell us about some of these girls in other ports,' suggested Reg with a glint in his eye, skilfully changing the subject back to my pre-war tour.

We carried on with this light-hearted banter till about midday, when we heard the gate-bell being rung. The whole yard went quiet at this sound. Should we be excited . . . or fearful?

27

Yanks to the Rescue!

September 1945

S everal of us went over to open the gate. Imagine our surprise
when we saw what was waiting to come in – an armoured car
with six American officers and NCOs in it.

'It's the Yanks!'

'The Yanks have come to get us!'

'Yippee!'

Well, we all just about went crazy when they drove through the
gate. I've never seen anything like it. Our men rushed up from all
over the camp and threw themselves on these soldiers. We'd never
met any of them, but they were our best friends and saviours. We
flung our arms around them with great enthusiasm and cried our
eyes out with happiness.

The Americans looked a little taken aback at first, but I
think they understood by then something of what we had been
through and it was a very heart-warming moment for both
sides.

'Well you Brits certainly know how to make a man feel
welcome!' laughed their senior officer, as Captain Wilkie strode
up, saluted, and shook him firmly by the hand.

This was the first time we had been in the company of civilised
and friendly people for three and a half years. The first warm
smiles and sympathetic hugs we had received from anyone from
the outside world. It was hard to believe, but a great boost to our
morale. We had felt like forgotten men for so long, and now we
knew our allies had never forgotten us, even though it had taken

them a long time to reach us. It was a glorious feeling and we were on top of the world. The Yanks too were overwhelmed by the moving reception we gave them.

While the officers spoke in a serious huddle, the NCOs came and sat with us, trying to answer our barrage of questions for about an hour, filling us in on all the recent news and the liberation of Europe a few months before. It was a great relief to know that our loved ones were no longer living in fear and that soon we could join them.

'Was it the death-ray bomb that won us the war in Japan?' I asked an American sergeant.

'Do you mean the atom bomb on Nagasaki?' he said.

'I don't know. What is an atom bomb?' I'd never heard of this before.

'It's a giant killer,' he explained. 'It was invented during the war, with the capability of killing a hundred thousand people if need be, and devastating a wide area.' He stopped to let me take that in.

I found it a shocking revelation.

'We dropped two mass-destruction bombs,' he continued. 'Both on Japan. The first was at Hiroshima and the second a few days later at Nagasaki.'

'So it was the second one we saw?'

'Yes. And that was what persuaded the Emperor that he might lose millions of his people if he didn't surrender.'

'So now the allies have won in Japan as well as Europe, and we can all live in a free world again?'

'Yes. That's about the size of it,' he agreed. 'And we can all go home to our folks.'

'It's like a dream come true,' I smiled. 'I know that seems a silly thing to say, but it's how we all feel.'

'Gee whizz. I'm glad we could come and give you guys a hand. But now we have to go and visit some of the other Fukuoka camps.'

'Are you leaving us here?' asked Walter.

'Yes,' said an officer as he came to collect the NCOs. 'But not for much longer. We'll do another drop of food and supplies in two or three days. I hope that will keep you guys going a little longer.'

'It will certainly help,' I said.

'Will there be more chocolate?' asked Stuart.

'And cigarettes?' asked one of the smokers.

'I'll make sure there will be,' he grinned. 'And we'll be back with some of our intelligence officers to debrief you.'

'How much longer . . .?'

'It won't be long now. We'll soon have you out of here and on your way home.'

'It can't be soon enough!'

Sure enough, the supplies came as promised, with all the things we had asked for, and the same group of friendly Americans returned a day or so later with two interrogation officers to ask some of us detailed questions about the things they needed to know, although they knew more than we did about most matters so I reckon we asked more questions than they did. But we did tell them about the factories and the docks, and also about our time on the railway of death.

One of the officers wanted to speak to some of our NCOs and I was one of those chosen.

'What do you know about the atom bomb dropped on Nagasaki?' he asked.

'Well, I didn't know it was an atom bomb. The Japs called it the death-ray bomb. But I didn't have any idea what it was. I was too far away to see the bomb itself drop, but I saw the planes fly directly over us at the carbon factory, on the docks, then out across the bay. We were supposed to be in the air-raid shelter, but some of us wriggled outside to watch the planes. Suddenly there was a terrible rumbling sound and I felt the earth shudder. I must have ducked my head down and closed my eyes, but when I looked up again, there was this enormous cloud growing outwards at the bottom and upwards in a sort of column. It rose like a giant, then it spread out all around at the top and kept on rising up, black, then grey with white at the top and lots of colours sparkling in it. We thought it must have hit some chemical plants or something. But the Japs told us it killed tens of thousands of people. That's hard to believe isn't it?'

'Yes. It was a good job you put your head down and closed your eyes, Sergeant. If you hadn't you would probably have permanent damage to your sight.'

'Like Bill Pask,' I said. 'He still has flashes and his eyes hurt. He says he can't see so well now.'

'He will need to see one of our medics as soon as we can arrange it.'

'I'll tell him.'

'And you all had a very lucky escape.'

'How do you mean, sir?'

'If the wind had been in the opposite direction, across the bay, the fallout could have caused you all a lot of trouble. In fact, it could have killed you.'

After the Americans had left, I mulled that over in my mind and realised how lucky we'd been. So my mother's nickname for me, Lucky Johnny, was still working. I'd definitely have to tell her when I got home.

Later, I told the lads what the officer had said to me.

'So do you think it was this atom bomb that made the Japs surrender, Sarge?'

'It seems like it.'

'Well, it certainly scared them stiff, the way they shouted about it,' agreed Geordie.

'But if instead of dropping the bombs, the American army had landed, and carried on the war across Japan . . .' I paused for us all to think. 'There would have been at least as many thousands of people killed, and probably more, including us.'

'Blimey! That's a thought,' said Stuart.

'The Japs would have shot us, like they promised,' added Reg. 'So the atom bomb saved our bacon for sure.'

'Please God they never use it again,' I added with a shudder. 'I can't stop thinking about all those people, the ordinary Nagasaki folk, going about their daily routines. The poor souls didn't have a chance did they?'

'They paid a terrible price.'

'The world has got to learn from this.'

'Bang on, Sarge,' nodded Walter and everyone agreed.

We thought we understood how bad this bomb was, but we had no idea yet just how devastating it had been.

Life carried on far too slowly over the next few days. We craved action.

'Why don't the Yanks come and rescue us from this hole?' moaned one of the boys. 'They need to get off their ruddy backsides and organise themselves.'

'Don't they know we've already been prisoners for too bloody long? How would they feel?'

'I know lads,' I tried to calm them down. We all felt their frustration of course. 'There must be a lot of camps around here. After all, we're camp 25. So they've got a big job on their hands to evacuate everyone. I'm sure it will be any day now. We won't have to be patient for much longer.'

'I don't want to be patient a day longer – I hate that bloody 'P' word!'

While awaiting our next move, Captain Wilkie gave us permission to leave the camp in small groups, as long as they were with a senior NCO.

'You can take some of your men out in parties of five or six to see if you can find fresh produce to buy or barter for, if you like,' he briefed us. 'But they have to stay with you. And you must tell all your men in no uncertain terms that it is imperative they behave themselves at all times. If they don't, I will hold you personally responsible. Is that clear?'

'Yes sir,' we all answered in unison.

'And anyone whose men get into any trouble whatsoever could find himself on a court martial when he gets home. Do you understand?'

'Yes sir.'

'And you must never forget that you are British. Hate, revenge and cruelty do not form any part of our make-up. We must not lower ourselves to their standards. I want you to drum that into your men. Anyone who doesn't agree must not be permitted to leave camp.'

So those were our orders and they were very clear.

I went through it all with my party and they did in fact behave themselves on that score. But it would have been a different story I'm sure if we had been fortunate enough to find any of our guards, or that beast of an interpreter . . . We would have been in real trouble then. So maybe it turned out for the best that we never saw any of them again.

So we wandered the streets and through the markets. All that my little party did wrong was to take a bit of food that was lying about here and there, and about ten chickens that we found, or maybe we stole. Take it from me – that evening, for the first time in a long while, we had a delicious chicken stew with our ration of rice.

Another party that went out the same day brought back thousands of pounds worth of Japanese yen. You should have seen the grins on their faces!

'Where the hell did you get that lot?' asked a wide-eyed lad as this group counted out their gains, with the seriousness of poker-players one minute, and the euphoria of pools-winners the next.

'We were just walking along, minding our own business,' said one of them. (I'd always thought he seemed like a bit of a spiv.)

'And we saw this bank with its doors open, so we walked in. There was nobody there, just lots of lovely money lying around on the counters, waiting for us to gather it up and bring it home.'

'Pull the other one!' Reg roared with laughter.

'We were just keeping it safe,' said his mate. 'If we hadn't taken it, somebody else would.'

'We believe you lads,' I grinned. 'But the officers might not be so understanding.'

We kept this to ourselves of course, knowing that our officers might have found their story difficult to swallow, so best not to chance it.

The next day, we were allowed out again for a stroll through Fukuoka, and it seemed the locals had heard about us. Lots of Japanese women and children came up to us. We thought at first this was just curiosity. But they looked distressed, pushing their children forward and speaking words we didn't know, but we quickly understood their hand to mouth gestures. A few of them had a little English.

'Please rice?' asked one young mother, her hollow cheeks mirroring ours.

'Children no food,' said another, pointing at three painfully thin waifs.

It melted my heart to see the beseeching expressions on those children's faces. They were obviously very hungry.

'What do you think, lads?' I asked. 'They're crying out for food. We've got to help them, haven't we?'

'Dead right,' agreed Reg. 'We know just what it feels like to be hungry.'

'I want to help them, but how can we?' protested Harry. 'We haven't got enough food in camp to feed ourselves properly yet, let alone all these people. There must be hundreds of them.'

'We'll find a way, don't you worry,' I reassured him. 'I've got an idea.' Then I turned to the women and tried to explain my plan. 'We go get rice,' I mimed with my hands. 'We come back give you rice.'

The women nearest me tried to grab my arms to stop me going away.

I was a bit worried. But one of the youngest women smiled and nodded at me, then spoke in a loud voice to the others. I couldn't tell what she was saying, but it seemed to have the right effect. The women holding on let go, their faces breaking into smiles, and several of the other women seemed to be cheering us.

'Thank you.' I bowed to the young woman who had brought about this transformation. 'We will be back soon.'

She gave me a little bow in return, with her hands together. 'Thank you British.'

'So what's this clever plan of yours?' asked Stuart out of the side of his mouth as we walked away.

'Where's that warehouse we passed on the way here?' I said.

'About half a mile or so down that street on the left,' he pointed.

'Didn't you notice them unloading some full rice sacks?'

'What are we waiting for?'

All the lads were as keen as I was to help these poor, starving women and children, so we found our way back there. The factory was now closed and locked up, so Walter stood cavy while the rest of us broke in and found the sacks of rice, which we dragged out to the yard. Then we commandeered a van that we found at the side of the road, loaded it up with the rice and drove it back to where the women were waiting. They started to line up as soon as we arrived and somebody handed us a pan to distribute our load.

Word had got around and, when we'd shared it all out, there were more people still coming. They looked pretty desperate when they saw we had nothing left, crying and wailing in despair, so we asked the English-speaking young woman to tell them that we would go and get some more.

After our return journey, we gave out another vanload and everyone seemed so pleased, thanking us profusely. We must have given at least thirty hundredweight away. The little children clamoured round, curious I suppose to see these odd, thin, white people that they'd never seen before.

It seemed so strange in a way, that we ourselves, almost starved to death by the Japs for three and a half years, should help their wives and children in a similar predicament. All I know is that we just felt we had to help them. Don't ask me why. Perhaps we are just a softer, more warm-hearted nation.

We made a real fuss of these dear little Japanese children, cuddling them and playing with them. After all, they were innocent souls and we couldn't blame them for the sadistic way we had been treated. Their mothers looked on in utter amazement. I have wondered, on reflection, whether their minds had perhaps been polluted against us. Who knows? Perhaps they had been brainwashed into thinking all POWs were monsters or bogeymen. Maybe we put the record straight for the women of Fukuoka that day. They certainly looked happy with us when we said our goodbyes.

Back at camp that evening, the lads had acquired an old pack of English playing cards, and it made me laugh to see them gambling large denominations of the yen that had been stolen from the Japanese bank. Some of them really believed it was valuable. I'm sure the winners were looking forward to an easy life when they got back home. What a shock they must have had when they were only allowed to exchange a very small amount on their return to England. I suppose they kept the rest as souvenirs.

Every day now we wondered if this would be our last at the camp. Surely the Americans would come and get us out soon. All I could think about as I fell asleep each night was getting back to Christine and the children. Would they come and meet me at the port? Would Christine still love me? Would Philip recognise me? How would the new little one, Sandra, take to me? I couldn't wait to see them all, to see their smiling faces on the dock. Would things go back to the happy way we were before? What about my mum and dad, and my ten brothers and sisters? Would they all have survived the war all right? As I drifted off it was Christine's beautiful face I would see, her voice I would hear, her smell, her touch . . . Surely it couldn't be long now? This wait was too much to bear.

28

Homeward Bound

September 1945

It was a bright September morning when the Americans arrived to evacuate us, and boy were we ready for it. They brought trucks for all our sick men and any who couldn't walk far. The rest of us marched to the station, where we boarded a passenger train and cheered like crazy as it pulled out of the station.

'Whoopee! At last!' cheered a lot of the lads. 'We're off!'

'About bloody time,' yelled Reg at the top of his voice.

'Hooray!' I threw my cap in the air. 'Thank God.'

So, after three and a half years of slavery and starvation, we were finally going home. We began our journey full of excitement and hope, but trepidation too. It was so long since we'd seen our homes and our loved ones. Would they have grown apart from us? Would anything ever go back to the way it was? And how much had our hellish experiences changed us from the men they remembered? I dreaded to think.

Though still thin and weak, with little energy, we were quite a lively crowd on that first leg of the journey, as we rattled along the track towards Nagasaki. But what a terrible shock we had when we saw the landscape change, becoming greyer and more barren, to a scene of utter devastation.

We all sat in silence, our mouths open in disbelief. I stared across the valley, where everything had been destroyed. How could this have happened?

Every building and landmark was burnt to the ground, to a thick carpet of rubble and ashes, with a few twisted girders, looking as brittle as matchsticks, protruding from the debris like starved arms reaching to the sky, and the charred remains of the odd blackened tree here and there, burnt to knee-high stumps and stripped bare.

Never before had I seen anything like this. I could hardly take it in. The whole valley where the city had been was like a scene from hell. There was no colour or life. Who could possibly have survived?

The train slowed down. We were all in shock, our emotions flayed so that we couldn't speak. I felt wracked inside. I know it left its mark on us all.

The aftermath of the bombing of Nagasaki.

Only a few minutes later, the train slowed again as we approached a station a little way from Nagasaki, near some docks. We were completely unprepared for the reception that awaited us. I can honestly tell you that never in my whole life have I witnessed anything so touching.

Coming into the platform, we all looked out of the windows as the train pulled to a standstill, next to a line of grinning American army officers and other officials, several American Red Cross girls waving British and American flags at us, and a Yankee band playing away for all they were worth. Can you imagine our feelings as we got off the train?

Talk about excited, this was such a happy welcome. I can't explain how moved I felt, laughing and crying at the same time, with my knees shaking beneath me. It was an unforgettable moment when the band changed their tune as we alighted from the train and they struck up with 'Take me back to dear old Blighty'. That did it! There was not a man among us with dry eyes. We threw our arms around those American Red Cross girls, kissing and cuddling them as if they were our sweethearts.

I think that's when it really hit us again, as we ran around in circles on the platform, crying like babies and shouting at the tops of our voices.

'We're free! We're FREE at last!'

'And we're on the way HOME!'

Up to this moment it had seemed like a dream, but now we knew it was really true. For three and a half years we had not known what kindness was, and now this! The Red Cross girls brought us tea and coffee, and plied us with tea-cakes, chocolates and American Camel cigarettes – as much as we wanted. These Yanks fussed over us like royalty. They knew the ordeals we had been through, without our even telling them much, and they overwhelmed us with their kindness and understanding. What a way to be welcomed back into the outside world, after our years of cruel slavery at the hands of the hated Japs.

At last it was time to go and board the ship that would take us on the first stage of our voyage home. We all had our own bunks, and tested them out for comfort.

'Gee whizz!' shouted Reg, in a mock American accent. 'It's like the Ritz.'

'How do you know?' asked Geordie. 'I bet you've never stepped inside the Ritz in your life.'

'I shan't need to now!' he replied with a grin. 'This is bliss.'

'Hey, have you felt these white sheets? They're the softest I've ever had.'

'And I've got two proper pillows. Not those awful rubber things in Fukuoka camp.'

'Well at least we had something there – I never had a pillow of any kind to lie my head on in the death camps.'

'No, none of us did.'

'Well boys,' I said. 'I think we're in for a good journey home. It's a long way, so we might as well enjoy a bit of Yank luxury on the way.'

I can't praise the Americans enough. From the moment we were on-board that ship, they waited on us as though we were children at a tea party, fetching us almost anything we wanted. And how they looked after our sick men was a credit to them all. Nothing – I repeat, nothing – was ever too much trouble for them.

Once the ship had left Nagasaki harbour, the medics started us off with a regime of soft foods, such as eggs, fish and milky rice pudding, building gradually on from our starvation diet. I must admit, most of us had the runs, because in spite of the care the Americans lavished on us they were inclined to be over-generous with tasters of rich food now and then, with dire results for our digestive systems. Had they ever allowed us to eat our fill of all the foods on offer on the ship, many of us would probably have died. So they had the difficult job of tempering kindness with firmness.

On arrival at our first port of call, Manila in the Philippines, we disembarked. I had been here before of course, playing matches on our world tour. I remember that match, when a whole ship full of British sailors filled a stand to cheer us on and we trounced the local team nine goals to nil. Little had I known then that I would be back in such different circumstances. It seemed so long ago, when I was young, fit and carefree. Now, compared to then, I was a wreck.

All our men who needed nursing or special care were carried or helped to the newly erected hospital tents, equipped with every modern facility available. Here, the nurses cared for them with great tenderness and understanding. Indeed, all us POWs were looked after with wonderful kindness and consideration. I know I can speak for all returned Far East POWs when I say: '*Thank you very much USA – you are a credit to the whole, free world.*'

Most of us were still little more than walking skeletons, but we had all been kitted out with American service clothes that fitted us as well as possible, and we still marvelled at the luxury of being able to bath and shower every day. We felt clean at last, and some of our minor ailments were beginning to disappear. It was wonderful to belong to the human race once more, and new life surged in us. Everything seemed exciting.

After a few days, our most seriously ill lads were flown home by the British and American branches of the Red Cross, where they were taken to various specialist hospitals to receive the care they needed. It really boosted our morale to know that at last these poor, sick men were being properly looked after.

As for us who stayed behind in Manila, with the wonderful food and care lavished on us we gradually built ourselves up into something like our former selves, albeit with a lot of health and weight still to make up. The Americans who looked after us were kindness itself – especially when they gave us cigarettes and a small allocation of beer each. But they always kept their eyes on us to make sure we didn't over-gorge ourselves or overdrink.

The strangest thing was that this was an enormous camp and . . . who do you think the Yanks had to do their donkey work? Yes, none other than Japanese prisoners of war! So the boot was now on the other foot. The Jap POWs were carefully guarded by US army guards with tommy-guns at all times. We often watched them from afar and felt a strong urge to kill the bastards, after what they had done to us, but the Yanks must have been warned to keep us well away from the Japs, and I'm sure they could see the hatred in our eyes, so they did just that. We were never allowed to get anywhere near them. It was probably just as well, or we would have been in real trouble.

While we were in the Philippines, we were taken out in groups to look around Manila on sightseeing trips, but we were always chaperoned by American soldiers to make sure we behaved ourselves, and mostly we did.

But all the time, we were impatient to move on.

29

A Welcome in America

October 1945

After three weeks of regaining the beginnings of our lost health and strength, we were shipped out on the second leg of our journey home, towards the west coast of America. The Yanks continued to do an excellent job of making sure we got all the nourishing food our bodies craved, but without abusing our digestive systems, which were still in a very bad state.

'Why do I always get the runs, almost every time I eat?' I asked one of the ship's doctors. 'And I feel full after only two or three mouthfuls.'

'Well Sergeant, that's because your stomach has shrunk to a fraction of the size it used to be. I'm afraid you may never get it completely back to normal. Your whole system is overworked by trying to digest such healthy food, after so long a period of malnutrition.'

'All the lads have diarrhoea,' I said. 'Will that ever get better, Doc?'

'Yes, but I'm not sure how long it will take. You will have to be very careful what and how much you eat for a long time, maybe for ever.'

'So won't I ever be able to eat my favourite foods?'

'Possibly, if you work up to them gently, over time, but it also depends on what your favourite foods were.' He smiled. 'What did you like best?'

'Before the war? Steak, I suppose, when I could get it. Or bangers and mash, or a Sunday roast, or . . . Mmm, it's making me hungry again just to think about it!'

258

'Well, hopefully you will be able to eat those things again by the time you reach England. But take it easy until then.'

As before, the American sailors were all exceptionally kind to us. Everyone seemed to understand what hell we'd been through, and this time they gave us the run of most of the ship. Each day we would look out from the deck-rail, across the wide, blue of the Pacific Ocean. It seemed so vast when we looked at it on the map, compared to the English Channel. But, of course, we had travelled the oceans before, both the Atlantic and the Indian Oceans, on our way to Singapore.

One day, I leaned over the bow-rail, watching dolphins play, darting to and fro in front of the ship. Next to me stood Bombardier Stuart Merritt, who'd been through the final year with me.

'Remember the last time we stood at a ship's rail together?' he asked.

'Yes, of course, the night we were torpedoed.'

'This is a bit different from the *Kachidoki Maru*. I don't remember dolphins in the South China Sea.'

'No. That bloody water was lethal, as we found out!'

'Have you ever been to America – maybe on that world football trip of yours?'

'Yes, in spring 1938. We went to San Francisco and Los Angeles.'

'What was it like?'

'Oh boy, did we have some fun there! Especially when we had a tour of the Hollywood film studios.'

'Did you see any film stars?'

'Have you heard of Charles Boyer? Now there's a real star.'

'Yes, he's French isn't he?'

'That's right. He was filming *Algiers* at the time.' I paused to think. 'And David Niven, the British film star? He was good fun. Then there was Robert Montgomerie and of course Victor McLaglan. He was a great guy and took us on to the set to meet all the actors. I was amazed they seemed almost as impressed to meet us as we were to meet them!'

'Any female stars?'

'Yes, quite a lot. Joan Woodbury – now she was beautiful, but unfortunately our team captain beat me to it. Heather Angel was another star that I remember well.'

'Was she as glamorous in real life as she was in *The Three Musketeers*?'

'You bet. She was beautiful, fabulous, and English too.'

Stuart gave me a look and I knew what he was thinking.

'No,' I laughed. 'She was too old, and married. But all of them gave me their signed photos, with messages to me on them. What an honour that was. And we did have a wonderful evening out with a group of starlets the studios had sent us, along with a couple of cases of champagne. Now, that was an evening to remember.'

'I bet!'

'There was one lovely young actress I met in Hollywood,' I reminisced. 'Charles Boyer introduced me to her and she seemed to fall for me, so we went out whenever I had any spare time.'

'Was she pretty? What was her name?'

'Jane. I don't remember her last name. She was absolutely stunning.'

'She drove me round all the best parts of Los Angeles, and took me home to meet her mother and father.'

'Oh yes?' laughed Stuart.

'In fact I stayed there a few times. To tell you the truth, I very soon realised I was falling in love with her.'

'Did anything happen?' he grinned.

'Yes, we did spend one whole night together at the hotel where the team were staying. Thanks to the kindness of my room-mate, Bill Whittaker, who moved in with a couple of the other lads for the night.'

'Were you sad to part when it was time to move on?'

'Yes, of course, I seem to remember we made all kinds of promises to each other, but we both knew we couldn't keep them. She was a special girl though.'

Pages from Johnny's scrapbook - Heather Angel and Charles Boyer
gave Johnny signed photos on the visit to Hollywood studios toward
the end of the Islington Corinthians world tour in April 1938,
Johnny is fourth from left.

'I bet they all were!'

'Well . . . you could be right!'

When we arrived in the United States of America, what a fantastic reception there was for us on the quayside. By now we had been consuming a lot of soft, high-nourishment food and we were all beginning to feel a bit more energetic, so we danced around to the music of the band as we disembarked.

We settled into our new camp and looked forward to the day we would finally leave for England. But first the American medics wanted us to get well. I think Captain Wilkie and all the other officers had received some orders about this too.

'Why do we have to stay here first, sir, before we go home?'

'You have to build yourself up, boys,' he told us.

'But we can do that just as easily in England.'

'Yes,' he paused. 'But just look at yourselves. I know we're all a lot stronger than we were, and getting better all the time, but how do you think your loved ones would feel if you went home now, under-weight, some of you still bloated with beriberi, others with recurring malaria, not to mention running to the lavatories all the time with diarrhoea. We don't want to frighten our womenfolk, do we?'

'I suppose not, sir,' I agreed, full of disappointment. 'But do you think it will be soon?'

'I'm sure it will be as soon as our friends the American medics think we're all fit enough to return.'

'But Captain,' pleaded one of the lads. 'Can't you persuade them?'

'I wish I could,' he sighed. 'I have a wife and family at home waiting for me too, and it's a very long time since I was home in the green fields of England, before the war started.'

So, we couldn't go back to our loved ones just yet, but we were at last permitted to send letters to them; letters that would be taken by plane to make sure they arrived before we did; letters to say that we would soon be coming home again.

While we stayed in America, we were billeted at a place called Tacoma, in Washington state.

'I've never heard of Tacoma,' said Stuart. 'Is it some sort of backwater?'

'No. It's where Bing Crosby was born and raised, and so was I,' one of the Yank soldiers told us with pride.

'Well if it's good enough for Bing, it's good enough for me,' said Reg.

'As long as they don't expect us to sing like him,' laughed Walter.

'No, I can't sing for toffee,' agreed another of the lads in our army billet.

'Reg can,' I said, grinning. 'You should have heard the songs he made up about the guards. You'd have laughed your heads off. We all did.'

'Even the guards laughed when he sang them in our camp concerts,' chuckled Geordie. 'They had no idea how rude his songs were about them!'

'Yes,' laughed Reg. 'That was a bit of fun. But I lost my dear old ukulele when we were torpedoed, and I can't sing a note without it.'

'Maybe somebody here has one they can lend you?' suggested Walter.

'Good idea,' I nodded. 'I'll ask around.'

Throughout the time we were in Tacoma, we were treated like gentlemen, even if we didn't always behave like them. The American officers gave us each an allowance of American dollars, and the freedom of the city, to do more or less as we pleased. So we did. Some of the lads went out and painted the town red, leaving quite a trail of mayhem behind them. But it was just high spirits, having money to spend on anything they wanted, and the chance to drink more than they had done since the war began.

The people of Tacoma were very understanding and let us get on with it. This really was quite remarkable and very tolerant of them. Some of them even stopped in their cars when they saw us walking on the sidewalk and invited us to join them for dinner.

I felt sure the citizens of Tacoma had been told of our sufferings, and they went out of their way to entertain us, welcoming us into their homes and treating us with a warmth and friendship that I will never forget. Geordie and I went to dinner with several of them, on our best behaviour, and had a wonderful time with these good people, getting to know their families, though they had a hard time understanding Geordie's accent!

Even after we returned home, many of us continued to receive food parcels from them, which helped out enormously to fill the gaps between our rationing coupons.

The time came for us to say our goodbyes to these marvellous people who had taken us into their hearts and homes and commence the final part of our journey, across the Atlantic Ocean to England and our loved ones.

Once again, we were played off the quay with a medley of lively tunes, a mixture of American and English songs, as we waved to our new friends and, with tears in our eyes, set sail for home.

After one day at sea, we were gathered on deck for an announcement.

'What do you reckon it will be?' asked Geordie as we lined up ready.

'A list of things we can't do,' suggested Stuart.

'Or that we can't go home after all, so they're taking us to Hawaii instead,' added one of the young lads with women on the brain. Well, not just the brain . . .

'I'm hoping it's something good,' I said with a smile. 'Though I can't think what.'

Within minutes we found out.

'Good morning men. The ship's captain tells me that we have more than a hundred sacks of mail, some of it quite old, which has finally caught up with us.'

'Hooray!' we all cheered.

'Terrific news!' I shouted to the lads. 'Letters from home.'

'About bloody time!' said Reg.

The last mail we had received was eighteen months before, in Singapore, and most of that was more than two years old then, so this was a wonderful prospect. I desperately hoped there were letters for me as I craved the love and inspiration they would give me, though at the same time I dreaded what else they might hold. My parents weren't getting any younger, and my brothers had been at war, like me. Then of course there was Christine, alone with the children for so long . . .

'The mail is being sorted now by the ship's crew and the captain informs me that it will all be handed out to you as soon as possible,' said our commanding officer, with a broad smile. I expect he was hoping for letters from his family too.

As soon as we were dismissed, we ran around like a lot of children in the playground, yelling and hugging each other, hoping against hope that there would be mail for all of us. I dreaded the thought that anybody would be left out. Just imagine . . .

Well, I had prayed for at least one letter but, much to my surprise, I was handed six of them, two or three of which were very old. I grabbed them with trembling excitement and ran away with them to hide in some little corner somewhere. I found the ideal place and began to read my mail, from the oldest letter first.

Four of these letters were from my wonderful wife, Christine. I needn't have worried – they were long and loving accounts of her life and the amusing escapades of our children. I couldn't wait to see them all. Not long now.

On the most recent envelope I recognised my beloved mother's handwriting and I opened this with trepidation. I don't know why, but I remember feeling worried that it might be bad news . . . and sure enough, it was terrible news, telling me that my younger brother Cyril had been killed in action, blown up driving an ammunition lorry to the front line in Antwerp.

This was a shattering blow to me, especially since it had happened several months before and I had not known till now. I tried to imagine my mother receiving that telegram, telling her the awful news. I could picture her shocked face and I'm sure she would have been overcome with grief for Cyril. She loved all of us so completely. And what a terrible death. I suppose the only thing to be grateful for was that it must have been immediate, and he wouldn't have known. My poor parents – this would have hit them both very hard. I wished I could have been there to comfort them.

The only consolation was to learn that, out of the five of us boys on active service, only one wouldn't be coming home, although they probably thought they had lost me too. As a family, I suppose we can consider ourselves very fortunate to lose only one brother.

I read and reread those letters, with tears of laughter and sorrow running down my cheeks, to catch up with everyone's news and to know they had never forgotten me, that I was loved and cherished. I must have read those letters at least a hundred times more on that last part of our journey home to dear old England.

The saddest thing was to see the sacks of undeliverable mail, letters to the thousands that had died on the railway of death, or in the South China Sea. Letters from loved ones who had lost their sons, husbands and sweethearts. If only the Japs had let us receive mail during our captivity, it would have helped us so much in our battle for survival, and perhaps saved a few lives along the way.

'Wake up, Johnny!' It was Geordie, shaking me awake. 'There's something going on. I'm going up to see. Are you coming?'

'You bet,' I said, leaping out of my cosy bunk into the cold morning air. I pulled on my trousers and jacket over the vest I had slept in and we rushed up the gangway together. It was a couple of weeks since we had left our friends in Tacoma, and for the last few days we had been crossing the cool Atlantic ocean, with the weather growing colder each day.

As we climbed up the steps, I could hear a great hullabaloo on deck and couldn't wait to see what it was all about.

As we reached topside, we spotted Reg already at the rails, waving and beckoning us over, so we went to join him. Stuart had followed us up as well.

'What's going on?' I asked excitedly as we approached the rail, already crowded with sailors and men alike.

'See for yourself,' said Reg with a huge grin, pointing at the horizon.

As soon as I could wriggle myself into a space I looked across the choppy grey waters and saw what all the fuss was about – a long white cloud that seemed to hover over the sea on the horizon.

'What is it?' asked Stuart, sounding disappointed.

'It's home, you chump!' shouted Reg in high spirits, and Stuart's face immediately broke into a smile.

'England,' I breathed. 'Our homeland.'

'The wanderers return,' grinned Geordie.

'Thank God!' I yelled. 'We've made it. We've all four made it!'

The four of us did a jig together to celebrate our first sighting of England, without yet actually seeing land at all, just the cloud. But we all knew what must be beneath it, and we couldn't wait. Other friends came up from their bunks and joined us in our jubilation – Walter, Harry, Bill, and many others who had lasted out the war with us.

Thank you God, I repeated to myself. *Thank you for returning us to our loved ones.*

We stood and watched then, in silent anticipation, waiting for that first glimpse of our familiar coastline, where our families would be waiting to greet us. And as I peered into the distance and watched that cloud slowly break up and the faint line of land materialising, my mind flashed back over the past four years of suffering, pain and fear. And I thought too of the past few months, during which I had experienced enough mental and physical stress, enough emotional anguish and joy, to last me a lifetime.

Lucky Johnny

And now, here we were, all of those who were left, on the last day of our long journey home, desperate to reunite with our loved ones. I cannot describe the feeling inside, knowing that in a matter of hours I would be embracing my beloved wife and children, my parents, brothers and sisters. Only now could I hope that, with their help, it might be possible to put behind me all the horrors and torments of that indescribable three and a half years of hell on the railway of death.

'Come on lads!' Reg broke into my thoughts. 'It will be hours before we get close enough to see anything. Who's going to join me for breakfast?'

Welcome home - troops arriving at Southampton, November 1945.

Later that day found us all leaning over the side of the ship again, this time waving and shouting like hell at the reception committee on the Southampton quayside. My heart was pounding and I couldn't stop laughing with joy. Gradually the details became more distinct and we all scanned the cheering crowds for our own families' familiar faces. Finally, I caught sight of the one I most wanted to see. Amazingly, she'd spotted me too, picking me out from so many of us along the rails. She waved and blew me kisses and I did the same back. I couldn't wait to hold her close in my arms, but it would not be long now.

30

Home Sweet Home – Scarred For Life

November 1945

They were all there to meet me. First my darling wife Christine, as beautiful as ever, with tears of joy running down her cheeks, my bonny new daughter Sandra, now nearly four years old, and five-year-old Philip, who of course didn't remember me. I embraced them all in turn. Then my mother and father, both looking older than when I last saw them, but well and happy to have the last of their surviving sons back home again. Most of my brothers and sisters had also made it down to Southampton, so we were a jolly party as we walked across the dockyard together in the November sunlight, Christine's arm in mine, like young sweethearts newly in love. I can't tell you how wonderful it was to be back in the heart of my family again after all those years apart.

We had all been told on the ship that we were expected to stay till we'd signed our forms, been debriefed and completed all the formalities, but after so much time apart, and now back in the heart of my family at last, I didn't want to waste another second.

'Let's go for a drink,' said one of my brothers.

So off we went in convoy, back to my dad's pub, the May Duke in Reading.

As soon as we got to the end of the street, I could see all the crowds and the banners. It looked like half of Reading had come out to welcome me home. I can tell you a few tears ran down my cheeks, tears of joy and thanksgiving, as I waved at everyone along the street.

'Welcome Home Johnny' read the banners, and there were Union Jacks around all the lampposts. I was back home at last. The pub was packed out with extended family, friends, ex-team-mates, and pub regulars, all wanting to shake my hand and give me a personal welcome home. It was a merry evening of celebration. My mum, Christine and some of my sisters had prepared lots of food, despite the rationing, and everyone wolfed it down, except me. Despite the occasion, I didn't dare eat or drink too much, fearing the effect it might have on me. But that didn't stop me having a wonderful time.

At the end of the evening, a friend drove Christine and me home where, as you might guess, the two happiest people in the world tumbled into bed and made love. Thank goodness that part still worked.

On my first Sunday home, I went down to my dad's pub to meet friends for a drink, while Christine was cooking my first Sunday dinner. I came home at about 2.30 in the afternoon and she had cooked a lovely joint of roast beef and Yorkshire pudding.

'That was good timing,' she laughed, as I tiptoed up behind and put my arm round her waist to surprise her. I watched her stir the gravy. Every movement she made was so graceful it fascinated me. I had so missed the company of women throughout those POW years, especially my own beautiful Christine, and loved watching her move around the house or play with the children.

'Mmm, that smells good,' I said.

'Well, it's ready and I've sharpened the knife, so do you want to carve the beef?'

I nodded and sliced it all up for her as she got the children ready for dinner.

'Come and sit at the table,' she called to the children and me. 'And I'll serve it up.'

We sat down together to this amazing meal that I had been

looking forward to for so long. I used to dream of this day, through all those years of starvation rations – my first Sunday roast. I had worked up to it throughout the long journey home from Japan, eating little and often and only gradually introducing richer foods. Christine brought me my plate, piled high with good food.

'What a huge portion,' I said, grinning from ear to ear. 'I hope I can manage it all.'

'Don't worry. Just leave what you can't eat.'

'Oh, I'll eat it all right. I've waited a very long time for this, and I'm not going to waste it!'

Now, at last, all my dreams had come true. I had my own precious family gathered around me in my own home and a delicious roast dinner to enjoy. I felt on top of the world.

Well, once I started this tasty feast, there was no stopping me. I had no trouble finishing every last morsel, so that my plate was almost licked clean.

'Thank you, darling,' I smiled, as I rubbed my bloated tummy in satisfaction. 'That was the best meal I've ever eaten. I feel really good.'

'I'm so glad,' she replied, her eyes sparkling with pleasure.

I watched Christine and the children finish their meals and helped her clear away the dishes.

'I'll do the washing up,' I said.

'Not yet. Aren't you going to have some dessert?'

'I'd love to, but I'm completely full. Can you save it for me to eat later?'

'Of course. But really, don't worry about the washing up. Why don't you go and relax in the sitting room?'

'Thanks, but I think I'll go and lie down on the bed. I feel like a nap.'

'Good idea,' she smiled, then looked a little concerned. 'Are you sure you're feeling all right?'

'Yes, I'm absolutely fine – never better. Just a little tired. Come and wake me if I don't come down by five o'clock.'

I felt a twinge or two in my tummy, but didn't let it worry me as I undressed and slid between the sheets. As soon as I lay my head on the pillow, I must have fallen straight to sleep . . . but not for long. I was woken by a sharp pain, and then another, until it became a constant spasm, a rumbling, churning sensation that quickly grew worse and worse. Soon the pain was like a sharp knife stuck into me – unbearable. I tried different positions, but none of them helped. I tossed and turned, rolling around all directions, writhing about in agony.

I had suffered many torments on the railway of death, but never anything that cut me in two like this.

'God, please help me,' I whispered hoarsely as I thrashed about. 'Am I going to die?'

I didn't realise it, but I must have started groaning and Christine heard me. Her footsteps ran lightly up the stairs.

'What is it darling?' she asked. 'Are you ill?' Then, as she came into the bedroom: 'You look awful. Where's the pain?'

The colour drained from her face and I could see the fear in her eyes as I tried to stay more still for her.

'Oh Johnny . . . what shall I do?' She stroked my sweating forehead. 'Maybe you've got a fever. I'll get you a drink of water.' She dashed back downstairs.

Will this be the end of me? I thought in the moments in between, as I tried desperately to regain control of myself. But it was no use. The pain was so awful that I couldn't stop struggling. I felt as if I was going to die, and it was so bad that I almost wanted to die.

As Christine came back with a glass of water, I managed to sip a little and the cool liquid slipping down my throat was a momentary relief. I sank back into the pillow and all I could hear was the US army medics' voices in my head, telling me not to eat too much, to be careful, not to have rich foods until I was ready – all the warnings they gave us. I knew then how stupid I had been to eat everything on my plate, and to scoff it all down so quickly. I had obviously eaten too much and now I was suffering for it.

Oh boy, was I suffering!

For several hours, I could do nothing to rid myself of this vice, squeezing and churning my insides, stabbing me with pain. I vowed to God that if I lived I would never again eat a whole, big meal like that.

Christine kept coming in and out for a bit, then her sister must have come over for the children so that she could sit with me, cooling my forehead with a wet flannel, holding my hand, her anxious face searching mine for any sign of improvement.

'Just leave me alone,' I said to her, feeling guilty that I'd caused her so much anxiety and trouble, merely through eating too much.

'I'm not going anywhere,' she said. 'So you'll have to put up with me here.'

'I probably just ate too much,' I winced.

'Yes, and you gobbled it down too quickly as well,' she nodded. 'You never used to eat that quickly, but I'll make sure you don't have such a big portion as that again.'

I tried to give her a smile to soothe her worries, but the vice squeezed me again and contorted my face.

'Oh, darling,' she sighed, stroking my forehead.

Finally, I either fainted or fell asleep. I have no idea how long I was out for the count, but when I woke up it must have been early morning and the pain had eased off quite a bit. It gradually disappeared through the next few hours, though my whole insides felt tender and sore for days.

As I lay next to Christine and listened to her gentle breathing that morning, I thanked God for my release.

I had learnt my lesson. Never again would I abuse my stomach so badly, and I've kept to that all these years. But my digestive system has never been right since the war, and my bowels have never worked as they should. I still suffer from chronic diarrhoea most days.

I can get very moody and depressed too, but the worst thing is the nightmares. I've had the most awful nightmares nearly every night of my life, ever since I came home from the war. But I have noticed that they are lessening, now that I have written it all down. Christine was always marvellous with me and never once complained about her broken sleep. Whenever I was woken by one of those nightmares, she sat up and stroked my forehead to calm me.

'Another bad dream?' she used to ask me, with genuine sympathy every time, without any hint of annoyance at being woken up yet again.

'Yes, I was back in the death camps,' I used to say as we got older, though for years I couldn't even talk about it with her, or with anyone.

'Well, you're here with me now.' Her soothing voice always wiped away the worst of my fear. 'Let's go downstairs and I'll make you a nice cup of tea. We can stoke up the fire in the sitting room and talk, with no interruptions from the children. How does that sound?'

'Just what I need.'

We would sit together in the glow of the fire, talking about pleasant things.

'Did I tell you what Sandra did today?' she might ask. We laughed at the antics of our young ones, or some funny story Christine had overheard on the bus, or maybe something on television.

It all helped me to stop trembling and feel normal again. Finally I'd say, 'Let's go back to bed,' and off we would go.

Many years ago, I went to my doctor about these nightmares.

'How often do you get them?' he asked.

'Nearly every night. Sometimes twice.' They used to be that frequent in those early days.

'Are they always the same?'

'Very similar.'

He looked down at his notes, then back up at me. 'Remind me, what did you do during the war?'

'I was in the Royal Artillery,' I replied. 'I was in the Siege of Singapore, then on the Burma railway.'

'Ah,' he said. 'A Japanese prisoner of war?'

'Yes, that's right. It was a terrible time.'

'So, your nightmares are about those years in the death camps?' he asked.

I nodded. 'They told us not to talk about our experiences when we came home, and I didn't, but I can't get them out of my mind. I want to be rid of all those terrible memories, but they never fade. They're almost as awful and vivid in my dreams as the day they happened, as if I was back there again.'

'I heard that you all had to sign something to say you wouldn't talk about your experiences on the Burma railway.'

'That's right. I think some POWs did, but I was never asked to. Probably because I didn't stay for the debriefing when we landed. Who could I talk to about it anyway? It would be too horrific for my wife and too shocking for anyone else.'

'Yes,' he started writing. 'I'll prescribe you some pills to help you sleep better.' He handed me the prescription, then sat back pondering for a moment.

I was about to get up and go, when he continued.

'The pills might help a little, but I'm afraid you will probably have to learn to live with these nightmares.'

'Really, doctor?' I asked in dismay. 'Will they never go away? Is that what you think?'

'I've seen it before. Your experiences have weakened your body and scarred your mind. Those scars in your mind are there for life. That's how things are, I'm afraid.'

'Thank you doctor,' I said in a gloomy state and left his surgery. These invisible scars were just another legacy of my three and a half years of hell and murder, as a guest of the mighty Japanese Empire.

I did try taking the pills, but he was right. They made very little difference for years, until finally I started to write about my experiences in this book. But even doing that brought back all those black and bloody memories, making me moody and introspective. I often sat in silence, shut away in the room where I wrote, but not writing at all. The scars are in my soul and will never go, but I think I am dealing with them better now.

One day, soon after this, I was surprised to receive a letter enclosing a five-pound note from one of the POWs I knew, a Sergeant Truscott who came from the West Country. He thanked me for helping him during a very bad time at Kanu camp, when we had all been so ill and weak, until I was given the job in the sweegie-bar, the Japanese cookhouse, and I smuggled out extra food for us all.

'Use the five pounds to take your wife out for a meal,' he wrote at the end of his letter, so I did. That five pounds paid for a feast for Christine and me, and there was still a bit left over.

Despite my enduring problems, I can't grumble. I'm alive, and at times I look and feel really well, unlike some I know, who are still suffering physically from various complaints, and mentally have never recovered from their dreadful ordeals.

I have met up with several of my old POW friends since the war and we've talked about our terrible times together in the death camps. It seems to help us to go back over our worst memories together, as if it somehow lessens our trauma and pain.

'Do you remember those cages?' I asked Reg one time when we met up in London.

'I'll never forget them,' he said, with emphasis on the 'never'.

'And the guards' sadistic cruelty?'

'Barbaric, I'd say.'

We sat with our pints of beer, in silent contemplation of our shared memory.

It was a 'punishment' that used to happen in most of the camps, and it still makes me shudder to remember it now. These brutal

Japanese and Korean guards used to build very small bamboo cages, and when anyone did anything that displeased them, he was thrown into one of them, just like you might do with an animal. The only difference was that an animal could walk about, but our poor fellows could only sit or kneel in one position, or lie down curled up on the filthy floor, covered in human excrement. These deliberately undersized cages were never cleaned out and were often in use.

A man would be caged like that, not even able to stretch his back, for several days at a time, and when he was finally released he could no longer stand up. It was an appalling sight. This poor chap had to be lifted and held up so that his blood could circulate through his limbs again, which gave him a lot of pain.

'Those bastards got a real kick out of seeing us suffer,' said Reg.

'It made me sick. I remember them laughing as they watched us help these half-crippled lads back to their quarters after a stint in the cage. Being cruel to us was like a sort of drug to them. They wanted more and more of it.'

'Inhuman, that's what they were. Damn and blast them to hell. That's where they belong.'

'My God,' I agreed, 'how I would have loved to smash my fist into those devils' sneering faces.'

After I got back, Reading were very keen to have the team up and running again, so I started training as soon as I could. I was never able to complete a whole match again, but I built up my stamina slowly. Only a few months after we got back home, Geordie came down from Newcastle with his wife for the weekend and we had a marvellous time. I got them tickets for the match at Elm Park and they sat with Christine to watch me play. Then we went back to the May Duke to have a drink and meet my parents.

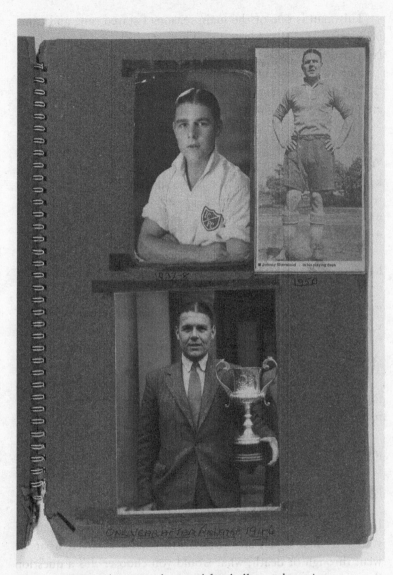

Lucky Johnny, professional footballer, and survivor.

'This man is one of the main reasons I stayed sane and came back safely,' I said as I introduced him. 'Geordie Ashbridge, from Newcastle.'

'Howay, Johnny,' laughed Geordie as he turned to my parents. 'I'm reet glad to meet you at last. Johnny hardly stopped talking about you all through the war . . . and the football too of course!'

'I'm not surprised about that,' laughed my dad.

'But I must tell you,' added Geordie, with a serious expression. 'You can both be very proud of your son. Johnny was the one who kept everyone sane. He never let us give up hope. That's what really kept us going. And there never was a better friend, or a more generous man,' he added. 'That's why I'm here now with my wife, to thank him.'

For once I was speechless. I was surprised and embarrassed to hear Geordie speak like this to my parents, in front of me.

'Thank you for being such a good friend to our Johnny,' smiled my mum. 'I can't call you Geordie,' she added in her usual, direct way. 'Do you have a name?'

'You can call me Sydney if you prefer, Mrs Sherwood,' he said. 'That's what my mum calls me.'

'Sydney,' I repeated in astonishment. 'All those years we spent together, all those troubles we shared, and I never even knew your real name!'

We had a wonderful weekend together, telling some of our more acceptable or funny stories to our wives, who got on together famously. If we had lived nearer to each other I'm sure we would have met up regularly. But we always kept in touch.

I sometimes ask my POW friends when I meet up with them: 'If you were there again and you had to choose between what we went through or death, what would you choose?' It's a question I've asked many Burma railway survivors since the war, and they've nearly all given the same answer.

'Death, definitely,' they say. I can understand why, but I don't think I would answer that myself, even now. I thank God that we survivors are here at all. The fact that we are shows miracles can happen.

Just ask any Japanese POW and they will tell you, 'It's a miracle that anyone came back from that Hell-on-Earth.'

I often think of those who didn't make it; I think of my old pals and their sacred graves, strewn throughout the jungles of Thailand and Burma, especially those who lie buried in unmarked graves and those who were drowned in the South China Sea. These brave men, both Brits and Australians, who suffered so much for their country, must be remembered for their courage. Take it from me, they were real men, and even as I write this my tears well up again and my heart aches with pain for them. At least they lie in peace, and God bless them all.

God bless the women too, the mothers, wives and sweethearts left behind, not knowing where we were, whether we were alive or dead, whether they would ever see us again, struggling on through the war, and still for months after it had ended, before any of us finally came back to them. They banded together to support each other, keeping up their morale . . . until the news filtered through of our appalling casualties and an inkling of what we were suffering. Many of them descended into an abyss of despair. They too were scarred for life by this experience. They were the unsung heroes – true heroines in my eyes.

This is my story, written from memory. Far from exaggerating the horrors, I have erred on the side of moderation. As events recede into the past, one tends to forget the most terrible details, and I'm sure that some events were much worse than I have described them here. Then again, some things were just too awful to relate. It's enough to thank God we somehow endured.

These memories have eaten away at me for years, urging me to talk about them, or write them down. Now that I have got a lot of it off my chest, I feel a great sense of relief. The Japanese guards had no pity on us whatsoever, no mercy for those unfortunate enough to be in their power. So I have no pity for them. I try to think of them as little as possible, because I do not want to pity them for the bombs or for their defeat. It all happened, but now it lives in the past alone, unlike those thousands of poor souls they murdered, whose memories live on in our hearts.

There is just one burning question I still have, that to my mind has never been answered. Why oh why was the 18th Division allowed to go into Singapore, only about eighteen days before capitulation, when it must have been so obvious to army chiefs that the fall of Singapore was inevitable? The only aircraft in the sky were Japanese planes, and they could do what they liked, strafing, dive-bombing and heavy bombing at will. The island was full of agents and fifth-columnists. Our chiefs, whether in the government or the army, were sending lambs to the slaughter. I often wonder if it was a panic move. Was it because they still really believed the old maxim that Singapore was an impregnable fortress? How wrong was that? Every unit in the 18th Division knew this was a major blunder, and later the worst sacrifice of the war as they handed us over to our desperate fate.

I certainly was 'Lucky Johnny' in many ways, and I have been all my life. Whenever I have felt depressed, as I still do from time to time, I think of my darling mum teasing me when I was young. She was the first to recognise something in me that perhaps helped me make my own luck and kept me positive pretty well throughout. Even now, that thought keeps me going with a smile.

My only regret is that I have never received my war medals, but I am blessed with two lovely married daughters and my son, six grandchildren, my darling mother, still alive at ninety-eight, and some marvellous brothers and sisters. They have all helped me through the last few years, since I lost my precious wife Christine in 1978. I have recovered from three major health threats since she died, but I am still going strong, enjoying the ups and enduring the downs with a smile. I consider myself a very lucky, fortunate man.

These days, I am not religious, but every VJ Day I say a solemn prayer for all my friends and comrades, who perished under the cruel rising sun. I shall never forget them. I can't. I was there.

Johnny Sherwood
Reading, 1984

by Johnny's daughter, Sandra Doe

Dad's real name was Henry William Sherwood, but his mother always called him 'Lucky Johnny', and it stuck. He married my mum, Christine, a few months before the war and bought a house near the Reading football ground. When Philip was born, Dad was in the army, training recruits up north, but I believe he came home for visits. Then, after a while, the army sent him overseas. He knew my mother was expecting me when he left.

One day, soon after I was born, Mum received a telegram that said my father was missing in action. She tried to find out more, but neither the army nor the Red Cross knew anything. I'm sure she must have been in a terrible state. They had always been so close, and Mum told me later that they were like best mates as well, so it must have been very hard not knowing.

It was ages after that, maybe two or three years, before she finally discovered he was a prisoner of the Japanese.

Philip had some health problems and it was difficult looking after him on her own, and she had no money coming in so it was all a struggle, until her sister Vashti moved in to help her with Philip and me and contribute to the housekeeping.

A few months after the war ended, they got their first letter from Dad, to say he was all right and he was coming home. Everyone was very excited, especially Mum and my grandma. The whole family went down to Southampton to meet him. Mum couldn't wait, after all those years, first thinking he was dead, then the relief of knowing he was alive, but a prisoner. Having no news about him must have been dreadful. Now, at last, six months after the end of the war in Europe, he was home. What a day that was!

When we got back, the whole of Great Knollys Street was full of banners, saying 'Welcome Home Johnny'. He was very popular before the war and my parents had lots of friends, so when he came back there were crowds of people along the street, waving and cheering. They had a massive, great party for him and everyone came, but I know they were all shocked to see him looking stick thin, when he'd always been quite a big man before the war, well-built and very fit from all the football training.

I don't remember my father much from when I was little. I was nearly four when he came home from the war, which was the first time I met him. We bonded, but he was always very strict with me and, like most men in those days, he left it to our mum to look after us.

Then, of course, my baby sister Susan was born when I was nearly ten. She was his favourite. I suppose that was because he was home when she was born and there throughout her childhood. He was never as strict with her as he was with me, but I think that always happens with the youngest child. I'm sure he loved us all. He and Mum always came to watch me swimming or doing things with the school.

Soon after he came back from the war, Reading FC gave him back his place in the team and he managed to get himself fit enough to play for most of their matches, but I believe he often had to go off before the end, because his starvation during the war had robbed him of his stamina. Mind you, he still scored plenty of goals.

During this time he took on running a pub with Mum. After Reading, he played as a professional for Aldershot, then finally for Crystal Palace, before he retired. It was such a shame he missed all those years. He could have been a top footballer if he hadn't been a Japanese prisoner of war. Mind you, even the most famous footballers didn't earn much in those days, not like now.

He carried on playing football for charity now and then. When

I was a little girl, I remember him taking me with him and I went round with the collecting tin. I used to watch him polishing his football boots with Dubbin every evening, keeping the leather soft. He was still playing in a charity league near Heathrow Airport when he was in his fifties.

After his retirement as a professional footballer, Dad took a job as a roofer for a while, and went to football practices, training youngsters in the evenings, though sadly my brother Philip was never well enough for football.

Next he gave up the roofing and became a bookie's runner and then a successful tipster for a while, under the name of 'Peter Lindley'. He used to do tic-tac at Ascot races.

I remember he was always cheerful and joking when he was with other people, in the bar of the pub or out on the racecourses, just like my mum told me he always used to be before the war. But she said the war had changed him. He was often moody when it was just us, and she told me he could get angry quicker too. It must have had a big effect on him, all that happened in the war, seeing his friends dying in front of him and not being able to help them. The scars never left him.

He used to have nightmares a lot, shouting out in the night. He would wake up in a terrible state and Mum had to sit with him and calm him down again. But he didn't usually wake me up, so I didn't know much about his nightmares.

If we went anywhere, he used to say, 'Don't buy anything Japanese.' Somebody came to collect him once in a Japanese car and he wouldn't get in it. But he never said much about the war. They'd been to hell and back, and survived. He was always a positive man, so although he resented what the Japanese had done to him and grieved for all his mates, I don't remember him being bitter, not when he was with us anyway. He was always positive about things. Once he'd made up his mind about something, that was it. He wouldn't change it.

Dad had a little room with a desk in it. I do remember him

shutting himself away a lot and Mum used to tell us not to disturb him. He was always in there doing something, but I didn't really know what to begin with. Then she said he was writing about his memories. It went on for years, but I suppose it helped him to write it all down.

I remember once, when my boys were small, Mum and Dad had them for the day when we went shopping, and when we got back he was quite cross with us because he couldn't get into his writing room. I was surprised to see Dad so upset about it, but then I realised he'd always been very protective of his sanctuary. My eldest, Sean, had taken all the screws out of the handle and put them in his pocket. He was always a rascal – just like his grandad. So we calmed Johnny down, and he saw the funny side of it in the end. My husband had to put the screws back in for him before we left.

Johnny was in the local papers quite a bit at one point, all about his war experiences, and they said that he was writing a book, but I never saw this at the time. I didn't know what sort of book it was, or what happened to it, until after he died.

Johnny liked going to the races and he always loved to gamble, whether it was the horses or the bingo. I remember he used to take our cousins down to the penny machines, and they often came back with bags of money. But he was a good gambler. He didn't care if he lost, and if he won he was always very generous, sharing his winnings with everyone. He won the pools once and he treated all the family. He always loved a flutter, and used to win on the horses quite a lot. He did know his horses well, so he knew what he was doing.

When he retired, Johnny still walked everywhere. He used to walk at least three or four miles every day. He liked being out in the open and going wherever he wanted. That kept him healthy and fit for years, but he still suffered some of the after-effects of his starvation and the vitamin deficiency illnesses he had. He always used to eat very quickly, as if he was afraid his plate would be taken away from him, or that he wouldn't get any more food. He ate some very strange things, like pigs' trotters and strong cheeses on Saturday nights. The boys used to sit watching him shake lots of pepper on everything. He loved strong tastes. Maybe that was because their rations in the prison camps were so tasteless.

I think when all the grandchildren came along, that helped Dad. He had an interest in them and everything they did. He used to kick a ball about with Michael and Sean. If they passed the ball to him, he would flip it up and do tricks with it. All their friends were mesmerised. I know they were very proud of their grandad. They loved their football and he was a big man in their lives.

He was quite a prankster with the children too. He used to come to all their parties, join in the hide-and-seek, and do crazy things to make them laugh. One time he put a stocking over his head and chased them. Most of the children screamed with fear, but he didn't mean to upset them. It was just his sense of fun.

My mum, Christine, died before Johnny. She died of lung cancer in 1978. After that he hated being on his own all the time, so he would have a weekend with me and a weekend with Susan, taking turns. Sean and Michael used to share a bedroom and he would be talking to them all night, telling them all these stories about his prisoner of war experiences. It went on for hours and hours.

I'm glad Johnny wrote this book and I'm delighted it is being published at last, and although he didn't live to see it, I know he would have been ecstatic.

After Christine died, he lived on for several years, surviving a serious stroke and heart attack. He always was a fighter, and believed he would survive.

He finally died of another heart attack in 1985, when he was seventy-two. Now that I have read his book, I can see how positive and brave he was, and I'm proud of all the help he gave people. He must have had a great deal of courage, and that was what kept him going through all those terrible times in the war. The one thing he wished for and never had was his war medals. We've never claimed them, but I know his grandchildren would like to have them.

Dad was a good man and achieved a lot in his life, especially with his football. He would have been thrilled to know that a few months ago his great-grandson, Lewis, was signed up by his old club Reading FC, joining their Elite Academy for promising young footballers. So now seventeen-year-old Lewis is carrying forward the family tradition, with the prospect of a bright future ahead of him in professional football, in the footsteps of Lucky Johnny Sherwood.

by Johnny's younger daughter, Susan Bark

My earliest memory of my father is of him taking me out in my shocking pink duffle coat, into Reading town centre to buy me an ice-cream. I was a proper Daddy's girl, born a good few years after he came home from the war. He was always kind to me, and to everyone – a bit of a softy really.

He often used to come and meet me when I was at infant school and walk me home. He was a popular man with a good personality and a lot of people knew him locally. They would call out to him as we went along. He always waved at them. Dad was a happy man most of the time, and generous to everybody – always with a beaming smile. Some of the older folks in the town still remember him and his football years, even now.

I didn't realise it much when I was a child, but I think his years as a prisoner of war did affect him quite a lot. I remember he always blamed the war for his rough, pock-marked skin, the result of his malnutrition for so long. I remember the scars he had from the Japanese beatings. Dad always said he wouldn't have survived being a prisoner of war on the Burma railway if he hadn't been so fit when he was captured. It was his football and being an army PE instructor that made him so fit and kept him alive.

For years, when I was still a child, I remember Dad was always at his writing bureau, writing his stories of the war. It was a big thing in his life, writing it all down for other people to read. Dad was my best friend when I was growing up. We had a very good relationship. He even taught me to count in Japanese, and how to say some of the words he had learnt. He loved his wife, his children and his grandchildren, but his book was always his obsession. All the years after he had finished the book, it was his dream to have it published one day. I admire Michael for making it happen. Johnny would have been chuffed to bits if he could have seen this day.

Acknowledgements

Special thanks to Jacquie Buttriss for her invaluable help in the preparation of this manuscript for publication. Also many thanks to agent Clare Hulton for believing in this book and making it happen, to Rupert Lancaster at Hodder for taking such a keen interest in the story and to Maddy Price and the whole Hodder team for all their hard work. Last but not least, I want to thank my wife Rebecca, who contacted Jacquie and got this whole project started.

Picture Acknowledgements

The publishers would like to thank all the family for permission to reproduce pages from Johnny Sherwood's scrapbook.

Australian War Memorial: p41 (PO2569.175), p112 (118879), p118 (P00406.027), p125 (P00406.031). Corbis Images: p 161, p236. Courtesy of David Downs/The Reading Football Club Ltd: p2. Getty Images: p226, p253, p268. TopFoto: p11, p213, p222.

Note on the Spellings of Camp Names

Please note that the spellings of the names of prisoner of war camps used in this book are amongst those most commonly used in Western historical sources. The Imperial War Museum's current curator of Far East POW and internee written records points out that:

> 'There is no such thing as a single "correct" spelling of the names of camps along the Burma-Thailand Railway, for most of which there is a greater or smaller number of possible variant spellings – almost every existing map or gazeteer of the camps will in this respect show variations from other maps and gazeteers. Often, the POWs themselves wrote the names as they heard them, and these spellings found their way into accepted use in the West. Modern Thai spellings are in some cases quite different from those used during and immediately after the war.'

Stephen Walton, IWM Duxford

Index

Page references in *italic* indicate illustrations.

An invitation from the publisher

Join us at www.hodder.co.uk, or follow us
on Twitter @hodderbooks to be a part of
our community of people who love the very
best in books and reading.

Whether you want to discover more about a book
or an author, watch trailers and interviews, have the
chance to win early limited editions, or simply browse
our expert readers' selection of the very best books,
we think you'll find what you're looking for.

And if you don't, that's the place to tell us what's missing.

We love what we do, and we'd love you to be a part of it.

www.hodder.co.uk

 @hodderbooks

 HodderBooks

HodderBooks